THE THIRD DUMA,
ELECTION AND PROFILE

THE THIRD DUMA, ELECTION AND PROFILE

BY
ALFRED LEVIN

ARCHON BOOKS
1973

Library of Congress Cataloging in Publication Data

Levin, Alfred.
   The Third Duma, Election and Profile

   Includes bibliographical references.
    1. Russia. Gosudarstvennaia Duma. 3rd, 1907-1912.
I. Title.

JN6554.L45   328.47   73-633
ISBN 0-208-01325-3

© 1973 by Alfred Levin
First published 1973 as an Archon Book
by The Shoe String Press, Inc., Hamden, Connecticut 06514
All rights reserved

Printed in the United States of America

TO FAY
For her full
appreciation
of an excursion
into the Russian scene

Contents

Foreword

The Duma Period, arising from the Revolution of 1905-1907, and blending with the upheaval a decade later, has become one of the foci of intensive historical analysis in modern Russian history. The Imperial Duma represented in fact, if not in intent, a serious deviation from the traditional, autocratic structure and offers us at least a glimpse into the capacity of the society of the Empire to assimilate an institution of a representative order and hence the potentiality of that institution for resolving Russia's accumulated ills. Its brief flutter, much of it in an atmosphere of crisis, cannot possibly provide definitive conclusions—except, perhaps that Russian society has always reverted to autocracy in acute or chronic crises. We can only assess its potentialities on the basis of the hard information available.

The basic problem of the Imperial Regime was the maintenance of stability in the framework of the parliamentary structure, yielded grudgingly under extreme social pressure. The essentially aristocratic, agrarian-oriented, ruling element and the bureaucracy supported or endured the new parliamentary system to the end of the Imperial Regime. They must have been sorely tempted to cashier the entire structure, particularly under the impact of the behavior of the first two Dumas. Instead, inhibited by what V. A. Maklakov anxiously dubbed "acheront," the destructive potential of mass revolutionary action, the "ruling circles" strictly interpreted the law to constrict the Duma's jurisdiction. And the boldest of the "constitutional" premiers, Peter Arkad'evich Stolypin, violated the law to assure a more moderate "popular representation," predominantly "cultured" and "Russian in spirit." The entire procedure recalls the experience of the local self-governments, the zemstvos, and town dumas.

This work is envisaged as the second of a series of studies (after *The Second Duma**) of the Duma Period, and as an introduction to further investigation into the nature and activities of the

*Alfred Levin, *The Second Duma: A Study of the Social-Democratic Party and the Russian Constitutional Experiment.* Yale Historical Publications, Vol. XXXVI (New Haven: Yale University Press, 1940); Second Edition, (Archon Books; Hamden, Connecticut, 1966).

Third Duma. The primary purpose of this study is to provide a basis for the evaluation of the Duma as an instrument for effective legislation in the wake of a major revolution; in a society with a six-century, statist tradition; with no modern parliamentary practice on a nationwide level; and consequently with little experience of, or taste for, political compromise. Hence, it examines in detail, the multiparty system represented in the Third Duma; the serious limitations, conditions, and procedures under which that system conducted elections; and its evolution in the course of the sessions of the Third Duma. Our study reveals, for instance, the strikingly conservative outsome of the elections to the Third Duma; not only where the Law of June 3, 1907, predetermined that coloration, but in those ranges of the electorate where a more liberal result was anticipated. We have attempted to analyze this development and offer it as a point of departure for the analysis of assumptions concerning the eventuality of an "inevitable" radicalization of Russian society.

In the completion of this effort I am particularly beholden to the Research Foundation of Oklahoma State University for the moral and material support offered me, especially in the microfilming of materials from the Slavic Division of the Helsinki University Library, and to the Oklahoma State University Library and the Kent State University Library for organizing these materials. I offer my deepest appreciation to the staffs of the International Research and Exchanges Board (IREX) and the Division of Foreign Studies, Institute of International Studies of the U.S. Office of Education, for making available funds and facilitating my research in the USSR. I also thank the Leningrad and Moscow Central State Historical Archives for making their resources available to me and to the Academy of Science offices in Leningrad and Moscow for providing a comfortable and uncomplicated atmosphere during my sojourn in the USSR. I cannot hope to repay my debt of gratitude to my long-suffering wife, Fay, for her patient understanding and encouragement of an effort which, in the nature of things, imposed severe limitations on normal social pursuits.

THE THIRD DUMA,
ELECTION AND PROFILE

I
The Loyal Support: The Reactionaries

The Electoral Law of June 3, 1907, and the Manifesto that accompanied it clearly reflected the purposes of the "governmental revolution." They sought to assure control of the hazardous parliamentary experiment by guaranteeing a predominance in it of "trustworthy elements"—those with a broad vested interest—and of the Orthodox Russians. The new electoral law represented the ultimate precipitation of bureaucratic experience with the operation of the first two Dumas.[1]

Belonging to that family of constitutional arrangements that were granted "from above" grudgingly, or as the better part of wisdom, after 1848, the Russian electoral laws of August 4, 1905, and December 11, 1905, could look back to a mixed Napoleonic, Prussian, German, and Austrian ancestry, adapted to established Russian concepts and practices; a lower house was to be based on wide popular suffrage and checked by a semi-appointive upper house within the framework of the Speransky and zemstvo system of indirect, class elections.[2] In the same tradition, the new law of June 3, 1907, also retained the principle of representation for broad categories of the population (national, economic, social) on an unequal basis. But now the representation was even more unequally distributed by an elaborate system of gerrymandering. The bureaucracy acted with decision on its negative attitude toward universal suffrage and on a positive need for the continuation of the zemstvo, property-curial system. The new law was distinguished from the old primarily by the multiplication of voter categories for the rather obvious purpose of assuring a majority for property owners, both rural and urban, and for Great Russians as against "aliens." More subtly, the new divisions might further restrict the suffrage of "untrustworthy" elements.[3]

To this end the lawmakers, thinking almost instinctively in terms of the traditional class-corporate structure, favored the rural landowner element, especially the large holders, who were primarily landed nobility. But this rural element also included small landholders, together with a large contingent of rural clergy, potentially sensitive to the demands of its upper hierarchy.

While the overall number of deputies was reduced from 524 to 444, the landowner category was increased by about 31 percent. It was assigned about 50 percent of the seats and given an absolute majority in twenty-seven of the fifty-one provinces of European Russia. In only eighteen were they a minority and they had one half of the vote in four others. With the richer townsmen they could control all provincial elections.[4] Some of the Senatorial interpretations of voting procedures made during the second campaign were incorporated in the new law and assured a more homogeneous opinion within the landowner category by excluding peasants who belonged to the rural communes, even if they had qualifications for voting as landowners. Moreover, the landowner assembly might be divided so as to separate the smaller from the larger categories.[5]

Weighting the vote in favor of the nobility was achieved primarily to the disadvantage of the peasantry who had provided the largest segment of deputies under the roughly representative Law of December 11, 1905. On June 3, 1907, their electoral strength was cut in half (from 43 percent to 22 percent of the electors) and their former majority in thirty provinces completely disappeared. Their suffrage right was limited to field peasantry; those who did not live on the land for a year could not vote with the village. This effectively excluded the semi-peasant workers with their newly acquired Populist, Marxist, and organizational furniture, as well as the rural intelligentsia.[6]

Another formidable insurance against intellectual and radical influences was provided by the new voting procedure in the village meetings and provincial assemblies. Heretofore the peasantry, at the first step of the election procedure, had selected representatives to a special *volost* electoral meeting—one from every ten households. Now the regular *volost* meeting for current business was called on to handle the election of delegates to the *uiezd* assembly—and such business could be brought up without previous notice, at any time during the early stages of the election campaign.[7] Moreover, the peasantry alone had been privileged, under the old law, to select their class deputies to the Duma at the *guberniia* assembly before the remaining deputies were elected. Now landowners and townsmen (in most *gubernii*) might also choose their class representative, who, like the deputies from the peasantry, were to be elected by the entire assembly. Given an absolute majority in most provincial assemblies, the landowners alone, or in combination with the wealthy city elements, could handpick many of the peasant representatives regardless of their popularity among the villagers.[8]

The town dwellers both gained and suffered under the changed electoral arrangements, depending on the size of their incomes which the lawmakers supposed determined their political coloration. The towns which had consistently sent the liberal and radical leadership to the first two Dumas actually acquired a nominal increase in voting strength, but it was artificially weighted on the conservative side. Although nineteen cities lost their privilege of directly seating their own deputies (rather than through the *guberniia* assembly), the townsmen enjoyed an increment of about 2 percent in their voting strength in relation to the total number of voters. In more than half of the provinces the town electors were to be selected by the numerically small upper middle class. And in all cities without direct representation the rich could, of course, count on assistance from the landowners at the provincial assemblies in the election of burgher deputies. For the city population was divided into two categories according to income: the large manufacturers, commercial people and property owners in the first; the rest of the eligible city population in the second. In twenty-five provinces these categories voted separately or together as they pleased, and in twenty-seven separate voting was mandatory. The seven largest cities with direct representation likewise elected deputies from each category separately. The usually conservative merchant-landowners could opt to vote with the city or landowner categories. As in the landowner category, the preponderance of voting power in the hands of the wealthier townsmen was emphatic.[9]

The worker representation was decreased by some 28 percent, and the period of continuous residence was limited to six months as against a full year for other categories, taking into account the fluid nature of Russian labor. But the significant reduction in the number of cities with direct representation made the worker vote quite insignificant in the sea of peasant and landowner electors at the *guberniia* assemblies. And except for the largest cities where he voted in the second curia the worker could vote only in the worker curia even if he had qualifications for the second curia or any other category. His influence was restricted like that of the peasantry to his own kind. And the conservative majority could handpick the few class deputies assigned him at the provincial assemblies. Yet the latter might have a relatively narrow range for their selection from the almost universally socialist labor vote.[10]

Still further to assure a conservative majority and that the new Duma would be truly "Russian in spirit," the Interior Minister was given the right to divide all assemblies at the *uiezd* and *volost* levels territorially and by nationalities. Heretofore such divisions had been on a territorial basis only, and were the responsibility of local electoral commissions. The nationality principle was entirely new.[11]

The national minorities were now dealt a stunning blow just when the resurgent national movements had begun to show tangible evidence of real and potential power in the 1905 period and the first two Dumas. As organized parties and groups, and in the liberal and revolutionary leadership, they entered the Duma and joined the opposition to gain equal rights with Great Russians or as members of the leftist fractions to change the political and social order. The Polish Kolo and the Moslem fraction at times had held the balance of power and the Kadets were materially strengthened by their support. They were just beginning to feel a sense of participation. But now the Tsar was committed to limiting their influence by severely reducing their representation to a point where they could not significantly affect legislation, specifically on Great Russian questions, actually on any issue except as the majority would accept their advice on local questions. And the new law implemented this purpose by reducing by two-thirds the number of seats allowed the "aliens," by assuring the Russians representation where they were in a minority, by instituting the above-mentioned divisive authority, and by excluding whole areas of Central Asia—old, populous centers of Moslem culture—"temporarily," on the grounds of political backwardness.[12]

Finally, to prevent the Duma from interfering in local, preliminary elections through its right to refuse a seat to an improperly elected deputy, it was limited to a review of provincial and direct city elections only. In the *volost* or *uiezd* the proper electoral commission alone had the power of investigation or annulment.[13]

After the successful dissolution of the First Duma—without undue popular disturbance—the confident government hardly concealed a program of control and manipulation of the electoral machinery. The bureaucracy could not be expected to shed ingrained behavioral patterns and attitudes—particularly in the severe crisis which continued to reverberate in scattered areas well into 1907. Parties were supported or harassed, legalized or refused legal status. And the Senatorial interpretations embodied in the new law were narrowly construed and copiously applied to hedge in the "untrustworthy" elements.

The exclusive company of the legalized parties included only those which stood to the right of the Kadets.[14] The extreme rightists numbered a melange of absolutist, nationalist, and monarchist elements (the Russian Assembly, the Monarchist Party, the Union of the Russian Folk [*Soiuz Russkikh Liudei*]), dominated by the hard-driving leadership of the Union of the Russian People *(Soiuz Russkago Naroda)*. The more moderate Nationalists and the Party of Legal Order stood between them and the Union of October 17 (Octobrists) and its leftwing splinter, the Party of Peaceful Renovation. This conservative cluster might command some respect at least among the liberals and their allies from the national minorities. But the favored position of the patently weak, potentially dangerous, sometimes scandalous extremists shaped the attitude of the non-legalized center and left toward the purposes and even morality of the regime.

The predominant position of the Union of the Russian People (URP) on the extreme right was largely the reward, paradoxically enough, for its adaptability to the constitutional regime, and for its capacity for developing a mass party which, if not comparable in size to those on the left, was the largest among the rightists. The Monarchist Party was too aristocratic in spirit, the Russian Assembly too amorphous ideologically, and the Union of the Russian Folk too idealistic, to attract wide followings. But the energetic crew of the URP which included the St. Petersburg physician, A. I. Dubrovin, the irrepressible Bessarabian public figure, V. M. Purishkevich, and the arch advocates of racial, largely anti-Jewish, violence, B. Nikolskii and M. L. Dezobri, proved effective in attracting a significant number of adherents— each in his special way. They shouldered aside the older, established bodies and absorbed a heterogeneous agglomeration of smaller elements—aristocratic, "democratic," and rowdy. They drew primarily from the lower middle class but to a degree from peasant and worker elements, predominantly Orthodox and Great Russian. Their aggressive, abusive, and sometimes satirical organ, *Russkaia Znamia* (the Russian Banner), popularized their program and tactics. Its editor, Vladimir Purishkevich, would create the illusion of uniting the lowly with the Tsar, and it incessantly stimulated racial and political violence. However distasteful their political antics might appear to allied elements, the URP (identified with the soubriquet "Black Hundreds") was to act and talk for the right in its moment of greatest strength and influence.[15]

The actual numerical weakness of the Union was obscured by its apparently strong position among the "ruling spheres." Sympathy, on occasion openly indicated by the Tsar, members of the royal family, court personages, privy councillors, governors general, and high clergy, was bound to leave an impression of strong, perhaps exaggerated influence at court.[16] Yet, during the third election campaign when the rightist appeal was probably at its zenith, the URP was concerned privately with the thinness of its ranks. It publicly claimed some 208 branches in large and provincial cities and in some villages. But at the end of June, 1907, the Union's central body, the Chief Staff, heard that its St. Petersburg membership numbered only 300. Grandiosely planned demonstrations and meetings attracted only small crowds. And its financial poverty was evident in the compulsion to seek support for its press and numerous odd enterprises projected by the center: patriotic funds, "True Russian" shops, and credit societies.[17]

Official reports bore out the Union's tendency to exaggerate its strength. The governors of Vladimir, Tver and Ekaterinoslav, for example, indicated that its figures "did not correspond with reality," or represented tens rather than hundreds, or that the branches were strong only on paper.[18] The Party did not exist at all, or only in name, in Poland, the Baltic Region, Central Asia, and the Amur Region, the Maritime Provinces, and Iakutsk. The reports noted its weakness in Western Siberia, Rostov Gubernia, and in Nikolaevsk on the Black Sea and Kerch in the Crimea. It was strongest in Astrakhan, Bessarabia, Vitebsk, Kiev, Mogilev, and Podolsk *Gubernii*—that is, in the border regions with a considerable Russian population—with over 10,000 members in each. The Ministry of the Interior ascribed it a total membership of 356,738.

Chronic internal bickering and factional strife, along with programmatic extremism, tended to repel otherwise potentially congenial elements from among the nobility, peasantry, and irregularly employed workers. These extremists were prone to develop sharp clashes of personality and dictatorial or oligarchical struggles marked by uninhibited personal abuse and wild accusations. And neither the leadership nor their cause went unscathed as squabbling revealed loose financial practices at all levels of the "True Russian" groupings.[19]

In a campaign begun with almost unseemly haste—within a week after the dissolution of the Second Duma—Dr. Dubrovin and Purishkevich were designated the chief URP candidates. The rightist tactics produced a negative impression on much of the electorate as being contradictory and morally questionable. While opposing the very idea of parliamentary government, they called for, and predicted, the election of their candidates. And their repeated resort to denunciation and espionage as self-appointed agents for officialdom generated considerable resentment. The "yellow shirts" in Odessa begot widespread notoriety with their physical attacks on a broad range of political opponents, from Social Democrats to Peaceful Renovationists, individuals bound for election meetings, and, of course, Jews and striking workers.[20]

More nearly in the manner of other parties, the rightists offered assistance to the public in registration and balloting, canvassed voters, held public meetings, distributed literature, and provided free legal and even medical advice. They concentrated primarily on the provincial population and the lower middle class, as the most promising fields for exploitation, and probably because of their limited resources. Much of the content of their agitation was eminently adapted to their illiterate or semiliterate targets. Unfortunately, at this stage of P. A. Stolypin's administration, subsidies were not readily granted the rightist press. At least one major newspaper, *Vieche* (the medieval town council) became defunct in mid-campaign, while *Russkaia Znamia* urgently solicited contributions.[21]

Normally the rightist campaign was facilitated by the provision for ethnic curias in the electoral law. Although the Black Hundreds frequently volunteered information to the Ministry of the Interior concerning advantageous arrangements, they did not always prove beneficial as political moods varied from place to place. Then, internal bickering and public hostility created unexpected difficulties, not only in seating candidates for deputy to the Duma, but in finding them. Dr. Dubrovin discreetly renounced his nomination and Purishkevich ultimately had to resort to his mother's holdings in Bessarabia as a safe constituency.[22]

Premier Stolypin had to steer a cautious course between utilizing and ignoring or repressing the rightists. He was sensitive to the sympathy the URP generated at court. Yet, for the prestige of the regime and the maintenance of public order he could not allow its excesses to go unchecked. Hence, he subjected its membership to a degree of repression while probing the possibilities for utilizing the right as a counter weight against revolutionary opposition. The Union was at times supported by local officialdom in its riotous proclivities and organizational efforts—as in Odessa and among the railway workers. But the "True Russians"

sometimes suffered severe restraints on civil or political counts
as individuals and groups. The Premier vigorously frustrated
efforts to establish relations between rightists and the crown. By
the end of July, 1907, *Russkaia Znamia* was openly assailing the
"Octobrist" Stolypin for patronizing "criminal-liberators" and
for reprehensible mildness toward the defunct Duma and toward
Finland while repressing "True Patriots."[23]

On July 15, 1907, some fifty delegates of "True Russian"
organizations, chiefly from St. Petersburg and Moscow, met in
executive session at the Monarchist Club in St. Petersburg to
write a platform for legislative action and propaganda. Their
program differed little from that of 1906. The only new element
was a clearer statement on participation in the Duma. It reiterated
the basic demands of the far right: the primacy and leadership of
the Russians, unfettered autocracy with power to limit the pretensions and arbitrary proclivities of the bureaucracy, and the
right to petition against the abuses of officialdom. The bureaucratic barrier between the Russian people and the royal ear and
action had to be dismantled. The lot of the peasant and worker
had to be improved but with full respect for private property—
without hurt to "other classes." There would be swift justice for
"True Russians," stern and effective punishment for political
crime and its abettors, especially in the press. And the program
called for "healthy" public schools quided by rightists, the state,
and the Church.[24]

The question that generated the greatest commotion, naturally
enough, concerned participation in the Duma. Some party officials, even candidates, vigorously opposed the idea in principle.
They would not traffic with a constitutional body. Rather, they
would await the dissolution of the oppositional Third Duma
and its replacement by an advisory Fourth. The majority argued
that it was unprincipled and criminal to oppose a Duma instituted by the Tsar's will. And the Congress held that it was the
duty of all "True Russians" to ensure the election of a rightist
parliament which would recommend the transformation of the
Duma into an advisory body.[25] The right found itself adopting
a gradualist approach toward their goals, not unlike that of the
liberals—perhaps a good omen for a parliamentary future.

But acceptance of parliament in principle in deference to the
Tsar's will was a far cry from approval of the institution. Rightist propaganda decried it as a hoax perpetrated on the Tsar by
crafty ministers. They held the institution to be indigestible by
the Russian cultural tradition and that it would bring only ruin

to the land and people. Through it shrewd, self-centered parties beholden to rich capitalists, landowners, spendthrift zemstvo figures, and Jews would only destroy "the Russian way of life." The rightists would agree at most to an advisory *zemskii sobor* (estates general) representing only Russians.[26] The Black Hundreds proposed, then, to enter the Duma to change its fundamental function and purpose.[27]

II
The Loyal Support: The Moderate Center

Like most Russian political parties the Union of October 17 consisted of an alliance of kindred political, if not cultural, currents which sprang from the catalyst of revolution in the years 1905-1907. And Russia's major conservative party was most heterogeneous in composition. Cultured, wealthy, country gentry from the zemstvo leadership; *nouveaux riches* from the aggressive, rising upper middle class; highly placed bureaucrats and scattered academic figures were united, as Professor M. Ia Kapustin had it, on matters which "concerned the life and autonomous strivings of the border regions and a definite attitude toward impatience and acts of violence. . . ."[1] More specifically, the merger of conservative and moderately liberal elements of country and town arose from a fear that, at the very least, the liberation movement might realize something far more drastic than limited monarchy and economic liberalism.

Each of the component elements that joined to form the Union of October 17 had its special emphasis and composition. The liberal minority of the zemstvo congresses of 1904-1905 was the most consistently constitutionalist, aristocratic, and intellectual of these groups. The "bourgeois" elements were not homogeneous. The Commercial and Industrial Union of St. Petersburg drew its membership from the retail merchants centered on the Gostinii Dvor and the Apraksin Market. They emphasized the need for a conservative Duma. The smaller Progressive Party of Moscow, somewhat more intellectual, was as liberal as the Kadets on all matters except national autonomy. Both groups were especially concerned with economic nationalism. The Industrial and Commercial Party, aware of its advantageous position in the domestic and foreign market, would not hear of the eight-hour day. Yet, reflecting the secondary, political position of the new entrepreneurs, it asserted its opposition to any class privilege.[2]

The formal program of the Octobrist Party reflected the influence of these varied currents.[3] As against the more militant liberals and socialists it emphasized cooperation between state and parliament to achieve social stability. And in this perspective it called for a monarchy limited by the provisions of the Fundamental Laws. The Octobrists would accept the upper chamber, the Imperial Council, but in the western, parliamentary tradition they assigned priority in financial matters to the lower house and called for a ministry answerable to parliament.

Emphasis on cooperation and fear of continued revolutionary activity begot a logical series of suggestions for ameliorative measures, a balm for the irritations which made for a restless society: the condemnation of repression, the immediate convocation of the Duma, publication of laws guaranteeing civil liberties, and the abrogation of all special states of security. The latter plank in the platform aroused considerable apprehension in the First Octobrist Congress and was balanced by an admonition against the abuse of civil liberties which were fully formulated in the program. The egalitarian temper of the middle class found expression in the demands for universal, free education uninhibited by official interference and for classless, independent courts accessible to all.

The conservative reaction to the revolutionary experience is perhaps best reflected in the Octobrist program on the vital land question. Emphasis had to be shifted from plans (at the constituent congress) to supplement the peasant land area to increased productivity on available land, land enclosure, easier credit, and emigration. While liberal and socialist programs were calling for partial or complete confiscation of landed estates, the bulk of the zemstvo gentry were offering a less painful alternative.

The labor plank, motivated, again, by the drive for social stability, would reinforce the worker's sense of security. He would be given social insurance and the right to organize and strike. But these programs were to be carried out with due regard for the capacity of Russian industry to compete in the world market and for the interests of the rural population. In short, he was not to drive prices upward by pressure for wage increases and an inflationary spiral—an alternative position that might well exacerbate unrest in the cities and contradict basic Octobrist purposes.

The essential nationalism of the Octobrists, which markedly differentiated them from other constitutionalists, found expression in their insistence on the traditional, conservative, and rightist demand for physical and administrative indivisibility of the Empire. Here, again, a fundamentally conservative, emotional attitude conflicted with a rational quest for stability. Yet they would recognize consistently enough the constitutional commitment to Finnish autonomy.

As official policy unfolded in the period of the first two Dumas, the Octobrist leadership reacted in much the same manner as other more committed constitutionalists to its various manifestations. They were concerned that the upper house would become a preserve for archaic, bureaucratic types. They sensed, in the official attitude toward interpellations, an effort to fend off challenges to administrative policy while hamstringing the Duma's efforts to evoke a desirable reaction from the bureaucracy.[4] They regarded the publication of the Fundamental Laws without previous parliamentary consent as an action opposed to the essential spirit of the October Manifesto, if not entirely illegal. Particularly, they questioned the provision for interim, administrative action under Article 87.[5] These attitudes represent the most advanced Octobrist positions reflecting the impact of the revolutionary upsurge on all constitutional elements. Their demands were consistently constitutionalist. But the weakness of the Octobrist Party lay in the patent lack of commitment to these ideas by a significant section of the leadership and, in all probability, most of the rank and file.

In the first two election campaigns the Octobrists were at a disadvantage. Repression of revolutionary activity was hardly the atmosphere for the flowering of a spirit of reconciliation. And the Octobrists were identified with their commercial-industrial elements. Thirty-eight candidates identified as Octobrists were elected to the First Duma and forty-four found seats in the Second. They were aided, especially in the second election, by senatorial interpretations and exclusions favoring conservative and reactionary elements. They generally followed the strong oppositional current in a reserved manner. With the liberals they strove to restrain excessive speech and action which might undermine the prestige, or even the existence, of parliament. But their tone was more nationalistic and they underscored their policy of cooperation with the regime. They roundly assailed the Kadets for their hesitation in condemning political crime. They applauded the ministerial benches while the opposition sat on their hands. And they would have no traffic, of course, with the demonstration at Vyborg.[6]

When the political dust settled on the schism in the conservative center in the late summer of 1906 as the more progressive elements took an independent direction,[7] the Octobrists assumed, outwardly, at least, a more stolid character. And they retained a colorful and generally capable leadership. The Guchkovs of Moscow symbolized the emergence of the new, aggressive entrepreneur element. Old Ritualist and but two generations removed from serfdom, Nikolai Ivanovich was designated mayor of Moscow and Aleksander Ivanovich was a restless, adventurous soul of the militant, conservative feather.[8] He might equal the far right in his ardent patriotism. But he proved a consistent, if restrained, constitutionalist. The administration would have done well to weigh seriously the admonition of the Octobrist organ *Golos Moskvy*, in August 1907 which expressed his confirmed sentiments. "The wave of reaction, if it should rise, would force the Union [of October 17] to carry on a definite and decisive oppositional mood."[9] Michael V. Rodzianko, another significant Octobrist figure, tended to dominate any assemblage in which he participated, with his massive figure and mighty voice. Basically, an "honest country tory," he experienced great difficulty in countering rightist elements in and out of the Octobrist Party. His sympathy with their anti-revolutionary proclivities conditioned his ponderous mastery of the parliamentary craft. But he, too, held doggedly to his constitutional principles as a dominant zemstvo and Duma figure.[10]

The basic problem of the moderate Octobrist leadership was largely to assure that their constitutionalism would not be diluted by too extensive compromise with official and public forces to the right. In the summer of 1906 the Party had to face the harsh reality of heterodoxy in its ranks. Its ideological instability and consequent looseness of organization should have proven costly were it not protected artificially by the Electoral Law of June 3, 1907. *Golos Moskvy* may have been entirely correct in arguing that internal Octobrist debates thought to be disruptive for the Party were normal, pre-election maneuvers. But the membership was not united, as *Golos Moskvy* had it, by internal ideological ties placing the group in a "solid, firm and definite position." For chronic schism inhibited or paralyzed efforts to arrive at firm decisions on many major issues.[11]

In the circumstances of the third election campaign a party (or a definable segment thereof) without a "definite tendency" (*nastroenie*) was positively abhorrent. D. N. Shipov noted that some Octobrists were repelled by this deficiency in the period of the First Duma. And M. O. Menshikov, an influential figure on the staff of the conservative *Novoe Vremia*, St. Petersburg's chief newspaper, excoriated the Octobrists for their general, loose, conciliatory position. He depicted them as "pale as if photographed with a poor negative, without an idolatry, mythology, or a martyrdom . . . catching cold at meetings is their greatest political suffering." Opponents, he held, should be irreconcilable, and the destruction of a foe was but self defense. All people kept their enemy helpless except hypocrites and fools. To seek equal conditions and weapons was not a serious political struggle but a sport. Compromise was not an especially acceptable virtue at this juncture of the Russian political scene, and ideological inflexibility influenced the behavior of every significant political party.[12]

Every major organizational consideration was affected by Octobrist intra-party differences. Internal discipline was deplorably weak or even non-existent. Provincial committees were sometimes entirely independent and arrangements could be made even with the URP. The branches in Minsk, Kursk, Ekaterinoslav, Tiflis, and Smolensk were at least as rightist as the URP. A leader of the liberal, St. Petersburg Octobrists, Bobrishchev-Pushkin, averred that only the Moscow-St. Petersburg organization could be called rightfully Octobrist. By mid-October, 1907, it was apparent that differences between the Central Committee and the local branches hinged more on the will of individuals than on ideological considerations.[13] Relations between the St. Petersburg organization and the Chief Center at Moscow were tenuous at best. During the period of the Second Duma these connections almost ceased to function and the St. Petersburg Octobrists were hardly informed of the meetings of the Zemstvo Congress in June, 1907.[14] Matters reached such a pass that the leadership of the autonomous German Octobrist Party in St. Petersburg found a more congenial response in the left wing of the local organization than in the Muscovite center. And these more liberal Octobrists were titillated by the idea of establishing a new political grouping—to include even the Peaceful Renovationists, intermediary between the Octobrists and the Kadets. In practice they stood aside from active campaigning.[15] In Dvinsk and St. Petersburg the Party could not even ascertain its membership which drifted in all directions.[16] Efforts to call a congress obviously needed to resolve internal differences were frustrated by the fear of exposing the centrifugal pull to the right and left.[17] In a sense the internal heterodoxy of the Octobrists and their central position (shared to a degree by the liberals) tended to develop some spirit of compromise, a commodity not generally abundant in Russian

political life. That which infuriated the conservative element
might well serve the parliamentary cause under the pressure of
the need for responsible action.[18]

It is evident from the official pronouncements of the Octobrist
Party and its leading figures that they sought to establish relatively specific standards of conservative constitutionalism. The
deviations from these standards were wide and legion, especially
in the course of an election campaign. And in their zeal to support Stolypin's dual policy of repression and reform, the Party
as a whole emphasized the former more frequently. Consequently,
in the early stages of Stolypin's administration they assumed
several highly questionable postures. But in the long perspective
of the Duma period, the effective leadership of the Party was
loyal to its concept of constitutionalism insofar as that was
realistically possible. And their standards did serve as the effective operating principles of the Party.

The Octobrists held as fundamental that Russian constitutionalism was *sui generis*. It would have to maintain a connection with
the old governmental tradition which served as the foundation
for the new structure.[19] Therefore it was not possible, for example, to introduce the parliamentary principle in complete
form at once and the people would have to be satisfied with a
ministry responsible to the Tsar.[20] Thus far their argument was
respectably substantial. But somewhat in the genre of their growing conviction that they were properly representative of Russian
public opinion, they tended to become entrapped by the ideological justification of their conservative convictions and temperament arising from their position in Russian society. One of
their cardinal postulates held that the constitution was granted
by the Tsar to seek support from the population after the bureaucracy revealed such woeful instability in 1904-1905. And the im-
plication was clear that the Tsar might modify or rescind what
he had granted. The more conservative currents would not hear
of the argument that the constitution was forced on the sovereign
by popular uprising, for they argued, and sufficiently convinced
themselves, that the population as such did not participate in
the disturbances. They held that this was the work of specially
interested opposition groups.[21]

Consistently pursuing the argument for popular support of
the throne, they would legalize the Kadets, promote the autonomy
of local self government, the judicial system, and creative, legislative work in the Duma. Thus there would be mutual cooperation between Tsar and people resting on the broadest possible
base.[22] Both the concepts of cooperation and representation

were severely jolted by the events of June 3, 1907. They could only call for a suspended judgement of the regime and a tolerant attitude toward the violation of constitutional guarantees in a moment of crisis. They maintained that the administration could not have tolerated a law under which it was impossible to eradicate class interests. They "sadly" acknowledged that the electoral law was not changed in the prescribed legal manner, "but we consider the necessity for it regrettable." In liberal and revolutionary circles the Octobrists were henceforth known as the "party of sad necessity."[23] The government, they held, had no other choice in the face of revolution and fell back on the ultimate right of the Tsar to alter the Fundamental Laws—an exceptional right to be used only rarely and carefully.[24]

Support for the Stolypin administration was eminently consistent with the views of the Octobrist leadership. Stolypin's attitudes, apart from his cabinet as a whole, differed little from those of Guchkov on basic issues: gradualism in constitutional practice, simultaneous repression and reform, enclosure of peasant holdings, the prior position of Russian interests in an indivisible Russian state but allowing for cultural autonomy for the minorities.[25] The Octobrist leadership was keenly aware of the pressures operating within the regime and the difficult adjustment of the bureaucracy to the new constitutional circumstances. They wanted to make their sympathy clear beyond question but they also warned against the traditional bureaucratic abuse of power and threatened to join the opposition if the regime moved in a reactionary direction. As one "powerful and sincere" Octobrist had it, "If they take the constitution away—I'll take my old rifle down from the wall."[26]

In connection with the direction of Russian constitutionalism, the Fifth All-Russian Zemstvo Congress meeting in Moscow in the summer of 1907 attracted special attention; for it might provide a preview of the conservative and rightist attitudes which were likely to prevail in the Third Duma.[27] The zemstvo movement had been in conservative, landlord hands since the turn of the year 1906-1907 and the Congress had been called before the dissolution of the Second Duma to counteract its possible impact on public opinion.[28]

The Congress met in two sessions, June 10-15 and August 25-29. The Octobrists sent the largest delegation (some 44 of a total of 107 delegates) which dominated the proceedings.[29] Thus it would limit middle class influence in the *uiezd* zemstvo by allowing only those who paid a tax on farmland to vote for delegates. Conversely, it rejected Stolypin's proposal to base voting qualifications on a designated, land tax—higher on urban property—rather than on acreage.[30] To prevent engulfment of the "cultured" nobility[31] by the rural population, the congress subordinated the projected *volost*, or small zemstvo, to the tutelage of the land captains and provincial administration.[32] And to avoid relatively heavy taxation of the nobility locally, the *uiezd* zemstvo was to supervise *volost* taxing power. *Volost* delegates to the *uiezd* zemstvo assembly were to sit only in an advisory capacity.[33] As an ultimate, exquisite precaution, the Congress proposed that installation of the *volost* zemstvo be made optative.[34] Characteristically, the Octobrist delegates supported a rightist resolution calling on the Congress to express as its sense that reform could never be realized until the government applied "the most resolute" measures to end terror and anarchy.[35]

The government could now gauge its allies in the active struggle with revolutionary violence. And in the perspective of the Fifth All-Russian Zemstvo Congress the Stolypin administration could be reasonably certain that as the political turmoil subsided and the "relationship of forces" emerged it enjoyed a rapport and coincidence of general views with a most important political element under the new electoral law. The premier expressed disappointment with the practical dilution of his small zemstvo project. But he could afford to await action in the Duma where he felt that his influence, and pressure, could be effectively directed.[36]

Besides its specific agenda, the August session of the Fifth Zemstvo Congress afforded almost the only opportunity for a nationwide meeting of Octobrist leadership. In view of the impending election campaign, a major convention was discussed throughout July and even a tentative agenda proposed. But difficulties arising from loose organization, financial stringency, and ideological differences between the conservative Moscow and "liberal" St. Petersburg organizations were apparent at once.[37] In lieu of a national convention the Central Committee had only two reasonable alternatives to avoid organizational and ideological confusion. It agreed to parleys with the provincial leadership at the zemstvo congress and called for a continuation of regional conferences being held since the end of June.[38]

Articulate statement of the Octobrist position during the election campaign came largely from the proclamations of the Moscow and St. Petersburg City Committees. Their basic ideas were wrapped neatly in a brief, preliminary proclamation issued by the St. Petersburg branch on September 1, 1907. It charged that the Kadets, Trudoviki and other, "non-Russian" groups were responsible for legislative inaction in the first two Dumas and for the threat to the very existence of the national representation. And it appealed to the voters to elect the "reasonable" and "conscientious" Octobrists who rejected both reaction and revolution.[39] Moscow and St. Petersburg proclamations, of September 16 and 20 respectively, enlarged on these thoughts and reflected basic Octobrist concern with restraint of revolution and the danger of provocation by extremists or by government action.[40] Specifically, the Octobrists asked that their candidates be elected to act speedily on government measures and to offer their own. Neither advocates of revolution, class hatred, nor ineffective bureaucrats should be elected. As an informal platform they offered Stolypin's enclosure act, improvement of labor-management relations, revision of local government (the *volost* zemstvo), reform of the armed services, a regime of enlightened economy, establishment of norms for the long-promised civil liberties, and the legalization of parties not practicing violence, elimination of futile security measures, and a regime "based on the force of law, not on the law of force." They would promote the interests of the minorities if they did not conflict with those of the *Velikorus* and the unity of the Empire. They promised to make no agreements with anti-constitutionalists and censured the Kadets for consorting with those on the left.

To cope with the practical problems of the election campaign, the Central Committee of the Octobrist Party moved to control, inform, and consult with the local organizations. It sought specifically to strengthen the Party's structure, ascertain the mood of the population, and devise tactics for elections. To this end it met with representatives of large regional branches and promoted conferences in the provinces, cities, and suburbs. It established election bureaus to arouse the apathetic electorate, especially during the summer months when a significant segment of its following tended to move to country homes and resort areas.[41]

The scene in the localities was not particularly encouraging and could only underscore the artificiality of the Party's position as a major contender for leadership in the new Duma. The Union of October 17 reported a membership of 14,035 to an inquiry by the Ministry of the Interior soon after the Third Duma opened its sessions.[42] It claimed a membership of over a thousand in Vitebsk, Kazan, Kaluga, Lifliand, Orenburg, and Tver *gubernii* and in Rostov-on-the Don. And while it proffered no information on Moscow and St. Petersburg, as the co-centers these were undoubtedly the largest organizations. The Octobrists apparently had no branches in forty-four *gubernii*. While the reportage is far from complete, it is apparent that much of the membership was concentrated in the provincial capitals. And the localities all too frequently submitted that the branches were inactive or declined in membership and lost influence in political life for lack of leadership. And some disappeared after the second or third election campaigns in such relatively large centers as Kerch and Nikolaevsk and in the major seaport of Odessa. The center seemed incapable of sustaining the energy generated for a brief period during the campaigns. Only Rostov-on-the-Don reported optimistically that its branch had grown one and a half times in 1907-1908. For the moment the Central Committee had to arouse and inspire the provinces to take uncommon action.

For their major propaganda effort the Party came to rely on a certain segment of the press. *Golos Moskvy* (The Voice of Moscow) and *Slovo* (The Word) spoke the loudest for them. But the conservative, independent daily, *Novoe Vremia* (The New Times) and *Rossiia* generally supported them, although at times they were critical to the point of frustration because of lax Octobrist organizational practices. And the Party was able to issue numerous brochures and leaflets for easy reading.[43]

Despite a keeness for political activity generated by their unusually favored position, it was not until late August and September, at the end of the summer vacation period, that the Octobrist leaders bestirred themselves to begin their campaign.[44] They directed most of their energies toward mobilizing the support of the landlords because of their preeminent position in Russian political and intellectual life, their influence among the peasantry, and their strong position under the new law. The Octobrists intended to nominate the most outstanding, congenial figures from among the landlordry and their liberal opposition identified them with it.[45] Urgent circulars were dispatched late in September appealing for a mandate for the Octobrist Party to justify the Tsar's "confidence" in parliament, to secure the whole future of Russian culture and especially the principle of private property. Defense of property was, again, the chief burden of signed and anonymous telegrams sent out on election day. Landowners with multiple holdings were importuned to vote in categories likely to strengthen the party most. Nonvoters, especially women, who might transfer voting qualifications of their property to relatives were urged to act.[46] And in the cities they called on constituents with a choice to vote in the second category where the liberal middle class would normally predominate. The fight against apathy involved pressure (especially on summer vacationists) to vote in the primary and intermediary stages of the campaign.[47]

While the Octobrists expected no great support from the peasants and workers, they created special committees to agitate among them. But their organization in the villages was sporadic, and they found the rural population more interested in commune property than private in the summer and fall of 1907. Among the workers Octobrist efforts were negligible, for they could find few agitators sufficiently acquainted with socialist programs and tactics to make effective appeals.[48]

As a constitutionalist party the Octobrists hoped to attract politically centrist elements among the minorities. But their conservatism, especially as reflected in a tempered, Russian nationalism, was likely to inhibit a real meeting of minds, and some Octobrist utterances were indistinguishable from those of the rightists. The Union of October 17 stood officially for cultural autonomy for the national and religious minorities, and in this respect they could oppose aggressive russification along with the Kadets. They supported a "merging not a swallowing of separate peoples." But they would not offer political autonomy to the nationalities and would promote the interests of the Orthodox Church "according to its significance."[49] The Octobrists might set up a committee to study legislation to lighten the burden of the Jews. But they were not behindhand in taking advantage of the division of voters by nationalities in the interest of the Russian population, especially in the border areas.[50]

Actually, the minorities, or elements thereof, who aligned themselves with the Octobrists were attracted by a complex of common economic interests, political views, prejudices, and temperament. The Octobrist program proved attractive to the scattered German enclaves in the Empire, particularly in the capital cities and along the Volga. But the German Octobrist organizations tended to operate autonomously while generally accepting the Party's program. In September, 1907, they published their own proclamation and program phrased to attract the German population. They reflected the Party's attitude toward the Jews: a cautious approach to the elimination of restrictive measures in deference to Russian sensibilities and economic interests, coupled with a demand for an end to "anti-Christian" activities. Yet they demanded a more definite stand on minority rights. And under no circumstances would the property-conscious German nobility and farmers accept obligatory expropriation.[51]

Even with their forces fully mobilized, it was characteristic of the Octobrists that in the capital cities, especially in St. Petersburg, they shunned public debate at pre-election meetings. They were loth to reveal and sharpen differences within the Party or to weaken their artificially favorable position in competition with the liberals. Meetings were urged and planned from early July, but no concrete action was taken until the height of the election campaign in mid-September.[52] In the summertime the St. Petersburg Octobrist following was largely vacationing and in the fall the Party's best oratorical talent had gone to its estates to vote. The organization found that it had to train students to meet the growing demand for propagandists.[53] At mid-September the Party Council of St. Petersburg could not decide whether to attend large Kadet meetings to counter liberal programs.[54] When the first gatherings were held at the end of the month, they met with a weak response—some twenty-four persons assembled on September 24. Further meetings called just before elections in early October were restricted to Octobrist speakers and one included a more or less "captive," clerical public.[55]

Of necessity, the selection of candidates generated a spurt of activity among the Octobrists. The Party's task was complicated by the dearth of popular figures and the effort to present at least an illusion of social variety among the candidates. Within the Party only the central figures could expect certain support from its members or adherents. And only A. I. Guchkov, Professor Kapustin, and Iu. N. Miliutin attracted wide attention in politically active circles.[56] In Moscow and St. Petersburg the Party Councils selected candidates from lists named by ward organizations for city-wide plebescites of the Party membership. These selections were usually confirmed.[57]

In the provinces the Octobrists faced approximately the same circumstances: a dearth of talent and few popular figures. But in the border areas they were favored (as the most predominant Russian party) by a division of slates according to nationalities.[58] By all political logic the new electoral arrangement favored the emergence of a strong Octobrist delegation in the Third Duma. But awareness of organizational instability and ideological diversity generated no inconsiderable degree of self-doubt in the "party of sad necessity."

III
The Reformist Opposition

As the increasing strength of the urban and rural conservative elements that adhered to the Union of October 17 endowed it with a cautiously conservative coloration, the moderately liberal intellectuals who founded the Party could not conscientiously continue to live with it and struck out in an independent direction. They could not bring themselves to cooperate with a regime committed to a policy of severe repression and progressive control over local and central representative bodies. The cause of stability, they felt, would be served better by legislating and enforcing regulations on the civil liberties promised in October, 1905.[1] When A. I. Guchkov emerged as the conservative leader, he emphasized the element of repression, and the liberals simply could not stomach his justification of courts-martial as a brutal necessity in a brutal struggle. D. N. Shipov and Prince E. P. Trubetskoi dubbed the Octobrists the "Party of the Lost Charter" and the "Party of the Latest Governmental Communication", and with Count P. A. Geiden and M. A. Stakhovich withdrew on September 9, 1906, to form the Party of Peaceful Renovation—*Mirnoe Obnovlenie*—dignified and sincere but confused and ineffective.[2]

The Peaceful Renovationist philosophy for action focused on the principle that the entire state structure was to be reformed along constitutional lines by peaceful means—by reconciliation of past differences. Hence they were fundamentally opposed to violence and arbitrary action from any quarter. Anti-constitutional action, they held, would sustain hatred and chaos, and prevent a peaceful reconstruction. "It will be the same to us whether there is a senseless reaction begetting a Pugachev plot or a Pugachev plot begetting a senseless reaction." The liberation movement had to rest on an ethical basis.[3] Their concrete program opposed extraordinary security measures and the repeated dissolutions of the Duma. They saw in the acts of June 3, 1907, grounds for lack of faith in the government, the source of class conflict, and ammunition for the socialists. On the one hand they were repelled by Octobrist vagueness and their rightist proclivities—particularly their Great Russian nationalism.

On the other hand they were concerned that the Kadets had dallied dangerously with the left in the first two Dumas—as at Vyborg—and in their persistent refusal to condemn political crime. They would support Stolypin if he ended his repressive policies and behaved constitutionally. They were indeed an intermediary blend in the political prism between the conservative and liberal constitutionalists. Like the Octobrists they felt the need for obligatory instruction in the Russian language, and with the Kadets they called for obligatory expropriation of excess farm land with just remuneration. Like all constitutionalist groups they demanded unfettered trade union activity and labor insurance.[4]

When the Peaceful Renovationists entered the party lists they found that most constitutionalists had already established party loyalties. Count Geiden's death in June, 1907, left them without leadership or direction until D. N. Shipov was elected president of the combined Moscow and St. Petersburg Central Committees in Moscow on August 29, and I. N. Efremov was named vice president. Given their organizational and political weakness, they fully realized that they might only further split the constitutionalists without hoping to attract a significant following. Accordingly they emphasized the need for a centrist coalition with the left Octobrists and the right wing of the Kadets, and sundry independent constitutionalists—a "Victorian compromise" of sorts. This sizeable nucleus was to act as a unit in parliament to assure the fulfillment of the promises of October, 1905. It would provide both an effective medium for the constitutionalist nobility and would relieve the Kadets of the need to seek the support of the Trudoviki.[5] The Moscow meeting promised to support worthy candidates selected from the constituent parties and groups. The Mirnoe Obvnovlentsy evinced a rapidly maturing capacity for parliamentary manoeuvering, but no significant coalition emerged during the election campaign.[6] They did appeal for sympathy from the Octobrists and the Kadets for their principles and plan of action in the face of popular apathy and mounting reaction. At the very best they tried to achieve their purposes by local arrangements to elect sincere constitutionalists regardless of their party affiliation. In the focal center, St. Petersburg, they attracted only a weak following from an electorate indifferent toward, or suspicious of, the old, rural, aristocratic liberalism, or from elements bent on more resolute action.[7]

By the end of June, 1907, the Constitutional Democrats, the Kadets, were fully committed to a policy of "correct seige." The impunity with which Stolypin had applied security measures and abruptly modified the composition of the Duma made it eminently clear that popular opposition was unthinkable. And the liberals were stunned by the vast scope of the changes of June 3, 1907.[8] Almost with a sense of disbelief they exclaimed that "that which the new electoral law represents surpasses all probability."[9] Salvation for Russian society, they averred, lay only in the reinforcement of the principle of government by law and they dubbed the violation of the Fundamental Laws a "state revolution" which could only lead to chaos. The class emphasis of the Act of June 3 and its disregard for the interests of the minorities were, in the Kadet view, a clear manifestation of the old bureaucratic spirit. These anachronistic attitudes would only weaken the state. The "130,000 landowners" would now rule and there was precious little from the conservative and rightist platforms and press to indicate that they could be expected to rise above their "class and racial egoism" to the level of statesmanship in enacting essential legislation. Only free and cooperative participation by all elements of the population could substantially strengthen the state both physically and morally. "The state must appear as a mother, not as a step-mother."[10]

The Kadets could console themselves with the argument that despite the administration's claims Russia remained a constitutional monarchy. In the October Manifesto and the Fundamental Laws the Emperor's power was indeed limited in legislative and financial matters. If the Manifesto of June 3 maintained that he who gave the law had the right to take it away, that was not abrogating the constitution but violating it.[11]

The liberals were now increasingly concerned for the operation of the party system. For they saw in the freedom of party activity and clash of party interests the only effective counterweights to bureaucratic arbitrariness and indifference toward, or ignorance of, the new political structure.[12] What had been won had to be defended and properly utilized to assure broader gains. They were fearful lest the constitutional limitations imposed on the Duma would render it more advisory than legislative—"a department of legislative affairs" rather than an effective organ of opposition to the government. And while Stolypin had proclaimed the Duma's right to differ, they were more impressed by his efforts to mould it to the government's purposes.[13] The promise of October—of vital change— seemed to be fading and the liberals uttered an insistent, plaintive plea for change. P. N. Miliukov invoked Michael Speransky's challenge to the ruling element to adapt itself to the "movement of the human spirit" and Count Witte's observation that "Russia has outgrown the forms of the existing structure [and] strives for a legal structure based on freedom."[14]

The changes in the nature and position of the popular representative body wrought by the new electoral law impelled the Kadets to evaluate the effectiveness of their constitutional program: the defense of the Duma as an instrument for reform. They had to define its functions and capabilities to a public likely to become disenchanted with, and dubious of, its possibilities as an organ that could provide concrete change to make life more attractive politically, economically, and culturally. And they had to convince themselves and public opinion that they could effectively promote their purposes.[15]

The constitutionalists had been challenged frequently during the second elections by skeptical intellectuals, workers, and peasants to show how the constitutional, legal struggle had benefitted them materially and politically; and they had not always been able to justify their course effectively with only the meager, legislative record of the excitable First Duma.[16] Now the Kadets mustered their arguments to justify the Duma as reflected in the activity of its more effective Second Session. They emphasized its creative and restraining function, notably in the committees and evening sittings. They argued that the maturity of the debates on famine relief, the budget, the recruit bill, and the bill on judicial reform revealed the Duma's capacity to restrain agitational tendencies and to counter servility to the regime as well as rebellion.[17] They denied the leftist charge that they harbored constitutional illusions. They were quite aware of the basic deficiencies and limitations of the Duma, and they had fought for their elimination within parliament as its powers would allow. The most telling agitation in any case would come from effective legislative activity. The Kadets contended that they also fully understood the need for agitation outside the Duma, but only for constitutional ends, not those of social revolution called for by Marxist strategy and purpose.[18] If the achievements of the Dumas were scanty because of official impatience and the hostility of the extremist groups, the Kadets held that they had, indeed, made fundamental progress in developing parliamentary experience and habits of work and thought. Miliukov compared the Duma to a ship that had weathered a heavy storm. It had been battered but its crew was more experienced. Participation in the Duma of elements that had once opposed it (Social Democrats and Social Revolutionaries) and deeper interest in public matters convinced the Kadets even in the face of evident apathy that popular representation had developed strong roots.[19]

Much of the strategy and manipulation of the Kadet Party was directed at resistance to any assault on, or diversion from, the legislative purpose of the Duma. The Party maintained that legislative power was a flexible, strategic instrument. It could arouse and inculcate public support and confidence. It could "unmask" the purposes of the government and it could expand the authority of the Duma "to make it an organic component of our state structure." But to these ends the Duma had to concentrate on attainable legislation—not extreme demands which only generated charges of irresponsibility. It had to avoid the "pangs of dissatisfaction, of dangerous disorder, of confused legal relationships and deceptive public hopes." And for the moment, the Duma had to inculcate in the bureaucratic structure a sense of respect for the law. "Defense of the law on a legal basis, that is the role of the Party in the Duma."[20]

As the Party of the liberal intelligentsia *par excellence,* the Kadets seemed to be a fair target for charges of "rootlessness"—lack of real support among the people. They could only point to the vitality of their program and ultimately to election results among "democratic" categories.[21] As for "deals" with the administration, the Kadets regarded discussions such as those of the moderate wing of the Party with Stolypin (in connection with the dissolution of the Second Duma) as a matter for party discipline. But they insisted that their goals remained what they always had been.[22] The Kadets lay charges of betraying the revolutionary cause to a misunderstanding of their tactics of adaptation to changing circumstances. This referred apparently to the Kadet position in the Second Duma on such matters as famine relief and unemployment. Liberal procedures in these debates were aimed at thwarting revolutionary and rightist manoeuvers regarded as dangerous to the very existence of the Duma.[23] But in this connection, the Constitutional Democrats had to be articulate in the matter of relations with the left. For this issue was always a source of potential cleavage within the Party.

From the evidence available it would not appear that there was any acute internal dissension in the period of the first two

Dumas and the summer of 1907. On the contrary, the public stand taken by V. A. Maklakov (identified with the right wing of the Kadet Party) in the period 1906-1907 reflects the general liberal attitude of suspicion of the regime's purposes. This is patent in his famous letter to Poincaré assailing the French loan of 1906, his pleas as an attorney in political cases, and his utterances in the Dumas.[24] Kadet debates on the nature of the Duma and the correct parliamentary strategy belong largely to the era of the emigré diaspora. Insofar as these arguments had any validity they are worth recording as the undercurrents of potential dissention within the Kadet Party which emerged in sharper relief later in the Duma period.

The highly critical minority view expressed by V. A. Maklakov emphasized the need for maintaining the zemstvo liberal tradition of the Alexandrine reform era of the 1860s as opposed to the current, inexperienced, more radical, publicist political leadership in the liberal movement.[25] It was characterized by a liberal-slavophile stress on cooperation with the government as most beneficial for gradual evolution toward true constitutionalism. Maklakov regarded as fatal any dallying with the left in consistent opposition to the regime since that was certain to bring a social upheaval or bureaucratic reaction. The revolution of 1905-07 seems to have stimulated the more conservative currents of Maklakov's mixed noble-intellectual tradition and aroused his concern for the direction of "acheront," the popular will and action. Nor does he seem to have grasped fully the profound nature of the revolutionary reaction and its relation to governmental policy of the preceding half century. He was quite sanguine about the readiness of the regime for compromise. And he was something less than enthusiastic about the more representative First and Second Dumas. Here he contrasted the Duma "amateurs" with government specialists and regarded majority decisions as the "autocracy of the majority."[26]

The majority liberal view was defined by P. N. Miliukov. It could not reconcile itself to the degree of centralism retained by the bureaucracy after 1905 and regarded cooperation with the regime, especially to the extent of participation in a cabinet, as unacceptable or unrealistic if the Kadet Party were to survive politically and ideologically. "We cannot grant credit because we will deprive ourselves of credit if we do this."[27] If the government could not compromise significantly, the Kadets felt that they had to unite all forces in opposition to it. Miliukov knew that the radical constitutionalists would be difficult to control.

He had given up efforts to reconcile sympathetic leftists and liberals by the winter of 1904 and now, in the summer of 1907, he was ready to define his friends and enemies on the left. He noted frankly that from the birth of the Kadet Party it had wanted to regard the left, the socialists, as its allies. But the Kadets were met only by hostility as "bourgeois liberals," with narrow class interests, "traitors," pursuers of ministerial portfolios. There was no question about the anarchists but more confusion about the "multicolored and varied group of social-political currents who came under the common title of Russian socialism." These squabbling elements who constantly read each other out of church for the slightest "bourgeois" predilictions were at one only against the Kadets. Doctrinally they had to reveal the Kadets as a socioeconomic category and they constantly split hairs over the social and political nature of the liberal party. For their part, the Kadets regarded those on the left as enemies who would replace political struggle with revolutionary destruction. Some leftists would form a temporary union with the "democrats," but Miliukov was irreconcilable toward those socialists who would have no traffic with the Kadets. And in an editorial in *Riech* of September 21, 1907, he aroused a furore among the leftists by postulating, in the vein of an old German folk tale, that the Kadets would be their own enemies if they were to carry an ass on their backs—that is, submit to opinions not their own. "An ass is an ass even though he temporarily finds himself on the back of a sage." The liberals could accept Plekhonov's position even though he would not vote directly for a Kadet but for a Social-Democrat who would support the Kadets. They could tolerate nothing further to the left.[28]

The Constitutional Democrats defined their current political attitudes at a conference held in mid-August, 1907. They issued a *Declaration* "to acquaint the country with the views of the Party on the current political situation and on the significance of the election campaign."[29] They proclaimed that despite the obstructionism of those who "tied their existence to the old structure" and their violation of the past revolutionary reforms, despite the interruption of considerable legislative work by two dissolutions and a new electoral law, the Kadets were optimistic about the triumph of the "popular cause." The new electoral law could not inhibit chronic social and economic disintegra-tion—only the implementation of true constitutional and democratic reforms could do that. And to this end the Kadets would enter the Third Duma standing on their program of

1906. They emphasized especially the articles on expropriation of unneeded land, true universal suffrage, local self-government resting on broad democratic principles to guarantee the welfare of the country, and broad support for the Duma. They would reveal the inadequacy and motivation of the government's measures, and as a minority fraction they obviously could not bear responsibility for the actions taken in the Third Duma.

While not treated extensively in the *Declaration*, the Kadet press enlarged on their philosophy concerning the national minorities. They maintained that the mechanism which bound mutual relationships in Russian society and promoted a feeling of solidarity in it were only weakly developed as compared to a more advanced society. And the impulses which specifically generated a feeling of national solidarity were in fact lacking in Russian life. There was no direct mutual relationship between Russians and nonRussians—competing peoples and political organizations. There was none of that sense of contrast or experience of direct struggle which promoted the feeling of social solidarity, especially among peoples defeated in a struggle. And in replacing the true products of popular activity with a counterfeit, official patriotism, popular creativity was poisoned at the source.[30]

Reformers of the early years of the century with bright and true goals which might be directly, if not easily, realized shrugged off the complexities of emotional, ethnic, and cultural chauvinism and provincialism in a society whose lagging cultural pace they acknowledged. And they placed considerable faith in the innate creativity of society by the simple process of eliminating the traditional "official patriotism" which found a hospitable environment among significant elements of that society.

The conference of mid August, like other central and local meetings, was a hazardous enterprise, hardly compatible with the dignity of the Party of the intellectual, liberal aristocracy and the liberal professions. But the government would simply not legalize one of its chief ideological opponents which had consorted frequently with the revolutionary left, and hence could not permit it to hold a national congress. Officially the regime explained that it could not afford to recognize a party which refused to condemn political terror in the Duma. Nor could the regime risk the impression that it would condone Kadet tactics and thus stimulate revolutionary action.[31]

In these circumstances the Kadet Party thrashed about for some procedure, short of an underground gathering, whereby it could reassess its tactics and marshal its forces in the wake of the recent "governmental revolution." Central councils and local committees, conveniently located, could always repair to Finland. And a gathering of provincial committees, held at Terioki within a week after the dissolution of the Second Duma, called for a national congress.[32] When it proved impossible to obtain official authorization for the gathering, the August Conference, after some heartsearching, allowed the Central Committee to continue in office without calling a general election.[33]

The Constitutional Democratic Party was structured, like Russian parties, with a Central Committee representing provincial and local units. These were a heterogeneous agglomeration of district organizations, small town committees, student and industrial-commercial fractions, and national groups.[34] And these local units felt the full burden of the non-legal position of the Kadet Party. Here, according to varying, local circumstances, the Party might carry on normally or be subjected to harassment as a "criminal" organization. In practical terms this meant that local district (*rayon*) organizations were unable to meet, even as the national congress, to elect their committees periodically. Consequently, these bodies continued to function of necessity beyond their designated term of service. Normally, the rank and file were only too willing to allow capable figures to hold office indefinitely—until such time as they could be officially reelected. But if a disagreement arose, as in the case of the Odessa organization, a squabble might ensue with attendant publicity. And the local officials, taking obvious advantage of the information proffered, fined newspapers which printed the Kadet ticket for the Duma and arrested the candidates.[35]

When unmolested, the local units engaged in routine organizational and agitational activities common to all parties. During the election campaign they held polls for local candidates, checked voter lists, distributed ballots, and mobilized the voters. Probably in connection with the restrictive laws of July 11, 1907, on student organizations, the Kadets made a concerted effort to challenge the strong position of socialist groups in the universities.[36]

In the third election campaign the Kadets understandably concentrated on the city categories, particularly the second. And their procedure for naming candidates varied with local political circumstances. Wherever it was apparent that they were weak, the liberals supported the non-Kadet figures whom they regarded as sympathetic. Normally a city committee canvassed the Party membership through the ward committees to determine the popularity of potential candidates.[37] It then submitted the names of the most popular figures to the Party rank and file, and those with the largest vote were selected as final candidates.[38]

A Kadet victory in the second category was almost a foregone conclusion in the largest cities and the procedure was somewhat less ad hoc. Candidates were proposed by plebescite in the wards and approved in the city committees. The strongest were submitted to a city-wide vote of the membership.[39] Yet, President of the Second Duma, F. A. Golovin, was offered as a candidate in Moscow without a plebescite, presumably because of his wide popularity. On the other hand, the St. Petersburg City Committee had to give considerable biographical publicity to A. M. Koliubakin, a rising Kadet luminary who was not so widely known in Party circles.[40] In the rural and small town areas the provincial committees named the Party lists.[41]

Fearing a natural tendency to boycott or shun elections, the Terioki Conference of June 10-11 called sharply for involvement in the balloting. A Volga-Ural Conference in the first half of August called attention to the "absurdity" of the argument that participation indicated an acceptance of the violation of the constitution and asserted that the membership was obliged to vote for Kadet candidates.[42] Electoral agitation in the cities was directed at elements likely to provide a reasonable turnout of liberal voters. After some investigation into the state of mind of the suffrage in the first category, the Kadets decided to rely heavily on their own membership and made a concerted effort to get their more affluent constituents to vote with the richer electorate.[43]

In the second city category the Kadets turned to every dissident group besides those strata on whose support they could normally count. They noted the striking apathy among the workers and warned the progressive parties to get the small apartment renters to the polls.[44] In this connection, the Kadets were, by every indication, inordinately optimistic or were snatching at propagandistic straws. They reasoned that trades unions had no desire to become political "vassals" of any one party because of the diversity of political currents within the labor organizations. They argued that the workers' chief interests were economic as reflected in the purely economic goals of the great majority of strikes. They were interested in the Duma primarily to get favorable economic legislation and relief from government repression of their economic activities. Hence the worker would support any program that furthered these interests.[45] There was, indeed, an element of unreality in the Kadet penchant for ignoring the intensive and fairly effective political efforts of the various socialist elements. Here the workers found their public heroes, and aside from congenial political leaflets or newspapers and the ideological disputations of the competing socialist groups they probably read little propaganda of any kind.

In the first two Dumas the liberal nationalist leaders of the minority peoples had stood hard by the Constitutional Democrats, and the liberals naturally strove to maintain this attachment. In the "basic" Russian area they would attract the not insignificant "alien" vote in the large centers. In the borderlands they formed blocs with minority organizations and manoeuvered to attract the Russian vote.[46]

In estimating their chances of victory the Kadets were deeply concerned and puzzled. The new law which divided the city electorate into richer and poorer categories certainly favored the more conservative constitutionalist elements who would cast their votes to the right of the Kadets. Then the socialists could be expected to make some inroads into the lower reaches of the second category. These were, in any case, demonstrably apathetic. And the Party's non-legalized position was fraught with unpredictable dangers. Fortunately for their morale, the Kadets were buoyed by a sincere enough spirit of optimism, maintained, however, by a considerable measure of self-deception. They argued that since there were no traces of reaction in mass public opinion it was evident that the constitutional idea was solidly embedded in the public consciousness; that a "paroxysm of leftist mood" now gave way to the acceptance of the liberal program as a basis for realistic reform. The liberals were certain that the oppositional mood would effectively counter official pressure in the provinces. There would be no youthful, passionate upsurge but a serious public movement for reform.[47]

At the moment the Kadets were grateful for the campaign itself. They would not hazard a prediction on the outcome of the elections but they were happy "only for this that despite the law of June 3, the population wants to vote and defend its interests and that is more important than results."[48] They were certain of the enhanced prestige of the Kadet Party and even envisaged a chance of victory in the elections if small landowners and clergy voted in considerable numbers.[49] There was certainly little in the brief, Russian constitutional experience to indicate any special inclination on the part of these elements to support the liberal view. And the tradition of clerical discipline was impressive.

Although it played no rôle in the Third Duma it is perhaps worthwhile mentioning the small intellectual Party of Democratic Reform. For its leadership was imposing and its legislative thought was broadly influential in constitutional circles. It was organized before the elections to the First Duma by the editors of *Viestnik Evropy* (European Messenger), and Professors V. D. Kuzmin-Karavaev and M. M. Kovalevsky, to attract liberal, non-party people (independents) and right-wing Kadets. Kadet Party discipline, its obvious political significance, along with the registration of Kadets to seats in the First Duma frustrated this effort. The program of Democratic Reformists was close to that of the Kadets, and its membership felt more nearly akin politically to their liberal left flank than any other group. Actually their agrarian program strongly influenced that of the Constitutional Democrats. They differed in their more conservative emphasis on the unity of the Empire and the protection of Russian interests in minority areas. They would make no demands for centralization and discipline within their party until it had proved its right to exist and with the *Mironoe Obnovlentsy*, renounced revolutionary methods and terror and would not consort with any parties which operated underground. Hence, they had some reservations about Kadet dealings with the left. They were not averse to effecting a compromise with the government or even joining a cabinet, but only if the major elements of their program were accepted by the administration. Professor Kuzmin-Karavaev favored direct elections to the Duma from the zemstvo and city governing bodies. But he feared that this might involve them too deeply in political manoeuverings and pervert their essential economic-administrative character.[50]

Another element that would appear strange in any but the Russian parliamentary environment were the "non-party" groups.[51] The varieties of "non-partisans" that bobbed up now and again were as numerous as the shades in the political prism and only a few were formally organized. The Kadets deplored the wasted effort of a group of non-party, gifted "Bersteinist" intellectuals who were torn between their socialist idealism and political realism. The former would not permit them to exchange their ideals for the mess of potage of daily politics. The latter kept them aloof from the left and caused them considerable concern about their estrangement from it—a charge frequently levelled at the Kadets themselves.[52] These intelligensia organized as a group of non-partisan progressives, and held talks with the Trudoviki and Popular Socialists to attack political apathy. Some delegates were elected in the provinces as "non-party" or "progressive" candidates.[53]

In St. Petersburg a group of distinguished figures, conservative constitutionalists, formed a special electoral committee at the end of October, 1907, to support individual non-party candidates who enjoyed more or less broad popularity but who otherwise might not be nominated. This group included Prince V. A. Obolenskii, I. E. Repin. and Baron de Ginsberg, among others. They were especially interested in countering rightist as well as Kadet interests in the first category of city voters. Their group proclamation noted the imbalance in favor of the right and Octobrists under the new electoral law. And they were anxious lest the Duma have a one-sided political complexion along with the Imperial Council and the Cabinet. Since these elements to the right of center were not likely to meet popular needs they warned that the danger of revolution would threaten again. The group consequently called on the voters to support independent progressives.[54]

Still another group, some workers in the industrial districts of St. Petersburg, were pleased to identify themselves as politically "non-party," and in circumstances where they felt it politically prudent to do so members of the Union of the Russian People used the same designation. Likewise some non-rightist delegates used the "non-party" soubriquet to avoid repression in the localities.[55] Given the temporary, even ephemeral, nature of their purposes and the lack of any coherent sense of organization, it was unlikely that an influential "non-partisan party" would emerge on the Russian scene. It was, of course, possible that political independents, especially among the peasantry, and the peasants (and worker-peasants) scattered through the various fractions might form a common group to consider peasant interests.

IV
The Disloyal Opposition

The militant revolutionary left was rendered considerably less significant in the Duma by law of June 3, 1907. But its spokesmen from the galaxy of populist and marxian socialist parties were the only articulate voices available to the peasantry and labor, and the leftists claimed to represent them exclusively even though they were not always organically connected with them. If their voice was small, in the Duma it was shrill. In their dogmatic or extremist fashion they managed to evoke an image of the world of the Russian peasant and worker. And they could always arouse considerable commotion among their ardent partisans. Some of these groups and parties were not represented in the Third Duma either from weakness or from ideological conviction. But the broad spectrum of Russian political leadership and certainly the political police had, perforce, to take notice of their activities.

The Popular Socialists at the populist far right formed around the editorial staff of the "thick journal," *Russkoe Bogatstvo* (Russian Wealth). N. F. Anenskii, V. A. Miakotin, N. N. Pieshekhonov, and A. B. Patrishchev very nearly represented their entire stock of talent. They had broken away from the Social Revolutionary movement in 1906 when its underground atmosphere proved too restrictive and its terroristic program repulsive. They attracted a scattered following in the provinces and in the institutions of higher learning in Moscow and St. Petersburg. In the Second Duma their small group of fourteen stood largely with the left. They were critical of Kadet preoccupation with "small issue" legislative activity yet they rather inconsistently assailed the regime for its aggressive legislative initiative.[1]

With only a formal commitment (in the revolutionary tradition) to the principle of parliamentary representation, the Popular Socialist Party searched its heart after June 3, 1907, and found itself irreparably divided on the question of participation in the Third Duma.[2] And by a small majority their controlling body, the Organizational Committee, went on record for participation. The boycottists warned that the government now counted on the Duma to reestablish the old regime. The majority claimed no great faith in parliamentarism to achieve their goals but considered that it had to face historic realities: the Popular Socialists were not qualified by temperament to lead an armed uprising.[3]

A five-day conference of central and provincial organizations and former deputies which opened July 28, 1907, called on the membership to participate actively in the election campaign.[4] They would join only with the socialists and Trudoviki at the first electoral stage. Thereafter they might even consort with the Kadets or withdraw from the campaign if the mood of the electorate proved boycottist.[5] The Organizational Committee offered candidates only in the second city category selected from those receiving the strongest support in a canvass of local organizations.[6]

The third campaign proved all but fatal for the Popular Socialist Party. In its quest for legality and more efficient organization the Organizational Committee decided on July 21 to publicize its membership for the information of those not already familiar with it. A month later the City Prefect of St. Petersburg called for the exclusion from the voting lists of Miakotin, Anenskii, and Pieshekhonov who had already been arrested "in the case of the Popular Socialist Committee."[7]

The Trudoviki were the largest cohesive element in the Second Duma and hence a force to be considered even after the excisions of June 3. They were a heterogeneous collection of moderate populist leaders and peasant deputies. They hesitated, accordingly, between liberal and socialist directions as their leadership tried to follow both its own inclinations and those of the peasant masses whom they more nearly represented in 1907 than any other group. They were rather a parliamentary group than a party, and had expected immediate relief and reform from the Duma. Hence, they originally followed the leadership of the Kadets as that political element best prepared for parliamentary activity. But they veered leftward in the face of parliamentary inaction and frustration and the programmatic and tactical moderation of the Kadets.

Like the Kadets, and quite remarkable for populists, the Trudoviki thought in terms of remunerating landowners for expropriated property. As the truly peasant "party" they reflected the attitudes of the peasantry with middle-sized holdings and incomes: the *sredniki* shoud get further increments from the land available. They were typical of the Populist "municipalizers" who would entrust the ownership of the lands to the state but divide them locally. They would (at least in theory) socialize agriculture while allowing capitalism to flourish in industry— likewise a general characteristic of the populists.[8]

The constriction of peasant voting power under the new electoral law had an especial impact on the Trudoviki as it severely damaged their political underpinning. Their frustration was balanced by a mood of resignation; a fatalistic attitude toward the official counteraction to the "liberation" movement. But the acts of June 3 stimulated their leftward drift and conditioned their ideology and tactics for the third election campaign. They openly challenged the parliamentary orientation of the Kadets and tried to restrict political action in common with them. The Trudovik campaign conference of mid-July emphasized that under the new law the Duma could no longer be regarded as the focal point of their activity. Rather they were to be concerned with organizational work among cooperatives and trade unions as well as propaganda in the villages.[9]

V. V. Vodovozov, Trudovik leader and legal expert, signalized the deepening schism with the Kadets in a debate on fundamental tactics. The Kadets had touched a particularly sensitive nerve by asserting that the Trudoviki were hardly representative of the peasantry which Vodovozov acknowledged in the sense that the peasants were too differentiated to unite at the moment in one party. But he held that with the satisfaction of their basic political and economic demands a separate peasant party would emerge from the welter of peasants, workers, and petty craftsmen who supported the Trudoviki. The Kadets were not likely to benefit from these contingencies since they were drifting rightwards and the peasants were not particularly concerned with people who did not represent their interests. They joined others further to left in maintaining that the peasantry now knew that Kadet hopes for action through the Duma had proven illusory. For the moment, the Trudoviki would concentrate on all those elements who had nothing to lose from the coming revolution. Their diffusion would be balanced by their mass.[10]

Despite strong reservations among the Trudoviki concerning their commitment to a parliamentary program, the July conference followed the normal leftist pattern of participation, especially in areas where there was a good chance of victory at the polls and their propaganda might prove effective. They would form blocs only with leftists in the primary elections and with the

Kadets if faced with a rightist challenge in the election of deputies. They would abstain entirely, and boycott elections if popular opinion was opposed to participation or was notably
apathetic. For all practical purposes this meant participation in
forty *gubernii* and the five largest cities.[11]

The Trudoviki had apparently lost heart after June 3 and
hobbled themselves psychologically with a negative attitude
toward the elections. Yet they feared that the peasant might vote
anyhow as he had in previous elections but that they would lose
political standing if he chose not to vote. Hence, they offered their
dualistic program, urging peasant participation to prevent the
government from getting the kind of Duma it wanted and emphasizing propagandistic activity outside the Duma.[12]

The Social Revolutionary Party did not even enter the third
campaign. It engaged in no electioneering and offered no candidates officially sponsored by the Party. Its leadership in the
Central Committee called for a boycott. But its membership was
not of one mind and the impact of its tactic was widely felt in
leftist, intellectual, worker, and "conscious" peasant circles. For
the Social Revolutionaries the "popular representation" was, at
best, a medium for nationwide agitation and, at worst, they were
suspicious of its potentiality as a liaison for cooperation with the
government. They had made it eminently clear that they had
entered the Second Duma primarily for agitational purposes.
They would consider the basic needs of the population and "reveal the government's crimes against the people" and its real
nature. To this end their strategy called for committees to examine the government's policies in the localities, among the
people. But their chief interest lay in agitational work, and this
included a strain of terrorism.[13]

With the revision of the electoral law the Social Revolutionaries
announced their return to the more congenial boycottist position.
In a pronouncement of mid July, 1907, they argued that since it
was possible to elect so few peasant and worker deputies it was
hardly worthwhile going to the Duma for agitational, not to
mention legislative, purposes. The voters had not recovered from
their disappointment over "constitutional illusions" promoted
by the liberals. And the socialists had not been able to control the
first two Dumas while the Third was being organized by counter-
revolutionaries. Participation in the new Duma would only seem
to sanction the acts of June 3, thus lending support to the regime
at home and abroad (where it sought financial aid). The conclusion was obvious enough: agitation for a boycott was needed to
disabuse the unenlightened.[14]

But the Social Revolutionaries still had some mental reservations and the Party was still divided on the matter. The essential
disunity on the issue of boycott only begot indecision and frustration while other leftists plunged wholeheartedly, even aggres-
sively, into the campaign. Confusion reigned as the capital cities
promoted a boycott while trade unions aligned with the Social
Revolutionaries were participating. And some branch organizations were concerned about the prestige of the Party with the
peasantry as it offered no firm decision. Their arguments hinged
largely on the powerlessness of the Duma to achieve "political
freedom" as against its unique position as a rallying point for the
people. And while the Party clung to an official boycottist position, at least one S. R. was elected deputy (from Voronezh) and
the Popular Socialists expected to benefit from those who decided
to vote.[15]

In the course of the third campaign the Social Revolutionary
leadership took a definite stand against political terror. The
Central Committee explained in detail just what it opposed:
agrarian and factory terror as a means of settling economic dis-
putes between labor and capital; terror even against the "ideological inspirers of reaction"; and against the destruction and
defacement of private property in the economic struggle. The
Central Committee threatened to oust the bomb throwers and
assassins, but it offered no binding resolutions.[18]

A decisive stand on terror at this political juncture seemed to
be the better part of wisdom politically and ideologically. It reflected the perennial difference in temperament between the
terrorists and the S. R. leadership. At a moment of falling political stamina the latter regarded terror as quixotic and potentially
lethal for the Party. And the Party center was certainly trying to
restrain moral and political anarchistic tendencies and fence itself from anarchism in the public mind.[17]

In the summer and fall of 1907 the Social Democratic Party was
in a deplorable state of disarray. The events of June 3 and their
aftermath only compounded the marxists' woes. The leaders of
the chief contending currents were largely in emigration. Lenin
had hardly touched Russian soil in November, 1905, when he
fled to Finland in the wake of the abortive December uprising.
Since August, 1906, he had been publishing *Proletarii* illegally,
and the government pressed its search for the "hereditary noble-
man by birth Vladimir I. Ulianov (N. Lenin)."[18] Despite strenuous efforts in the preceding spring Lenin had not been able to
achieve decisive control in the Central Committee. The Bolsheviki could outvote the Mensheviki and their Bundist allies—but

only with the aid of the Poles and Letts.[19] Lenin complained that
the Central Committee's proposals (on the establishment of a
central organ, first steps in the Duma, and participation in the
"bourgeois" press) were never implemented because of the
hostility or neutrality of the non-Bolsheviki and it was impossible to get a resolution on them.[20]

Pressure from the regime was well-nigh unbearable. It was
general knowledge that the Social Democrats along with other
parties on the extreme left were suffering mass destruction. Only
scattered individuals operated in Kazan, and remnant organizations clung grimly to their political lives in Kursk, Tambov, and
other provinces. Only in Perm were the Social Democratic organizations growing stronger.[21] In Moscow the Party Committee
was bound over to the district military court on charges of maintaining a secret, revolutionary press and arsenal. In Warsaw,
Polish and Jewish S. D. leaders were arrested and the Polish Socialist Party was without funds.[22]

Continued factional strife only brought into relief the mythology and futility of Party unity. The basic differences between the
Bolsheviki and the Mensheviki were essentially the same as those
that crystallized at the Third and Fourth Party Congresses.[23]
The ultimate goal was still the political and social revolution, but
the Mensheviki now emphasized that they could not imagine a
"proletarian" victory in the immediate future with Russian
political life at the tender mercies of the Stolypin regime—especially after the dissolution of two oppositional Dumas. The
Social Democrats had first to create the conditions for victory
within the framework of a bourgeois revolution and at the moment the country was headed for a constitutional, not a revolutionary crisis. Hence, the Mensheviki saw no purpose in underground conspirative action which the Stolypin administration
could easily destroy and which failed to attract the great body of
the workers. They would "liquidate" underground activity and
called for a broad, open worker's party which would know how
to operate within the framework of a legal press and legal labor
organizations. They proposed that the proper course for the
proletariat was to act as an extreme opposition and avoid a pre-
mature strike for power in both the strategic and marxist senses.[24]

Lenin and his acolytes fiercely opposed these "liquidator"
tendencies. They counterposed the need for Bolshevik leadership
of the revolution over the "democratic" petty bourgeoisie, the
peasantry, in competition with tsarism (i.e., the potential attraction of Stolypin's program) and with the insidious and treacher-

ous liberal bourgeoisie with their appeal for a constitutional as against a revolutionary social and economic solution.[25] In his opposition to the Mensheviki, Lenin posed all questions four-square within the rigid confines of the marxian dialectic. And he found sufficient grounding—at least to his own satisfaction—for his more opportunistic pirouetting.

These theoretical disputations were hardly interfactional alone. They represented the temperamental and basic sociopolitical differences of two politically opposed parties under the single Social Democratic roof. Both claimed marxist legitimacy, yet both found it neither practically nor psychologically expedient to strike off independently. The implications of their differences motivated their every major theoretical and practical decision. At the moment, the factions clashed vigorously in the areas of "partisan" (terroristic) struggle, trade union activities, participation in the legal press, and instructions to future deputies to the Third Duma.

The emotional debate on terror concretely brought into relief the implications of illegal operations. Neither wing of the Party was in a position to condemn terror in the Second Duma, and each differed vastly on its implementation. Lenin had already expressed himself on terror in his classic, "realistic" manner.[26] He found the dialectic conveniently flexible, and resting on marxian text he held that under certain circumstances the true Social Democrat had to resort to "expropriation." It was unavoidable within the framework of his conception of the current scene at a moment when mass insurrection was imminent and intervals between big battles were briefer. Expropriation proved demoralizing to class consciousness only when there was no proper leadership (as that of the proletarian party). He assumed an idealistic purpose for "partisan" activity and that it could be controlled and directed. For he insisted that it had to be strictly in accordance with ideological and organizational conditions. The Fourth and Fifth Congresses of the Social Democratic Party condemned Lenin's arguments as anarchistic and disorganizational and ordered the fighting units disbanded. But the Bolshevik-inspired Tiflis raid on a treasury wagon (which netted 250,000 rubles) renewed the fracas.[27]

The borderland party organizations (in whose territory expropriation incidents gained widest notoriety) stridently demanded the suppression of terror. Polish (Polish Socialist Party), Ukrainian, and Jewish organizations (the Jewish Bund) called for the expulsion of the terrorists. In Poland, Party conferences demanded intensive agitation among the masses to prevent arson and political assassination.[28] The "Bernsteinists" remarked dryly that the "government had finally gotten a condemnation of terror such as it vainly tried to win from the Duma, and most significantly of all, it has been expressed by the extreme left."[29]

In the vital area of trade union connections and leadership the Social Democratic factions likewise were torn by the argument for and against legal operations. Their political control of the workers was generally recognized as unassailable.[30] But the direction of the control was in question during the third campaign. The Fifth Party Congress adopted a Bolshevik-motivated resolution calling for stronger ties with the trade unions because labor organizations obviously had to be dominated by the marxists along with labor. The Mensheviki insisted on politically neutral trade unions to avoid internal strife and were certain that labor would follow the Social Democrats in any case.[31] When the Moscow Bolsheviki resolved to create illegal trade unions in September, 1907, the St. Petersburg Mensheviki protested vigorously that the unions might be decimated and only reaction would benefit. They could point to police orders to destroy unions with active Social Democratic membership. And they stirred the Bolsheviki by calling for all means to preserve trade unions in order to guarantee them at least a semi-legal existence.[32]

It is evident from the contemporary press that except for a few hesitant acts in reaction to the events of June 3, trade union activities were limited primarily to economic interests. The agenda for the Moscow trade union congress reflected a concern for organization and labor economics. But the heavy repression of the post-1905 period hardly allowed for a demarcation between economic and political action. The trade union congress and conferences and meetings of trade union organizations had to be concerned with political terror, relationships with political parties, city and zemstvo governments and their personnel. And these gatherings were usually held without benefit of "administrative observation"—illegally.[33] If the current mood òf the rank and file seemed to favor the Menshevik position, the condition of trade union activity offered a congenial field of operation for the Bolsheviki.[34]

The rigidity of the Bolshevik position on legal operations emerged starkly in a noisy exchange over Plekhanov's article "Groundless Fears" in *Tovarishch* in mid-September, 1907. The journal of the "Bernsteinist intelligentsia" was distasteful by itself for the Bolsheviki and for Lenin this was a major issue. But the article challenged the Bolshevik position on party alliances. The Central Committee charged Plekhanov with insubordination and activity disrupting Party unity in the midst of the election campaign.[35] Plekhanov pointedly used the columns of *Tovarishch* to reply that he could not submit through fear but only through conscience. And since, in his opinion, the order of the Central Committee was illegal, it but made "competent bodies incompetent."[36]

The question of participation in the Third Duma was the most immediately significant interfactional issue among the marxists and it produced the strongest alignments. The great body of the Social Democrats argued for participation and Lenin assumed a position relatively close to the Mensheviki. But he was generally opposed in the Bolshevik ranks, and he was himself largely responsible for his peculiar position. He still suffered the consequences of the Social Democratic tactical error in boycotting the First Duma and his stand seemed inconsistent with his own attitude toward parliamentary activity—particularly after the "state revolution" of June 3, 1907. He had been wrathfully contemptuous of the popular representation. "The Duma is only a toy addition to the bureaucratic and police structure . . . it's all that same Russian police precinct in broadened form."[37] On September 30, 1903, in *Proletarii* he sounded one of the earliest notes of a familiar, almost aristocratic, theme: without Party control "parliament becomes a brothel where gangs of bourgeois politicians are bargaining wholesale and retail about 'people's freedom,' 'liberalism,' 'democracy,' 'republicanism' and other popular commodities."[38]

But ever a *realpolitiker*, Lenin was never fully convinced of the wisdom of boycotting an obvious propaganda forum and the abdication of marxist places to the populists and bourgeois liberals. When the disorientation of the worker suffrage and a resounding Social Democratic victory in the Caucasus became apparent, Lenin voted with the Menshevik majority of the Stockholm Congress in April, 1906, to abandon the boycott and form a Social Democratic fraction.[39] In August, 1906, he came out stoutly for participation in the Duma ("realistically," without exaggerating its significance) to incite economic and political uprising.[40] But as emphatically he defended the boycott of the First Duma as the only means available to counter "constitutional illusions" and expose the "trickery" of Kadets. And it was not until the spring of 1920 that he admitted that "Russian experience has given us . . . one erroneous (1906) application of the boycott by the Bolsheviki."[41]

After June 3, 1907, Lenin was deeply concerned over a strong boycottist current in key Social Democratic organizations. The Central Committee refused to commit itself in the face of moves to boycott the elections in Moscow and St. Petersburg. In the borderlands the Polish Socialist Party was markedly boycottist, but Menshevik allies, the Baltic S. D. Parties, and the Bund decided for participation along with the major Kiev organization.[42] Lenin felt that it was imperative that the tide be turned and he raised a shrill minority voice to warn his fellow Bolsheviki that they would be engulfed ideologically and politically if they would not make even their limited influence felt in a major political campaign. In a speech delivered (probably in Finland) on June 8, he pronounced his basic theses against abstention from the campaign.[43] He called for flexibility of tactics to serve the revolutionary purpose. And he felt impelled again to justify the boycott of 1906 as a successful means of dispelling illusions about reform by constitutional methods in a period of revolutionary upsurge.[44] Then, there was the practical matter of political survival. "When circumstances forced us to do so we had to consider compromise, to enter the Second Duma or suffer defeat."[45] The Duma was not, of course, to be taken seriously. At this juncture it was not to be used even as a revolutionary instrument but only to demonstrate that the government would continue to violate the constitution in the absence of a mass rebellion, to demonstrate the connection between the failure of the December, 1905, uprising and the event of June 3, 1907. In this strange twist of circumstances Lenin's tactical and theoretical thinking coincided in large measure not only with that of the Mensheviki but of the Kadets as well. Like the latter he was calling for a major tactical compromise to serve his ultimate goals.[46]

The opposing Bolshevik viewpoint, offered at a St. Petersburg Social Democratic conference in mid July, held to the standard boycottist arguments: participation in the Duma would mean that the Party sanctioned the events of June 3 while the popular mood was boycottist, and there was little point to electing deputies who would never be heard.[47]

The most powerful Bolshevik counterblast was delivered by I. Kamenev in his brochure "For a Boycott."[48] He bore down on Lenin's admission that the Duma was a convenient, if secondary, arena of action. For Kamenev the question was not when the boycott was more or less useful, but given the weakness of the revolution, whether the boycott or the elections were more harmful to the revolutionary cause. He held that no basic matter of principle was concerned, for the Duma was a second and third rate arena for the cause of the proletariat and the revolution, and no undue attention should be focused on it. "Any attempt to connect the question of boycott and election with the question of development or liquidation of revolution is scholastic."[49] Boycott might seem too elementary a tactic but participation would prove even more so. To go through the motions of election without hope of electing candidates would appear to the masses as something akin to performing a police obligation. The Party's real task at the moment was to choose the proper place to apply the proletariat's limited energy and that was in a boycott campaign. For that would define precisely its proper attitude toward the Duma. It would not distract, as electioneering might, from the campaign to attract the least politically conscious and least revolutionary elements. It was necessary to fight Stolypin's Duma and that was what the boycott was all about.

Lenin's arguments were apparently forceful enough to sway the St. Petersburg organization which opposed boycott by a narrow majority. But the Moscow organization under Bolshevik control stood staunchly for abstention.[50]

The split in the Bolshevik ranks allowed the Mensheviki easy victories in most S. D. *oblast* conferences. In general, the central, northern, Volga, and Ural organizations, dominated by the Bolsheviki, were boycottist, while the southern and border S. D. organizations were participationist.[51] It became apparent from the reports of the *oblast* conferences that official S. D. participation was a foregone conclusion. This position was formally adopted at a national conference held late in July. The balloting, at first close, was decided by the border parties, particularly as the Polish Social Democrats were won over to a definite participationist position and the anti-boycottists triumphed by a vote of 15 to 9. But the motivating resolution passed by only two votes.[52] The latter reflected some evident Leninist influences. The indifferentism of the electorate was offered as proof of the destruction of constitutional illusions and a true, popular perspective of the new Duma. The boycott was justified as a weapon against these illusions, including the idea of a "Duma ministry." And despite the new electoral law, the Social Democrats saw no real change in the nature of the Duma. The Second Duma was Kadet, the Third would be Octobrist. Thus it was reasonable and necessary to join in the third campaign to popularize the S. D. program and to oppose liberal domination of the liberation movement.[53]

The same reasoning permeated the Social Democratic platform for the third campaign which appeared early in August. It was offered by the Central Committee as a compromise between Bolshevik and Menshevik projects. Its first section (a further explanation of the decision to participate in elections) was marked by an appeal to mobilize all revolutionary forces in the campaign. It noted that the rural and urban rich were in a position to select the Duma's deputies; however, if true fighters were elected in the primary elections, the range from which the conservatives might choose would be constricted. Every non-socialist party was declared anathema: the "bloodthirsty, coarse, ignorant and foul" Black Hundreds, the essentially counterrevolutionary Octobrists, and the "double-dealing," anti-popular Kadets who acted as a restraint on revolutionary forces corrupted the revolutionary consciousness of the people and were thus, in fact, accomplices in the perpetration of the crime of June 3. Only the Social Democrats remained the consistent, implacable enemies of the government.[54]

The actual planks of the Party platform were appended briefly to the long policy statement. The Social Democrats would propagate socialism, arouse the population under the leadership of the proletariat to overthrow tsarism, develop the economic and political struggle of the proletariat and "tell the whole truth to the country from the Duma tribune." They would fight reaction and the "counterrevolutionary influences" of the Kadets, the hypocrisy of bills offered by the bureaucracy and the rich in their own interests. The Social Democrats would offer their own democratic demands. These included, besides socialism, a constituent assembly to establish a democratic republic; popular election of officials; civil liberties; a standing army instead of universal military service; equality of nationalities; public education; democratic zemstvos and town dumas; confiscation of all royal, landlord, and public lands to be given over to elected organs and distributed locally. Labor legislation would include an eight-hour day, weekly holidays, state insurance paid for by the capitalists, prohibition of overtime work, an elected factory inspectorate, and a public works program for the unemployed.

V. I. Lenin was probably not enchanted by the planks on land distribution and the "trade union" elements of the labor program.

But his political style is unmistakable in the summation of the argument against boycott and the characterization of the Kadets.

After the Party conference and the promulgation of its program, some organizations shifted their positions and others intensified their anti-boycott activities. The Elizavetgrad organization disclaimed any original intention of remaining inactive.[55] The Kharkov organization scolded its membership for ignoring organizational efforts in connection with the campaign and limiting their "mass activities" to destruction of voter lists, breaking up election meetings, making a considerable noise and other "intensive actions"—enough "to make a rooster laugh."[56]

The St. Petersburg organization oscillated sharply.[57] With some of its primary committees holding out for a boycott, a city conference held early in August, decided to sound out all workers and permit freedom of action for factories and shops which voted against participation. The Party Central Committee annuled the action as contrary to the decisions of the last Party conference. And the St. Petersburg committee fell back into line with the weak explanation that it had offered only a suggestion and not a resolution.[58] Its actions may have been conditioned by the troublesome competition from the anarchistic, independent Workers Party and the Makhaevist "Workers' Plot." Their challenge forced it willy-nilly to hold numerous meetings and gatherings to debate the boycott issue.[59]

In Poland the socialist bloc fell apart. The Polish Socialist Party (PPS) boycotted the third campaign as it had the second. Yet it was the chief hope of the socialists in the "Kingdom" because of its nationalist attraction. The PPS entered the primary elections and named 70 of the 90 delegates in the workers' curia but would not move beyond that stage. They wanted only to prove that the workers more or less disregarded the agitation of the nationalist Christian Democratic and National Democratic Parties. The Jewish Bund and the Social Democrats of Lithuania and Poland were altogether too weak, and neither the nationalists nor the government would allow them a forum.[60] Dogmatism, political inexperience, and weakness compounded to frustrate and further aggravate ethnic and economic minorities.

V
The Restless Borderlands

The peoples of the Russian borderlands had at least in common with the Social Democrats that they experienced a deep
sense of frustration and injustice in the wake of the "governmental revolution" of June 3. But, insofar as they were not
enlisted in the ranks of the boycottist *narodniki,* they decided to
make the most of their diminished political strength that they
might at least be heard. The irritating, sometimes humiliating,
disabilities which the national minorities endured under the
new electoral law contrasted sharply with the favored position
of the Russian population in their midst. But the impact of the
new law was not entirely felicitous from the perspective of its
designers. In some localities, Dvinsk, for example, the changes
actually redounded to the benefit of the Russian liberals. Their
political experience and program seemed to offer the only
visible ray of hope for segments of the local population. With
their strong showing in the first two elections, their candidates
seemed to stand a good chance of reaching the Duma.[1] And in
the Baltic Region with its conservative, vested German gentry
and middle class, the government apparently felt no strong compulsion to enhance the position of the Russian community to
the considerable annoyance and consternation of the latter. The
Riga Octobrists pleaded pitifully with Stolypin for a Russian
curia and a separate Russian deputy. For the nonce, the most
they could expect was a union with the German and Lettish
Octobrists, thereby running the risk of electing a Lettish nationalist.[2]

But generally the administration, central and local, aggressive-
ly favored the interests of the Russians in the border areas. Property qualifications might serve their purposes here as elsewhere
in the Empire. But it was more likely than not that the Russian
viceroy, governor general, or governor would set off the Russian
population in a special electoral category and guarantee its
representation in the Duma no matter how patently disproportionate that might be.

In Poland, Russian strength resided in Warsaw with its

separate Russian deputy. Here the strong Octobrist Party decided to enter the lists against both the Kadets and the Union of the Russian People. They could best the extremists only by attracting the conservative and liberal vote and they presented an image of greater moderation than the party as a whole, particularly on the national question. They opposed autonomy for the Poles, not as Russian nationalists but for the good of the Poles themselves, for Polish autonomy, they were certain, would lead to bloody adventures. They were indeed for self-determination for the Poles—through the establishment of zemstvo organizations in Poland. In mid July they forsook the editorial board of the chief Russian journal, *Varshavskii Viestnik,* when its right-wing majority refused to adopt an Octobrist attitude. And they even placed themselves on record as not opposed to the elimination of the Jewish Pale of Settlement.[3]

But there were some weaknesses in their strategy, perhaps not entirely forseen. For one thing they risked the support of some 22,000 polonized evangelical Russians whose interests might prove more indigenous than Russian. Then, they offered as their candidate Professor Filovich, widely known as a constitutionalist. And they dropped their support for Professor Espiov as too rightist for their tastes. The latter indignantly moved to split the Octobrists by forming a new "Governmental Party" dedicated to the support of every governmental measure, and it attracted the considerable *chinovnik* vote in the Russian curia.[4]

The more conservative and rightist Russian elements had only one purpose: to further increase Russian parliamentary representation in Poland and the western borderlands and reduce still further that of the Polish majority. *Novoe Vremia* suggested that predominance of Polish interests might be countered by limiting all non-Russians to one deputy per province in the "Vistula provinces" while the Russians elected a number of deputies proportionate to their strength in the population of each province.[5] For the moment, the largest Russian community in the borderlands was badly fractionalized—along much the same lines as were the Russians in the heart-land.

The political activity of all of the national minorities in the election campaign presented a characteristic weakness arising from the new electoral law and internal cleavages. Yet the Russian public mind, as reflected in its press, was fascinated by the large Polish electorate and the Jewish minority with their articulate leadership and their potentiality for strengthening nationalist and liberal elements in the western territories of the Empire. The problems confronting both ethnic groups were typical for the electorates of the national minorities.

The first political reaction of the indigenous peoples of the Polish provinces and the western borderlands to the assault on their representation was an almost spontaneous closing of ranks. It seemed that the breach between the Polish nationalists and the "progressives" might be mended. But it was also apparent that if the strong Polish position in the landlord curia (among large and middle landowners) could be joined with the Jewish town vote at the provincial level in the western regions a strong, if multinational, voice for local interests might emerge.[6] The concept was given theoretical precision by Professor A. Lednitski. He declared that all candidates from Poland and the west should represent, and speak for, all social groups. And he proposed the election of an all-national bloc, including the socialists, which should hold to the common principle of the defense of the constitution and Polish rights.[7]

But the non-Polish nationalities dissented vigorously to the emphasis on Polish rights. The constitutionalist Polish-Lithuanian-Bielorussian Party, largely a political community of regional Polish aristocrats which was established after the promulgation of the new electoral law, held with Professor Lednitski in emphasizing local interests. A preamble to the Party's program called for especial attention to the needs and special interests of the "Lithuanians and Bielorussians because of their historical development and economic, ethnographic, and cultural peculiarities." It rejected any "narrow chauvinism" and insisted that the welfare of the region demanded "the common work of all of its inhabitants without exception, of all nationalities living there. The task of our Party is the realization of the possibility of common work, the creation of necessary conditions for a common, cultural life and activity."[8] Here there was obviously a clash with the metropolitan Poles of landlord-ethnic interests and a call for its resolution in a moment of crisis. The program naturally called for national equality, including the Jews; broad, religious toleration; and the "preservation of a Christian spirit in life and learning." The Polish-Lithuanian-Bielorussians identified themselves as limited monarchists, and they held strongly to the fostering and protection of private property as the basis of agrarian reform.[9]

In much the same vein the Polish Krai (Regional) Party, likewise dominated by large landowners, disavowed nationalist

policies emanating from Warsaw, placed local interests above
Polish national matters, and would oppose any union of the
Bielorussian and Lithuanian Northwest Krai with the Polish,
or "Vistula," Region.[10] A meeting of the landowners from the
western (Lithuanian) and southwestern provinces early in
September reiterated the Kraevist emphasis on local interest and
voted to form a regional Kolo (bloc). This body would support
the Polish Kolo, the nationalist Duma fraction, insofar as it did
not contradict regional interests.[11]

At the other end of the political spectrum the marxist Jewish
Bund would have no traffic with elements of the Polish Kolo.
The Bund considered that the Polish nationalists were motivated
entirely by their own advantage and would always remain anti-
semitic and concerned exclusively with Polish national interests. The moderates in the Polish Socialist Party and the Polish
Social Democratic Party stood with them.[12]

The key ingredient in any successful alliance of nationalities
in Poland was the National Democratic Party. From the beginning of the Duma period the "Endeki" dominated a Kolo including moderate progressives (the Realpolitikers and the Polish
Progressives).[13] So certain were they of their preeminent political
position in Poland that they were apparently little concerned
for the cohesion of the Kolo. They would grant the Polish Progressives no representation in its presidium and would coun-
tenance no deviation by the Realpolitikers and Kraevists. Hence
the Polish Progressives and the Realpolitik Party withdrew
from the Kolo. The former maintained that they would avoid
the impression of civil strife in Poland. But they bemoaned the
impossibility of releasing the N. D. grip on the peasantry which
could not understand the difficulties posed by their politically
"monopolistic;" nationalistic program.[14]

For all purposes, the withdrawal of small, liberal and landlord
elements (along with the usual division among the socialists)
meant that the National Democrats were practically unchallenged.
Yet their self assurance represented almost a forlorn, futile gesture.
The Polish delegation had been reduced from forty-six deputies
directly representing Poland in the Duma to ten.[15] And they
sought to make this fistful of nationalists as nearly effective in
the Third Duma as the Kolo was in the Second. Hence, they
would stand as a single monolithic group in order, at the least,
to get representation in committees that counted for them.[16]
Since they would have no influence in Russian affairs, they
renounced all responsibility for participating in them. And they

bitterly pointed to the self defeating nature of the administration's policy. Heretofore they had been willing to compromise with the Russian parties and the government to establish a constitutional regime. But, given the nature of the new law, they would make an important difference between compromise and "penitence." And now they could make no compromises which would not weaken the bureaucratic regime.[17] They observed that the Russian liberals had accused them of taking an equivocal position on the agrarian issue to retain both peasant and landlord vote. In turn they charged these liberals with vagueness on the reduction of Polish representation, the creation of Kholm gubernia, and the educational program in Poland. Yet both Poles and Kadets noted their common appeal to reason: their common moderate temperament.[18]

The most aggressive and capable leadership from the Russian extreme right had come from the western border regions. And this experience haunted all of the indigenous minorities, particularly the Jews. Hence the possibility of a Polish—Jewish bloc, or at least some action to assure mutual support naturally emerged. The first inclination of the Jewish political leadership, like the Polish, was to urge a closing of ranks to assure the election of an exclusively Jewish deputy in the Duma, if possible. But they were resigned to indirect representation, through moderately liberal Poles, since they were aware that the National Democrats could not control nationalist and anti-Jewish sentiment among the landowners, peasantry, and clergy.[19] But the longstanding ideological differences among the Jews resting on philosophical and religious grounds and class sustained a habitual state of disunity which rendered them politically ineffective. All groups were united in their opposition to restrictive legislation on domicile, occupation, and education. And they would unite spontaneously in the face of pogrom activity and the administration's lacksadaisical (or even sympathetic) attitude toward it.

The greater part of the Jewish community in Poland and the western borderlands supported the Society For Equal Rights For Jews (*Obshchestvo Polnopraviia Evreev*) and its splinter, the Jewish Popular Group (*Evreiskaia Narodnaia Gruppa*).[20] In the third campaign both organizations accepted the Kadet program along with planks for specifically Jewish concerns.[21] The Jewish Popular Group firmly supported the Kadet slate and condemned the formation of infinitesimal groups each speaking in the name of the Jewish population. Some spokesmen of the

Society For Equal Rights seemed to question Kadet sincerity in matters of concern for the Jews, and they brought upon themselves the wrath of the Popular Group and the liberals by polling the various candidates on the question of self-determination for the Jews.[22] The Kadets mobilized their best oratorical forces from among their Jewish membership (G. B. Sliozberg, M. M. Vinaver) to emphasize that in the entire Duma period the Jewish question had been one of their main concerns. And they listed speeches, bills, interpellations, and expert organizational effort devoted to Jewish rights and anti-pogrom activity.[23] The Kadet concern was superfluous. The plebescite of sorts, conducted among the Jewish electorate by the Society for Equal Rights in mid October, indicated a clear choice for Kadet candidates.[24]

Conservative and nationalist groups and, in a sense, the Jewish Bund were opposed to coordination of efforts with non-Jews, or concentration of effort on purely Jewish problems. Ultraconservatives (like the Khassidic sect) feared liberal and revolutionary influences that made for religious indifferentism or godlessness among the Jewish youth.[25] But it was the Zionists who were largely responsible for the fragmentation of the political efforts of the Society for Equal Rights by their insistence on a separate fraction in the Duma concerned with Jewish, and particularly national interests. In 1910 they carried on a separate campaign with their own candidates attacking the Equal Rightists as assimilationists. They charged that, like the Kadets, the Equal Rightists were really not representative of Jewish interests.[26] But it was always apparent that they would play only a limited political role. In the first two Dumas the Zionists were more or less identified with the Kadets, and in the third elections they were hopelessly dispersed among the "bourgeois nationalists" and various minute socialist factions.[27] And except for relatively small proletarian groups the Jewish voters in the third election campaign continued to favor urban liberal candidates.

The position of the Bund in the matter of cooperation with non-Jewish elements was somewhat anomalous. Like other Social Democrats among the national minorities, they would join with non-marxist elements only insofar as that was practical and with the Populists and liberals when necessary. Their chief concern lay with the Jewish proletariat, and they warned specifically against traffic with the Polish Endeki for fear that Polish nationalists would disregard Jewish interests in general and particularly those of the workers. Like the Jewish nationalists they were too weak politically to play a significant, independent role in the elections in Poland and the western border-lands.[28]

Other ethnic electorates were confronted by problems identical with those which weakened the Polish and Jewish vote. Their strength was shattered by the Law of June 3, and they further diluted their political force by forming into numerous splinter groups. United action was inhibited by ideological, economic, and traditional, often irrational, hostilities within and among the various minorities.

These factors were nowhere more evident than in the backing and filling that accompanied the formation of blocs among the ethnic minorities. In Lifliand (Livland), for example, the Letts considered various proposals to counter or nullify German strength. Their first inclination was to ignore the Balts in the first category where they were particularly strong. But any effort to elect Lettish nationals would require the help of other nation-alities. Since the Letts insisted that only their candidates sit in the Duma, projected coalitions with Poles, Jews, Lithuanians, and Russians proved chimerical.[29] Lithuanians and Bielorus-sians, we saw, could not accept analogous demands by the Poles.[30]

Again, as with the Jews and Poles, other significant minority electorates were severally sundered from within and poised against each other by differences among nationalists, socialists, and liberals. In the Trans-caucasus the Armenians clung staunchly to the nationalist Social Revolutionary Dashnaktsut-iun leadership.[31] The Moslems of the region had been finely splintered in the second elections but managed to lead a Moslem fraction in the Second Duma. And in the third elections Men-sheviki, Kadets, and Octobrists struggled for predominance among them under the new electoral law.[32]

The Moslem Union, a focal organization in the Caucasus, was constitutionalist, and its application for legalization raised fundamental questions concerning the nature of the post-October regime.[33] The St. Petersburg Special Office for Society and Union Affairs allowed it to register after due consideration. The Chairman of the Office, City Prefect General D. V. Drachev-skii, annulled the decision. He argued that the Moslem Union sought to establish a constitutional monarchy and according to article 99 of the Criminal Code any deprivation of the Tsar's authority or the limitation of his rights was punishable by death. Hence, the goal of the Moslem party was criminal. Four members of the Office disagreed. They saw in the Union's action no contradiction of the Fundamental Laws since the monarch was limited now constitutionally by Articles 86 and 87 of the Fundamental Laws and principles announced in the Manifesto of October 17, 1905. General Drachevskii, burdened with bureaucratic responsibility and the attitudes it begot, protested to the Ministry of the Interior that Articles 1, 4, and 222 of the Fundamental Laws established the unlimited authority of the Tsar. He asserted that the Articles (86 and 87) establishing the Imperial Duma and the Imperial Council in no way limited the Supreme Authority since it could both order and annual these Articles. The "Tsar-Emperor" ordered them as a "standing rule" as stated in the October Manifesto. He contended that the Moslem Union would change the Fundamental Laws, and only the Tsar could do that according to Article 87 of these Laws. The City Prefect rested his case on Article 6 Section I of the Provisional Rules of March 4, 1906, on Societies and Unions.[34]

The case was remanded to the Ministry of the Interior and Assistant Minister Kryzhanovskii's report simply evaded the basic issues of principle. It did not consider whether the Fundamental Laws limited autocratic power and whether a constitutional monarchy did in fact exist. The Moslems were refused registration because their application was not sufficiently definite in indicating how the measures they proposed to establish a constitutional monarchy corresponded with the Fundamental Laws. The Ministry took another tack in arguing against legalization of the Moslem Union on political grounds. It held that this organization would serve only to further arouse national animosities, especially in areas with large Moslem populations as in Kazan, Ufa, Orenburg, and other places. Hence, harking back to Article 6, Section I of the Provisional Rules, the decision held that the Moslem Union might threaten public and state security and its request for registration was rejected. The Ruling Senate concurred with the findings of the Ministry of the Interior on October 24, 1907.[35]

The issue of the registration of the Moslem Union vividly reflected an almost crass insensitivity to, and perhaps a psychological alienation from, broad strata of public opinion still recovering from the blows of June 3, 1907. The government did not consider, much less challenge, General Drachevskii's unliteral interpretation of the nature of imperial authority. And regardless of the administration's effort to avoid the issue, the essential nature of the modified regime was in question. Rejection of the Moslem application on largely putative grounds,

straining the interpretation of criminal law, was bound to produce profound disquiet not only among liberal and revolutionary elements but in that "other third" of the population that was
non-Russian. For them, as for the opposition as a whole, the
regime seemed to be violating its own rules for the political
game.[36]

VI
The Blocs:
The Potential for Political Cooperation

The "continental" multiparty system with its attendant ideological nuances and the manipulation of the suffrage by the Election Law of June 3, 1907, practically constrained the various political elements to join in election blocs. These had proved relatively effective in the first and second campaigns. But the prevalence of loose party structure and discipline and a penchant for ideological rigidity tended to frustrate carefully planned agreements.

The extreme ideology and propaganda of the rightists, chiefly of the Union of the Russian People and its semi-autonomous satellites, seemed to preclude a voting bloc with other elements, including even the more moderate nationalists.[1] Given the constant factor of clashing, unstable personalities, it was difficult enough for the URP to corral M. L. Dezobri and his "Active Struggle" and the more intellectual and moderate "Russian Assembly" into a single bloc. It was the position of the URP as the source of some funds and effective speakers that ultimately produced an agreement of sorts on campaign tactics.[2] But differences of purpose and temperament effectively obstructed the formation of a single "Russian National Party" which would include the Octobrists and the Party of Legal Reform along with the rightists. The conservative groups placed considerable emphasis on Russian nationalism but they were likewise constitutionalists of a conditional order.

The normal and first tendency of the right and conservative center was to arrange for joint action wherever that was considered necessary and feasible—as in Warsaw, Kiev, Poltava, Kremenchug, and Moscow. The URP actually advanced to the point of considering the circumstances under which all blocs with the center could operate, that is, only for runoff elections. And in some places, at least, it was apparent that some of the Octobrists were attracted by the program and tactics of the extreme right. Rightist Octobrists complained (almost in a Bolshevik vein) that the Octobrist Central Committee was trying to blur sharp differences with the Kadets and that its hesitancy paralyzed efforts to conclude political alliances.[3] But the general incompatibility of the extreme right and the conservatives begot a concrete reaction relatively early in the campaign. The Rightist July Congress had expressly forbidden any arrangements with parties which would limit autocracy. And in repeated statements the Octobrist Central Committee explained that its Party was making arrangements only with rightists who approximated the Octobrist stand for the purpose of countering liberals and leftists. They would never accommodate themselves to extremist elements.[4] The URP branches in the capitals and other large centers (Elets, Tula, Vilno, Saratov) moved toward the Octobrists, but rifts seem to have sprung, in some cases from local squabbles, concerning procedure and candidates. And the Chief Council had to remind its branches at the end of September of the July decision.[5]

In numerous localities and in some of the main centers of the borderlands where national consciousness was naturally exaggerated, neither the Black Hundreds nor the Octobrists paid much heed to the central directives while consulting their immediate interests. Blocs jelled in Kiev, Minsk, Vilno, Smolensk, and Vladikavkaz to "elect only Russians," to propose "True Russian candidates," or to "oppose progressives."[6] But in Warsaw an interparty committee disintegrated soon after its formation on June 3, 1907 as both the URP and the Octobrists refused to yield on the matter of candidates. The URP, considering itself favored by local officialdom, regarded the Octobrists somewhat haughtily and addressed them sharply for any concessions they might propose in the areas of self government and cultural autonomy.[7]

When the campaign reached the crucial point of balloting, both rightist and Octobrist discipline tended to disintegrate throughout the country and illegitimate blocs had to be sanctioned by central organs. This was especially true in the central and southern provinces—at such widely scattered points as Tula, Pavlograd, Samara, and Voronezh—where the attractive power of the Kadets posed a threat of growing, but sometimes exaggerated, proportions. The Octobrists were at times embarrassed by rightist excesses, as in Voronezh and Kharkov where they were hard pressed to justify the "constitutionalism" of their rightist allies.[8] But in the capitals and many major provincial centers the Octobrists and right joined almost spontaneously to counter the liberal opposition and revolutionary left.[9]

In the course of the third campaign in the summer and fall of 1907 both the Union of October 17 and the Constitutional Democrats were called upon, and felt impelled, to define their respective relations with neighboring political elements. The credentials of both were challenged, and a clear call to combine their efforts for the constitutional cause brought the usual recriminations. But more important, it afforded each an opportunity to define its position in the Russian political spectrum with some precision and offer justification for that position. The Octobrists would defend their constitutionalism; the Kadets, the nature of their relationships with the Octobrists and the left.

The Octobrists, it seemed, were driving hard to elect their own candidates, but the rank and file in the provinces looked to the right which provided aid and alternative, more congenial figures to pit against the liberal constitutionalists and the socialist left. But some widely known moderates, chiefly from the Party of Peaceful Renovation,[10] were moved by what they regarded as imperative necessity to unite all constitutionalists against any threat to their cause. They believed that if they could but mobilize the electorate behind all constitutionalist candidates they would be able to endow the Duma with a content "unforseen" by the Law of June 3, 1907. In the realm of practical politics the small, intellectual Peaceful Renovationist Party would search out channels through which its influence might be exerted most effectively.

The formidable hurdles, political and psychological, obstructing any Octobrist-Kadet union became apparent at once. Intellectual habits and political practices of a negative order inhibited and, at times, paralyzed efforts at political combination. These attitudes and stratagems arose from the long doctrinaire struggle between Russian political groupings and the absence of a tradition of compromise in the unrelenting battle for political liberalization and social change under autocracy. And they were not easily cast off. Programmatic differences, particularly in the area of agricultural legislation, could only arouse misgivings among the conservatives and impatience and frustration among the liberals. These differences could only exacerbate conflict arising from clashes of temperament and political attitudes. Then there were practical considerations. The Octobrists were in a favorable position which they would not abandon lightly. The Kadets, for their part, were not likely to cast any shadow on their constitutionalism, always under the critical scrutiny of the excitable left.

In an open letter to A. I. Guchkov and P. N. Miliukov, a Peaceful Renovationist spokesman, Prince E. P. Trubetskoi, argued his cause with obvious feeling and a sense of frustration.[11] He stressed the need to unite their respective parties and warned that failure to join forces would only weaken their representation, especially in the city categories. Together they might deflect the intent of the electoral law. In the face of Kadet emphasis on ideological incompatibility with the Octobrists, he stressed the matter of winning elections. He sought to counter the rigid Kadet posture by an appeal to evaluate the position of the Octobrists in relation to the right. If they supported the Octobrists, the Kadets would be deceiving no one about the nature of the Duma but might begin to transform it into a truly effective body. He observed that all constitutionalists had worked together in the zemstvos where there was no hint of aristocracy in spirit or act. The liberals might "democratize" the "destructive" left and the Octobrists could fashion a conservatism that was "peaceful, cultured, democratic." The alternative might be a "*pugachevshchina* that will flick the Kadet constitution and culture from the face of the earth."

M. A. Stakhovich, another prominent "mediator" from the Party of Peaceful Renovation, appealed largely to the Kadets (in the final weeks of the campaign) as one "thoroughly familiar . . . with the shades of party moods of the *pomiestchiki.*"[12] He noted the diffusion of the landlords in small groups on the right and the need to draw more moderate elements toward a conservative-liberal center. He advised the Kadets to mobilize the peasantry among whom he was certain they enjoyed prestige as evidenced by the large vote they attracted in the first two elections. Then they might join this combination in a bloc with the Octobrists to offer constitutionalist candidates. He predicted that this bloc might seat a core group of 150 constitutionalists in the Duma to keep the rightists under control.

The isolation of these moderately liberal, intellectual aristocrats from the mood and purposes of the political scramble in the liberal and revolutionary arenas is evident. They hardly gauged the compulsion which the Kadets felt constantly to justify their position (to articulate populist, labor, and ethnic elements) as true leaders in the constitutional struggle for achieving basic reform. They did not seem to sense the acute suspicion among the marxists and populists of the "bourgeois" intellectuals who might cloud their dogmas and express reservations on, and alternatives for, the means chosen to attain their ends. They did not perceive that there could be no easy communication of spirit between Kadets and the leftist leadership or the bulk of those they represented. And with the extremists in the revolutionary tradition there was hardly a chance for mutual understanding.

Nor were the conservative and liberal targets of the Peaceful Renovationist campaign likely to be moved sensibly. If Prince Trubetskoi's appeal was launched early in the electoral campaign, Stakhovich's came too late in the political day to have any palpable effect. The call for coordination only seemed to harden positions already assumed. The Kadet leader, Professor Miliukov, doubted that any combination could counter the reactionary opposition to reform[13] or that the Kadets could mobilize the peasantry and intelligentsia. A bloc with the Octobrists would only indicate Kadet support of the new electoral law while it was their purpose to utilize whatever attraction they had to demonstrate that there was no real support for those political elements on which the government relied. For this the Kadets had to appear alone. Their political strength rested on their ideology and reform program, and Prince Trubetskoi's proposal could only tear them from their political base now decimated by the new law. Further while Miliukov saw some virtues of a practical nature in the "lesser evil" concept (avoidance of control by extremists) offered by those who proposed a constitutionalist bloc, he was doubtful that the Octobrists were able to cooperate with the Kadets in the Duma. The conservatives had always held too narrow a view of the franchise and could not accept the Kadet agrarian program, the real basis for their popular authority.

As was their wont, the Kadets remained equivocal in discussing their relations with the left. They recognized the threat to parliamentary government from the revolutionaries but they shrank from the prospect of complete isolation from this significant segment of the opposition. Miliukov argued that G. A. Aleksinskii, the leader of the Social Democratic Fraction in the Second Duma, represented a real electorate as opposed to political diletantism among the Octobrists. Yet his explicit preference for Social Democrats in the Duma to Social Democrats in the streets implied an element of control that contradicted his professions of little or no influence on the left.[14]

The Octobrists were no less adamant and somewhat more belligerent than the Kadets. They, too, saw little prospect of communication with their projected partners, given their ideological and programmatic inflexibility. A. I. Guchkov sharply resented Miliukov's exposition of the Kadet stand. He saw it as an "unexampled, crude, party egoism" which would divide the Duma, leaving it without a defined majority. The Kadets, he charged, refused to regard anything not Kadet as constitutional. And *Golos Moskvy* characterized Miliukov and his ilk as persons with great pretensions and impatience who preferred select "crowds" and designated hostile "antipodes."

For the Octobrists, the Kadets strongly resembled the left and were altogether too close to it. Like the revolutionaries, the liberals aroused popular dissatisfaction to bring pressure on the government. They had effective control over left-wing elements in the first two Dumas and were largely responsible for the obstructionism of these bodies. Their program insisted on autonomy for the national minorities and perhaps, most dangerous of all, their agrarian project called for the obligatory expropriation of some landlord property. Before they would deign to deal with the Kadets the Octobrists demanded that they break completely from the left.[16]

In the realm of political manoeuvering, the Octobrists could see little advantage for themselves in a union with the Kadets. An agreement between them would only disturb their congenial relationship with the regime which favored them and the moderate rightists. The electoral law could not but benefit them, and in the provinces the rank and file was not likely to obey directives from the party leadership to look away from non-constitutionalist elements.[17] Hence on October 4, 1907, the Octobrist Central Committee rejected any general agreement with the Kadets on the grounds that they were politically unreliable. They proposed instead a coalition with the monarchists and those rightists who would support the Party because it would work with the government for reform. They would, in fact, direct their efforts to defeat the Kadets in the *guberniia* elections.[18] In the last stages of the provincial and city elections neither the Octobrists nor the extreme right needed nudging to form alliances of convenience—official and unofficial—in such major centers as Warsaw, St. Petersburg, Moscow, Kharkov, Ekaterinoslav, and Grodno.[19]

Novoe Vremia placed its finger on the essence of the Kadet-Octobrist relationships (and a characteristic attitude in Russian party relations) with the observation that "opening bargaining by bidding between Kadets and Octobrists can by itself hardly serve to shame one party or the other. The question leads chiefly to *kto kogo obedet i na chem* (who can overtake whom and on what)."[20]

There were no real grounds for serious concern about a formal election arrangement between the liberals and leftists despite the government's attitude and Octobrist and rightist charges of collusion with the revolutionaries. Here was a significant factor

insufficiently appreciated by moderate administrative and political elements. For the Kadets now had neither the interest nor
the capacity to join with a left bloc, although they would not, of
course, reject any proffered support from the various leftist parties
and fractions. Relations with the left begot no heart-searching by
the Kadets and no compulsion to explain why practical combinations were, or were not, made. The Kadets were far more concerned that their image as an oppositional, and not a revolutionary, element be crystal clear.

The fact was that neither side, the liberals or leftist grouping,
particularly wanted political collusion. There were those on the
left who were relatively close to the Kadets and those who would
not hear of any relations whatever with the liberals. Thus, as
with the Octobrists, there could be only practical arrangements
in the localities as the possibility or need for them arose or was
regarded as imperative.

Professor Miliukov and a number of editorial statements in
Riech berated the government and both the right and left for
consistent misconceptions concerning the Kadet position.[21]
Since the formation of the Constitutional Democratic Party and
especially since the participation of much of the Kadet leadership
in the proceeding at Vyborg in the preceding summer, it had
been exasperated by the government's refusal to differentiate
between the chief liberal organization and the revolutionary
left. And the Kadets faced the perennial difficulty of intellectuals
in identifying themselves with causes and attitudes at wide vari-
ance from those generally held by the socioeconomic strata from
which they stemmed; in the case of the Kadets, chiefly from the
liberal professions and landlords. The Kadets complained that
the administration and the political opponents of the liberals
simply would not understand that there was no connection between the nature of Kadet relations with the left and with the
popular masses. The right was certain that the source of Kadet
authority was in the political left. And the leftists were as certain
that the Kadets depended on them because they had no mass
support. It was simply impossible, the Kadets held, to influence
the views of the government and the rightists, and the left was
incurably doctrinaire. It saw only capitalists and proletariat and
ignored that highly complex intermediary element (even in the
face of Karl Marx's social analysis) which included the peasantry
and was extremely difficult to organize because of its complexity.
The Kadets maintained that the source of their authority was in
their program and consistent democracy and they were not con-

cerned that the left would cut them off from the masses. For the revolutionaries promised only distant "perspectives" while the Kadets would get tangible results for them. They would always remain oppositional (as opposed to revolutionary) and efforts to define the degree of their opposition were meaningless and contradicted the seriousness and breath of their purposes.[22]

The Constitutional Democrats readily understood why misconceptions concerning their relations with the left might arise. For liberals and leftists did have certain characteristics in common which might provide facile proof of their common purposes. The authority of both rested on mass support. Both professed principles which "differentiate a citizen from a subject," principles of "universal human citizenship" based on natural rights as against historic rights. With considerable indulgence the Kadets were able to contend that the left as well as the liberals rested on law while their common opponents would ultimately resort to force.[23] The Kadets acknowledged that their practical, political, and social program approached that of the socialists at many points. And it was only natural to identify liberals and socialists when they were subjected to common and persistent repression by the authorities.[24]

But the Kadets were as certain that their differences with the revolutionaries were fundamental and were emphatically acknowledged by the left as a normal part of their political propaganda. For one thing, the Kadets were confident that the leftists had come to regard them as dangerous competitors since the liberals recognized the leftist mood of the population and tailored their programs accordingly. In the Second Duma it was quite evident that, except on the question of the election of the presidium, Kadets and socialists were always opposed to each other. They had differed profoundly on their respective evaluations of the real "relationship of forces" and the potential strength of the Duma. The constitutionalism of the Kadets, their "consistent democracy," and their competing programs predetermined a clash of interests.[25] In this connection they acknowledged that the leftists had harmed the liberals to a degree by portraying them variously as bourgeoisie, *pomietchiki,* and "official" reformists of the Stolypin stripe, all opposed to popular interests.[26]

Finally, the Kadets observed that there were basic tactical differences between the Kadets and the left. A close analysis of leftist tactics would indicate that they ranged from near-Kadet to extremist. And the fate of those like the Popular Socialists whose program and tactics approximated those of the liberals would seem to indicate that no intermediary position could be maintained between the predominant socialist elements and the liberal party. The great body of "non-party leftists," the true intermediary elements, could not create a code of unified principles of action while vaccilating between the center and left.[27]

Moderate liberals and even some socialists reacted to the unbending position of the Kadet and socialist leadership in much the same manner as had the Peaceful Renovationists. As the excitement of the campaign mounted and the possibility of a conservative-rightist landslide emerged, moderate circles importuned everyone in opposition to the regime to face realities. *Tovarishch* (on election day for deputies from chief centers) insisted that the left and the Kadets simply had to unite in the face of demonstrated reactionary tendencies by the Octobrists and rightists and the realities of local politics. And the liberal *Russkie Viedomosti* asserted that as long as the constitutional structure was not firmly established, the left and the Kadets would be logical allies.[28] Then, G. V. Plekhanov aroused a considerable stir by publicly advocating a liberal-socialist union in the struggle against the "Black Hundreds." And he characterized the silence of those who failed to support him as "harmful" and "incomprehensible."[29]

Along with the debate on the boycott, and in large measure related it, the question of electoral agreements offered the marxists still another area for sharp intra-party strife. With slight variations this was but a continuation of the argument in the second elections and hinged largely on the attitude of the Bolsheviki toward the Kadets. Reports from a number of conferences of Social Democratic organizations indicated that the old pattern was favored. They would keep apart from all others in the primary balloting and propaganda in city elections, and in runoff elections it would be necessary to support "sharply oppositional" parties, especially the socialist. The conference left open the question of relations with the Kadets until the liberals took a definite stand on alliances with the Octobrists.[30]

Early in June the Central Committee published a project of "the basic regulations on agreements of the RSDLP with other parties in elections to the Duma." This, too, was a compromise pronouncement. In cities voting directly for deputies to the Duma, the Social Democrats were to appear independently and enter into no agreements. In runoff elections they were to seek agreements only with parties to the left of the Kadets. At the second stage of elections, in the provinces, the Kadets might be included in the agreements, presumably to counter the conservatives and rightists. But, in the order of their priority, the Social Democrats were to ally themselves with the Social Revolutionaries, the Trudoviki, the Popular Socialists, and Kadets. There were to be no blocs with parties which made agreements with Octobrists, Peaceful Renovationists, and rightist elements. In the workers' curia there were to be no agreements except with the national Social Democratic organizations (the Bund, the Polish Socialist Party etc.). Agreements had to be non-ideological and were subject to the veto of the highest party organ in a given electoral district.[31]

Ideologically, temperamentally, and emotionally, Lenin could find no virtue whatever in blocs which included the Kadets. Even before the promulgation of the projected rules on agreements, and with a party conference impending, he offered his predictable views in a lengthy article.[32] The key issue, he asserted, was the attitude toward the bourgeois parties. The Bolsheviki would lead the peasantry in a struggle against tsarism and the liberals. The Mensheviki would abdicate the lead to the bourgeoisie in a bourgeois revolution. They would forego a struggle to establish a dictatorship of the proletariat and the peasantry and limit the proletariat to a role of extreme opposition. In the current campaign this meant that the Bolsheviki might form a bloc only with the Populists while the Mensheviki would make arrangements "case by case" with socialist and liberals. But the Kadets would never yield landlord holdings to the peasants and these conflicting interests had to be clarified to free the peasantry from the influence of the bourgeois intellectuals. Yet Menshevik tactics blurred just these differences. Lenin argued that agreements with the Kadets violated the decisions of the London (Fifth) Congress which permitted election alliances only with the revolutionaries in a "left bloc." With his intensely ideological, perhaps psychological, aversion for the Kadets, he apparently discarded as insincere their program for obligatory expropriation. And in this connection he certainly identified the practitioners of the liberal professions with his bourgeois stereotypes.

Later, in August of 1907, Lenin offered several supplementary thoughts.[33] He averred that the Mensheviki, with numerous bourgeois intellectuals in their ranks, had a compulsion to subordinate the peasantry to the liberals and give ultimate priority to landlord interests. Yet, alliance with the Kadets would enhance the liberal campaign to prevent utilization of the Duma as a podium for revolutionary propaganda. In a bloc with them, the proletariat would become only their sorry appendage. Lenin was pressing his basic argument against the "tail" (*khvost*) role for the Marxists.

After the usual, prolonged bickering, the Party conference emerged with a paste-pot pronouncement differing little from that offered by the Central Committee earlier in the month. The Bolsheviki would get their socialist bloc and the Mensheviki their broad alliances—all in good time. The Party would consort only with socialists in the cities but might vote for Kadet candidates to defeat the rightists in the provincial assemblies. In the worker curia where they expected no challenge, the Social Democrats would act independently at all stages.[34]

Compromise resolutions had never satisfied either wing of the Social Democratic Party and arguments and recriminations continued. As the moment of final decision approached, the Mensheviki were particularly concerned about the requirement that there be no alliance with the Kadets in the cities. They feared a fatal split in the ranks of the opposition, and their spokesman, L. Martov, incisively expounded his views in an article-letter to all Party organizations.[35] The logic of the conference resolution escaped him. He could not understand why it was forbidden to vote with the Kadets in the cities in either primary or runoff elections and yet join with them in the final stage of voting elsewhere—as in the *guberniia* electoral assemblies. The Social Democrats could make their point, could contrast their program as sharply as possible, with those of all other parties on the first ballot in cities. But a division of leftist and opposition votes in runoff elections in cities might mean victory for the reactionaries. In Martov's opinion the Party was not confined to this impossible position. The conference decision had not considered specifically how the Party was to act if the Social Democratic candidates for the elector received neither first nor second place in the primary elections and a runoff was required. Martov's shrewd solution was only likely to infuriate the Bolsheviki as a manoeuvre to avoid the direct issue—in the manner of the Kadets: he would make agreements with no one on voting or the distribution of seats but would carry on an intensive propaganda campaign to impress on the Social Democratic suffrage that if they could not elect their own candidates they had to defeat the rightists by all means. And he appealed to the Party not to assume the view generally held by the Bolsheviki that it was all the same whether a reactionary or a Kadet was elected.

The Bolshevik and Menshevik positions subtly reflected their respective commitments to parliamentary procedure. The Mensheviki felt the need for a predominantly bourgeois, reformist deputation. And for all his concern for socialist representation in the Duma, Lenin did not place so high a value on it that he would tolerate support for the ideologically dangerous and "untrustworthy" liberal intellectuals.

Some significant areas and local party organizations actually began to move toward Martov's position. A resolution by the Ukrainian Spilka reflected his views.[36] And the St. Petersburg organization decided to join with the Kadets and related parties in runoff elections in the second city category, where the Social Democrats were obviously weak.[37] But in practice, the St. Petersburg Social Democrats could reach no general agreement on firm action. They apparently sensed no real danger from the right, at least to their own candidates, and they tended to take various, independent directions. Some abstained; some formed a common list with other leftists—to demonstrate the strength of the "democratic" elements; and others, especially the Bolsheviki, drew up independent lists to demonstrate their own strength.

At the beginning of July the Central Committee declared the campaign opened and called on low income voters to register. The direction of the appeal to the electorate was given to a central election committee consisting of the Central Committee and three members of the St. Petersburg Committee. After considerable discussion the machinery for the campaign was set up at the end of July and early August.[38] Important local organizations, like the St. Petersburg city election committee were not actually operative until mid or late August.[39] Ward election committees came into being at about the same time, although their functions had been defined during the preceding month. They were to mobilize the electorate by political agitation, assist it in the complex electoral procedures, especially those imposed on the low income groups, and study the strength and leadership of the various political groupings in the localities.[40] At an even lower level they were assisted by "non-party" factory committees and even street committees.[41]

Given the centralized structure of the Social Democratic Party, it was quite natural for the city and provincial committees to name candidates for deputy to the Duma from their respective areas. Lenin noted that the St. Petersburg Committee had no other alternative because of the difficulty of calling a city conference.[42] Yet, a city-wide meeting was called for in St. Petersburg

at the beginning of September which named six Bolsheviki as
the Social Democratic electors.[43]

With propaganda as their stock in trade, the election campaign
offered no problems for the Social Democrats other than assuring
its effectiveness and coping with the usual intra-party differences.
They had to be watchful of government interference but this did
not seem to inhibit the "flying groups" of orators or prevent the
calling of meetings in shops and factories.[44] The Central Committee proposed to establish a central organ with Lenin as editor
but the membership would not hear of it. Hence the Party published a campaign leaflet, *Pravitel'stvo*, and collected speeches
of eminent social democrats for the edification of the electorate.[45]

With the approach of the final elections to the Duma, political
considerations became paramount. Arrangements between the
liberals and socialists were made as quickly as necessity dictated,
in both categories and in such widely separated localities as
Kiev, Voronezh, and Baku. At times, failure to combine and the
resultant splintered vote (as in Vologda) begot, at the least, defeat for opposition candidates on the first ballot and a belated
sense of urgency to combine against conservatives and rightists.[46]

But the great body of leftist voters sought to establish a bloc
of sorts to forestall a Kadet victory where possible. Yet, they
would join the liberals to prevent Octobrist and rightist success-
es. The Trudoviki took the initiative to broach a merger of all
Populists and Social Democrats, and the "progressive non-partisans" were gradually drawn into the select circle. The Social
Revolutionaries took themselves out of consideration by voting
to boycott the elections. And the Social Democrats, after some
vaccilation, decided to enter a common list only in the second
category. This, after all, was their only chance of obtaining seats
from elections in the major centers. They were certain that the
Kadets would allow the leftists, perforce, a seat if they felt that
the combined Octobrist-"left bloc" opposition would forestall
an absolute Kadet majority in a given election.[47] They motivated their insistence on differentiating themselves from the
Narodniki by pointing to the varying interests of their respective
proletarian and peasant bases.[48]

On September 25, the central bodies of the Popular Socialists
and Trudoviki took concrete steps to include the leftist non-
partisan voters, trade union organizations, and nationality groups
in the leftist bloc, and they offered a common list of candidates
for the second category in St. Petersburg. It included some of the
most outstanding figures of the component elements—L. I. Lut-

iugen, the Popular Socialist, A. A. Dermianov of the Trudoviki, and the "Progressive Non-Partisan," A. D. Zarudny.[49] Stubbornly and consistently dogmatic, the Social Democrats qualified their participation in runoff elections. They would join with the left bloc only if there were a chance of defeating the Octobrists. And only after a Kadet sweep in the first ballot in St. Petersburg was N. D. Sokolov joined with Lutiugen for the bloc.[50]

The propaganda campaign of the Narodniki was negative and inept. They could see little fruitful work in the Duma but would assure a rostrum for some leftists.[51] They appealed to the Jews to vote for Zarudny and Sokolov to reward their services as lawyers in the Kishinev pogrom trial. And to the Poles they offered the opportunity to fight for the right of all citizens.[52] Their imaginative level was aptly reflected in Zarudny's call to vote with the left "because the heart is on the left side."[53]

VII
The Designation of the Russian Voter*

The election period, broadly speaking, began with the publication of the new law. The largest cities responded almost at once, but to ensure a universally orderly procedure the Ministry of the Interior required the publication of all registration lists by July 25, 1907. Governors and governors-general originally established dates in mid July which they had to extend later to less optimistic deadlines ranging into early August in major population centers.[1]

The capitals set up registration within a week after June 3— Moscow on June 5 and St. Petersburg on June 7. In St. Petersburg all city employees assigned to registration work had to forego vacations, and by June 25 the city administration had increased its staff by 115. Preference was given to persons with previous experience, most of whom were students. In Moscow, Mayor P. I. Guchkov assigned the task of compiling lists to the Statistical Department of the city administration. Procedures in the rural areas apparently kept pace with the larger centers.[2] By mid July lists were compiled for St. Petersburg *uiezd* and for the city on August 4; all temporary employees were released (with a bonus of 25 rubles) on October 26. In Moscow registration was completed by August 16, but in Odessa not until the end of August.[3] To the officials involved, the work appeared to progress slowly enough. Funds for the operation were readily provided although not officially confirmed until the end of July, when Stolypin's request for 400,000 rubles for preparatory work and registration was granted.[4]

It became apparent at once that the lists compiled for the Bulygin Duma were hopelessly outdated in their information on landowners and wealthier elements. The lists of second category voters had also been considerably disarranged since the Second Duma, because many persons had moved or were in arrears in their taxes. Since it would be costly to compile new lists, the local officialdom turned to agencies designated in the law for information: financial offices, governmental agencies, and city and zemstvo administra-

*The greater part of the materials in this chapter appeared in author's article "The Russian Voter in the Elections to the Third Duma", *The Slavic Review*, December, 1962, pp. 663-677.

tions. In Moscow, the Statistical Department made a house-to-house canvass to examine apartment registries and to question voters individually.[5]

Unforeseen difficulties constantly arose, since the complex and hastily written electoral law required interpretation at every step, and the inexperience and cultural level of the officials and the electorate made accurate compilation difficult. The routine task of rooting out ineligible voters was, in itself, formidable enough. And the effort to supplement woefully inadequate data from semiliterate voters, janitors, and policemen only yielded long, tedious police reports, frequently colored by a presumption of suspicion. Bureaucratic agencies and employers were slow in proferring necessary information. Struggling registrants endured constant revisions and delays, while the administration's intentions in the matter of subdividing curiae provided a continuing element of uncertainty. With the vacation period at hand, it seemed that some city voters would never be registered.[6]

St. Petersburg and other important administrative and military centers faced a special problem in enrolling civil service workers and those employed in military installations. The law clearly excluded members of the armed forces, police, and other categories.[7] Local election boards not only had to establish exactly which civil service workers were allowed to vote (in St. Petersburg these numbered some 35,000), but they also had to make impromptu interpretations of the law which were not likely to satisfy the broad constructionists in public circles and the narrow interpretationists of the bureaucracy. In the second elections, boards had been criticized for unwittingly permitting certain types of police officials (bookkeepers and passport issuers) to enroll. To avoid this pitfall, the St. Petersburg election board ventured to request from the governor general a list of all police officials as it normally would from any other bureau, and was impressed by General Drachevskii's prompt compliance.[8] Conversely, election officials made certain that the lists included employees of independent agencies such as state theaters (largely intellectuals) who had been excluded inadvertently in the last elections.[9]

Other agencies offered more delicate and complex situations. When the press noted that the Nikolaevskaia Railway office in St. Petersburg had excluded some 12,000 of its lower category workers, the line's administration replied that it was adhering exactly to the construction by the St. Petersburg city administration of the Law of June 3.[10] The city election office was probably aware that its interpretation excluded many workers from the vote. Its justification rested on the exclusion of higher salaried categories. On the other hand, despite the clear statements by the St. Petersburg city election authorities that in military installations only uniformed personnel were excluded from the vote, they could not always satisfy the complaints of civil employees that their suffrage privileges were being violated. The election authorities could only enroll those certified by their superiors and felt that they had no right to question officials of institutions presenting lists of eligible employees. Since appeal of actions of the military command was extremely difficult, many could expect to be excluded permanently.[11]

From the reports of the watchful opposition press, it appears that charges of illegalities arose chiefly from rigid official interpretation of the law and that there were relatively few flagrant violations by officialdom of procedures for registration. Those that occurred were mainly illegal enrollments or arbitrary exclusions. Military agencies were known to list officers who obviously had no right to vote. The Smolensk police checked and eliminated some 345 of 3,600 odd voters, chiefly from the second category. In Kishinev the *uiezd* election committee checked the documents of persons required to register, although the law allowed them control only of the officials compiling the lists. The Elizavetgrad committee permitted no revision of inaccuracies noted by the city administration after the legal two-week period for complaints. Unduly narrow construction, perhaps misunderstanding, of the law resulted in wholesale illegal eliminations of registrants on the last day of enrollment in Kazan, and clerks were asked to offer more documentation than the required professional certification. These were second category elements likely to vote for opposition candidates.[12]

The unfolding pattern of the registration period indicated all too clearly that in the cities the bureaucracy was realizing some of the expected benefits of its artificial manipulation of the electorate. Everywhere the number of voters dropped considerably below the level of the past election. From incomplete but adequate data it was apparent that the lists were at least a third smaller than those for the second election, and in many localities were considerably lower. In comparison with an overall participation of approximately 55.7 percent of city voters in the second elections, a report on July 25 covering 67 cities (about 10 percent of all cities in European Russia) indicated that there were 36.6 percent fewer voters in the third elections, or about 19.1 percent of the qualified town electorate. And it was just here that the constitutionalists rested their hopes. The greatest decline, some 40 percent, appeared in the central *gubernii,* while in the border provinces and the south the rate of decline was somewhat lower, ranging from 33.5 percent to 35 percent, respectively.[13] Losses in some large provincial centers (Ekaterinburg, Poltava, Samara, Sevastopol, Stavropol, and Viatka) ran to 50 percent or more, and some registered a decline of 40 percent (Iaroslavl, Vologda, and Kremenchug). Other towns (Dvinsk, Kishinev, Kazan) had about average losses as compared with previous elections, and a number of small provincial centers (Bobruisk, Borisov, Mozyr, Pinsk) indicated a somewhat greater interest, with the registration only some 25 percent lower than in preceding elections.[14] In some fairly large centers, such as Nizhni Novgorod, Saratov, Riazan, the registration was miniscule, and others reported only that the number of voters was "considerably greater" in the last election.[15] The major cities fitted the general pattern. The Odessa lists were half as large as in the second election, the Minsk enrollment was one-third as large, Kiev was less than one-sixth, Moscow one-fifth, and St. Petersburg under one-third.[16]

The formidable limitations and excisions of the Law of June 3 were obviously a major factor in generating a spirit of indifference toward the impending elections. The brief period allowed for registration followed hard on the dissolution of the Second Duma and the promulgation of the new law in the first wave of defeatism and exhaustion that gripped broad sections of the population. And, aside from the rigorous repression, the petty and major impediments offered the city voter had an especially deleterious effect. Embodiment in the new law of the interpretations of the summer of 1906 which narrowly delimited the qualifications for voting in the low income categories had a serious effect in many centers. In Stavropol, for example, feldshers, veterinarians, *volost* elders and judges, and clergy as well as peasants owning property or residing in towns were ruled out of any city category, with the result that the total registration was reduced by 35 percent. In Poltava it was the cossack and peasant elements and in Dvinsk the peasantry alone that were eliminated. Everywhere the reluctance to enroll on the part of those classified as nontaxpaying apartment renters appeared quite early as the chief contributing factor to the smaller registration in the third elections.[17] The requirements that nontaxpaying apartment renters and state pensioners submit written statements of intention of enrollment offered a psychological impediment which may have deepened the prevailing apathetic mood. The voter who realized, if only vaguely, that the law allocated him only 10 to 20 percent of the electoral strength of his wealthier compatriots across the town would need more than a little reserve of spirit and conviction to expend the time and energy required to register.[18]

Even when the nontaxpaying apartment renter was inclined to register, he faced obstacles at the first stage of the procedure. The law required that his place of residence be confirmed by the house superintendent and witnessed by the police. Petitioners for enrollment were frequently refused police certification on grounds that the governor had given no instructions, or even worse, the police certified that the applicant was untrustworthy politically. In Kiev, Odessa, and Kremenchug refusal of certification by the police assumed serious proportions. In Kremenchug alone 3,000 voters were eliminated by this procedure. In some cases the unwary or impatient petitioners offered only the superintendent's signature. And since a great many persons submitted documents at a late date there was hardly the time, and not always the inclination, to fulfill procedural requirements. The provincial and local bureaucracy reacted at a snail's pace.[19] In some places notices on the dates of elections for the various categories and stages were posted only a relatively short time before the stipulated terminal dates for registration, and in others the local administration made no effort to inform the public of these dates.[20]

Official telegraphic agency reports from the provinces stressed the general apathy, making invidious comparisons with past elections and suggesting a tendency toward boycott. The opposition press countered by explaining that there had been only one city category in past elections and no requirement to submit requests for registration—which the electorate in all probability understood in the first place. Moreover, caught in the mood of the moment, and under the impact of a rigid censorship, the provincial press—even in the larger centers like Odessa—made little effort to arouse the public to excercise its electoral right.[21]

The inevitable result of these accumulated factors was a relatively slow pace of registration and a generally light response by the nontaxpaying apartment renters. On June 27, the Statistical Department of the Moscow city administration reported an "extremely weak interest" on the part of this category. Similar reports came from all over the country at the end of June and early July—close to the deadlines originally established. Moscow, where the response of these elements had been weak even in the second election, recorded only 150 registrants and in St. Petersburg only 166 out of a total of 30,000 qualified to vote as small renters. Smolensk reported 178 small apartment registrants as against 5,000 in the comparable stage of registration in the last election; Vilno registered 16 in this category as against 5,000 in the second election; Tula, 2 in comparison with 914; and Mogilev one as against 400. Kamenets-Podolsk and Sevastopol reported no small apartment registrants by June 29.[22]

There appeared to be a flurry of activity during the next two weeks in widely scattered areas as the final date for registration approached and after some extensions were permitted.[23] But the overall reaction was decidedly weak. In final tabulations Minsk lost over 5,000 voters who did not pay an apartment tax as compared with the second elections; and the smaller Ekaterinoslav fell by 2,500. St. Petersburg, Moscow, and Kiev, the three largest cities, lost 70 percent of these voters.[24]

Pensioners, another category required to request enrollment in the voter lists, faced the same difficulties and reacted identically. And they faced an additional bureaucratic hazard in that the *guberniia* zemstvo boards in some instances refused to honor their pension books as evidence that they had been pensioners for at least a year. This legally questionable procedure would force them to apply to *guberniia* treasury officials for confirmation of their status.[25]

Alarmed at the apathy of an element of the population that had contributed heavily to the liberal vote in the past elections, the Kadet Party, lawyers, individual political figures, and newspapers made a determined effort to assure an effective vote from the small income city electorate. In St. Petersburg one of the lawyers' consultation groups established, in the manner of preceding campaigns, to guide the confused electorate through the legal maze of electoral requirements, appealed to the city Office of Electoral Affairs to extend the deadline for registration beyond June 30. The limit had been originally established to allow time for publication of voter lists at dates in mid July required by the Ministry of Interior, and the election chancellery replied that those omitted could call on the *guberniia* election committee to include their names. The city administration announced on July 1 that enrollment would be accepted up to July 10. Two days later the deadline was indefinitely postponed. On July 12 it was announced that since the Ministry of the Interior had decided not to require publication of registration lists until September 12, the voters might submit requests for inclusion as long as work of preliminary compilation continued.[26] Moscow likewise pushed its enrollment period toward a publication date of September 10, and in Kiev the period for registration was extended to the end of July.[27]

To counteract the inertia of those who had to request enrollment as voters, the legal aid groups in the capitals undertook a wide distribution of forms for registration and for insertion or for correction of omissions. From June 27 to 30 inclusive, *Riech*, the chief Kadet organ in St. Petersburg, prominently published the addresses of all consultation points, warned its readers of the terminal date for registration, and publicized later extensions of the registration period. The Kadet Party and the Jewish Election Committee in St. Petersburg and the "most important progressive voters" in Orsha visited the small apartment voters and instructed them in the proper procedure for registering and correcting errors.[28]

The position of voters in the worker category was, to say the least, anomalous. In this category, which had been the only city category designated by the Law of December 11, 1905, and was now carried over into the new law, the worker was not registered in lists of voters but was merely allowed to vote in enterprises with fifty or more workers. Located in city and *uiezd* and closely tied to the peasantry, the workers were definitely not allowed to vote with the latter. Yet it was estimated that some 24,000 workers (14 percent of the labor electorate) were employed in establishments with less than fifty workers. The question immediately arose as to whether these workers might vote as small apartment renters. But to qualify for this category, the apartment had to be rented in the worker's name and most city workers lived in dormitories or "squatted in corners or separate rooms."[29] Finally, interpretations defining apartment residence were refined and a number of exclusions from the polls followed. Those who occupied small apartments for their services could not vote as apartment renters, and apartment renters who voted with the workers were excluded from their lists.[30]

At the end of July the Mayor of Moscow protested to the City Prefect *(grandonachal'nik)* against the "elimination" of the worker curia as a contradiction of the Law and Manifesto of June 3, which promised continued representation to all elements of the population. The cautious prefect petitioned for an extension of worker registration until September 4—the final date for submission of complaints concerning the voter lists. But the Vice Minister of the Interior in mid August refused to go beyond the regulations already established, and few workers could or did qualify as apartment renters.[31] The labor vote was also subjected to harassments not unlike those experienced by other low income categories.[32]

The first city category, one of those favored by the new electoral law, experienced almost no complications except those arising from the vagueness of the decree. There was no prerequisite for registration; names were automatically inscribed on the lists in accordance with specific qualifications.[33] In the largest cities the question of excluding all but a single co-owner of industrial and commercial establishments arose. Action by the city election office in this connection was finally resolved in favor of the inclusion of all co-owners.[14]

A few salient characteristics of the first city category—none of them particularly surprising—were evident from the registers. Aside from the remarkably small constituencies, the predominance of city duma elements and the paucity of "public figures" was evident. First category figures of the stature of Attorney Pergament of Odessa were rare.[35]

In the rural categories the large landowners were the most favored by the law, which sought to assure their maximum representation. Yet in widely scattered areas the registration in this category declined some 30 to 40 percent as compared with previous elections. This was due, for the most part, to the exclusion of peasants with large landholdings from the landowner classification. Sale of landed property evidently played some role, but indifference was evident even in this stratum. Those who were excluded from suffrage because of sex, military status, or state service but might offer qualified substitutes failed to take action— largely because they, too, had to submit special documents.[36]

Regulations on substitution allowed women, who were themselves not enfranchised, to transfer to their husbands or their sons any property they held which might provide a voting qualification. This article of the law was obviously intended to mobilize all stray elements of the "dependable" strata. And it was just for this reason that the authorities had expected an increase in this category. In the cities there had been little resort to this privilege in the first two elections largely because it had no special attraction to persons of little substance, and most persons who qualified as substitutes had their own personal service or apartment qualifications. Only ninety-five substitute voters registered in St. Petersburg, although those seeking to qualify were given until the end of July—a month longer than the original time limit established for small apartment renters.[37]

The senatorial interpretations of the summer of 1906 that were incorporated into the Electoral Law of June 3, 1907, decimated the list of small landowners who had voted lightly even in the first two elections.[38] A sampling of the counties throughout European Russia revealed a uniform picture of significant decline. Losses of 70 percent between the second and third elections were not uncommon (Smolensk, 69 percent; Odessa *Uiezd*, 73 percent; Orshansk, 69 percent; Chizhegorod, 59 percent; Bobruisk, 57 percent; and Pinsk 25 percent; and in thirty-nine scattered *uiezdi* the small landowner vote fell by 76.2 percent). In Poltava *uiezd* the registration of these voters was entirely negligible: they declined from 16,000 in the first elections to 575 in the third. The prime cause for the decline was the exclusion from the landowning category of all commune peasants with land apart from their commune holdings. And in areas with heavy losses, particularly in the Poltava region, indifference seems to have played no little role. The majority of the small landowners in all probability quickly sensed the significant diminution in their voting strength, noted the strong leaven of clergy added to their category, and reacted with indignation, indifference, or apathy.[39]

In contrast to the small landowners, the commune peasants had voted heavily in past elections—some 72 percent in the second.[40] But the resident village homeowners were automatically registered as members; hence their voting interest would become evident in their *volost* and *uiezd* elections.[41] Some peasants, a significant number in some localities, were excluded, nevertheless, from the suffrage by the operation of the law. Authorities (for example, the Governor General of Moscow, Dzhunkovsky) assured city dwellers of peasant origin excluded from the city vote by Article 62 of the new law (on the ground that they were registered in the commune) that they would be able to vote in the communes as holders of allotment land. Yet many so registered were urban workers who had long broken all connection with the countryside and had held no allotment land during the preceding year, and few were likely to be classified as homeowners. Under a strict interpretation of Article 37 of the Electoral Law of June 3, 1907, they could be, and were, excluded from the suffrage in the village.[42]

Registration among the national minorities followed the same general trends evident in country and town among the "basic" Russians. But both mechanical and psychological difficulties were further complicated by the purposes and provisions of the law: to make the Duma "Russian in spirit" and to regroup the electorate therefor.[43]

When the compilation of lists was completed in the course of July, they were published (some were printed by private firms) by city and zemstvo boards. Most of them were forwarded to local and central administrative offices for posting during the two-week period following publication, when voters might check them for possible errors and omissions. A limited number were offered for sale.[44]

The provincial and county election committees were formed in July and the machinery for complaints and appeals began to function early in August. Minister of Justice G. I. Shcheglovitov, characteristically enough, felt impelled to intervene in the process to remind the circuit (okrug) courts that not all of them had elected their representatives to the commissions. They were to proceed with that business and in addition duly inform him of any difficulty they experienced in applying the electoral law.[45]

The first editions of the lists reflected the novelty of the election experience and the relatively brief period for the registration of voters and compilation of lists. They were generously punctuated with inaccuracies; in some cases they included duplications and women, as in Novgorod, or the names of deceased, some widely known in public circles, as in St. Petersburg.[46]

Reports from the major centers seemed to indicate that the greater part of the complaints submitted soon after the lists appeared were honored by the appropriate committees. These were presented, in all probability, chiefly to rectify inaccuracies in voter records.[47]

That was before the voting began. But with the completion of the first stages of the election procedure, the bureaucracy (governors and city prefects) and some rightist elements entered into what appeared to be a concerted, if belated, attack on opposition candidates to disqualify them—usually on the basis of faulty residence qualifications, but whenever possible, on political grounds. Shifting the burden of proof increasingly to the registrants, the bureaucracy, as was its wont, interpreted the letter of the law with remarkable rigidity. Prominent local leaders and some of the most imposing figures in the opposition, including former deputies, were involved. And in some cases the electorate supported a candidate with questionable qualifications.[48] In numerous instances, city candidates or popular gentry were excluded from the registration lists by election committees—usually at the provincial level—because they did not occupy apartments for which they were taxed. In Stavropol some five opposition electors were "interpreted" on the eve of the elections.[49] Late in the campaign, Professor P. N. Miliukov, charged with nonoccupancy of his apartment, was allowed to remain on the lists after a hearing by the Ruling Senate because of his professional qualifications as a journalist.[50] And in connection with their residence qualifications, an attempt was made to disfranchise Instructor M. P. Bobin of the Iaroslavl Demidovskii Lyceum and the prominent Kadet, Professor V. M. Gessen of the St. Petersburg Polytechnical Institute. The suffrage qualifications of these former deputies was challenged on the grounds that they were government officials. In Gessen's case, the provincial committee ruled that residence outside the Institute housing preserved his franchise. Bobin was stricken from the lists.[51] A further variation of the same theme which, again, involved V. M. Gessen as well as the former president of the Second Duma, F. A. Golovin, was the bold argument that these men had lost their residence qualification while in attendance at the Second Duma. Both the Moscow and St. Petersburg provincial committees recognized the patent illogic of this official premise.[52]

At the very least, the campaign to challenge individual qualifications created widespread uncertainty as the process of review dragged on into October. Professor Gessen barely escaped elimination as a candidate, and the liberal, former Cossack deputy Karaulov, was not cleared in time for elections to the provincial assembly.[53] Governors and city prefects not only eliminated potential candidates during the registration period but frequently struck just before elections. By this procedure the Popular Socialist leadership in St. Petersburg was eliminated in the competition for Duma seats.[54] And public suspicion of official motives was heightened when the pattern of charges and committee action revealed what appeared to be a bias in favor of the rightist elements—as in the "Shmid affair."[55]

Gustav Karlovich Shmid was sentenced in 1891 under Article 253 and 257 of the Criminal Code on "Russian subjects who inform foreign powers of secret documents, drawings, plans of Russian fortifications." Specifically he had been charged with receiving 10,000 rubles for plans of fortifications. In accordance with the law he was deprived of his rank as captain in the navy and of his orders and noble status, and was exiled to Tomsk for life. He was subsequently pardoned by the Tsar.[56] An organizer of the Minsk branch of the Union of the Russian People, Shmid had been elected as a candidate of the "Episcopal Bloc" to the *uiezd* and *guberniia* assemblies in September, 1907. Before the *guberniia* assembly met, a group of Minsk city voters submitted the number of *Pravitel'stvennyi Vestnik* of 1891 containing the facts of Shmid's conviction and dismissal from the service and protested that according to Article 10 of the Electoral Law of June 3, 1907, anyone so deprived of rank and status and sentenced —even though pardoned—had to be stricken from the voter lists. And the *uiezd* committee so ruled. Shmid appealed to the *guberniia* committee, which set a hearing for September 27.

On the eve of the meeting of the *guberniia* committee, the "True Russians" gathered to emphasize Shmid's services in promoting patriotism and to ask the committee "to meet the demands of Russian society." But on the same day more decisive pressure was exerted by no less a figure than the Assistant Minister of the Interior S. E. Kryzhanovsky. In a telegram to the Minsk committee he declared that he had been ordered by Stolypin to state "for information and guidance" that Shmid had been reestablished in all his rights, that the proper documents were available, and that his electoral right was incontrovertible. The committee thereupon reinstated Shmid. The reactionary border Russians jubilantly celebrated and claimed God's special protection for their cause in the election campaign. But the articulate opposition was so astonished at the obvious contradiction between the administration's conclusions and the provisions of Article 10 of the electoral law that several newspapers took pains to ascertain that the G. K. Shmid of 1891 and 1907 were identical. "The government," declared *Riech* in a leader assessing the administration's efforts to influence the campaign," "has the right to 'interpret' as it pleases," but asked that it refrain from "naked provocation of the voters."[57]

VIII
The Voting Process

The mood of the population on the eve of the final elections was subdued, verging on the indifferent in widely scattered areas. Characterization of the popular temperament by newspaper correspondents in Simferopol, Taritsyn, Kazan, Tula, and Zhitomir, Kiev, and Riga ranged from "quiet" and "sluggish" to "automatic" and "prosaic." They noted a marked contrast with the spirited, generally good natured argumentation and exchange of opinion during the preceding elections.[1] A. N. Brianchaninov, a liberal zemstvo leader, observed succinctly that, at the moment, sensitive and informed people did not have the slightest idea of regarding elections as an act of political significance. They had not moved to the right, but into themselves. In his opinion the landlords mobilized not around any government formula but around the negative idea of defeating reformists; and the progressives, having lost faith in progress after June 3, acted sluggishly and indecisively, on a feeling of heavy duty.[2] Local correspondents in St. Petersburg and the provinces noted the difficulty of arousing the electorate, particularly in the face of rigid restrictions by the authorities. Significantly, the Polish voters in St. Petersburg had to be told that no one could be held for a vote cast as a secret ballot.[3]

The liberals squeezed what optimism they might from the circumstances. *Riech* was confident that if the small landowners, including the clerical component, voted the great landowners would be defeated. And Professor M. M. Kovalevskii, interviewed in Paris, expected that the government would be greatly surprised and that the Duma majority would not be reactionary.[4] A number of Kadet leaders agreed, after touring various parts of European Russia, that the general mood was oppositional.[5] And after the first ballot for the Duma deputies, *Riech* felt reassured that the public had spoken for peaceful transition to a democratic-constitutional structure.[6]

But the Kadets also observed a disquieting movement to the left. Student and faculty elections in St. Petersburg University and the Technical Institute were dominated by the Social Democrats and Populists. The liberals complained that the Kadets were fully supported by the opposition press in the elections to the First Duma, that the press was divided on their support in the second campaign and that it opposed them in the third. And some election meetings in St. Petersburg reflected a marked strain of hostility towards the Kadets.[7]

Nor were the constitutionalists entirely reassured by the stream of official circulars which sought to define electoral procedures and regulations in the light of the new electoral law. The administration felt a compulsion to remind voting officials that all senatorial interpretations which did not contradict the law of June 3 were to remain in force as a part of that law. The government emphasized, in particular, that voters registered in the communes, including *volost* officials and village teachers, were never to be entered in the second city category.[8] Warnings to ward administrators to take measures against "scandals" by revolutionaries at the polling places portended a measure of police interference.[9]

Major pre-election "instructions" issued by Premier Stolypin on the "order of holding elections" stressed a careful check on documents and the lists of eligible voters in every precinct. They were particularly concerned that no one voted twice if he had more than one qualification in the same or different precincts. They indicated that the procedure for voting had not changed measurably and had been liberalized to a degree.[10] Specifically the new regulations provided that in cities with an ethnic mix, representatives of the predominant nationalities were to sit on the election committees. In closer adherence to the electoral law, ballots, other than those prepared by the city committees, might be used and could be distributed to the voters before the elections. Voting for too many candidates no longer invalidated a ballot. Names which appeared more than once and superfluous names were simply to be cancelled. As in preceding elections, voting districts were established for every 2,000 voters. A week before elections each voter was to receive two official envelopes (one for runoff elections), identification papers for voting with coupon attached (likewise for runoff elections), and an official ballot which, as noted, he need not use. These were to be delivered directly by the police whenever possible or could be procured from the election committees. At the polls, the voter's identification was to be checked against the lists of voters. He would place his ballot in an envelope and drop it in the ballot box in full view of the local precinct committee. Public check on all boxes and careful security for ballots was provided for. The results were to be entered on record cards for each candidate and published by the committee. The record card was also an innovation to adhere more closely to the legal requirements. Heretofore, the count had been accomplished with coupons torn from the ballot.[11]

With the advent of elections the realities emerging from the accumulating complexities of electoral regulations began to take on real meaning. The rigid application and multiplication of rules governing the voting by categories was a new experience. Now the suffrage waited uncertainly as officialdom utilized its new powers to divide the electorate by nationalities and property qualifications within each category. And governors and the Ministry of the Interior made full and, on occasion, almost uninhibited use of their authority to assure a predominance of Russian and propertied elements at the polls.

For the Imperial bureaucracy the intricate play of division and subdivision of categories followed naturally from the purpose of the law of June 3, and the overreaching opposition of the preceding Dumas. For the seasoned observer "all this scandalous manoeuvering" reflected a "passion for manipulation" which might again violate the Fundamental Laws.[12] For the opposition the mandate to divide was but a legal extension of official pressures felt in the first two elections.[13] While the practice of dividing constituencies was not universally applied, directives issued, often late in the campaign, assured the regime of safe margins where they were needed. Now the Ministry of the Interior established a special bureau under Assistant Minister S. E. Kryzhanovskii to investigate local materials from city and *uiezd* electoral agencies. The official purpose of the study was to avoid "errors" made in the second elections but the data could be especially useful for dividing categories.[14]

Divisions conjured up for the preliminary *volost* and *uiezd* elections were almost fantastic in their intricacy.[15] Rural voters were assigned to three to six groups according to landed, real estate, class, ethnic, and religious qualifications. Typical decrees designated divisions for small and large landowners and clergy.[16] The number of delegates from the small landowners to the *uiezd* election meeting was based on the number of qualifying areas of varying dimensions. Thus the small landowners with holdings which were usually less than a complete qualification enjoyed considerably weaker voting power than the middle or large landholders.[17]

The position of the clergy in the landowner category was exceptional. Either out of self interest or under pressure from the upper heirarchy they were the single category that swarmed to the polls and their number formed a considerable leaven among the voters at each stage in the non urban electorate. In the *uiezdi* on which the governors reported, they sent 453 delegates from the landowner curia to the *guberniia* assemblies of a total of 2366 landowner electors, or 16.6 percent of the landowner electors from the *uiezdi* listed.[18] The governor of Penza *Guberniia* estimated that they were sending twenty to twenty-two electors from each *uiezd* meeting. He decried the clanishness of the clerical electors and maintained that "the greatest danger at elections is that clique numerically powerful and extremely untrustworthy in their views that the priests send to the electoral assemblies."[19] In the elections and by-elections to the Third Duma local official-dom showed concern for the control of this element, particularly if the provincial bishops were politically ineffective due to lack of interest, senility, or ideological hostility.[20]

A similar multiplicity of categories marked the voting pro-cedure for the cities. The most commonplace divisions grouped the voters by real estate holdings, business, craft, and apartment taxpayers (or nontaxpayers) as well as recipients of pensions and grants from the central and local governmental agencies, class institutions, or railroad services. The second city category was occasionally divided to isolate intellectuals from small property owners, traders, and craftsmen. In Vladimir the subcategories were decreed just before elections in an effort to undermine the Kadets. In Tver the first category was so defined as to include most intellectuals where they would vote in a minority. Geo-graphic divisions were frequently designated, usually for admin-istrative convenience but the ethnic and religious factors were significant in urban as in all voting arrangements.[21]

The most spectacular, sometimes bizarre, manipulations of categories were designed to further weaken the position of those national and religious minorities who could still hope for a de-gree of representation in the Duma. Every stage of the electoral process was affected. In the preliminary (including peasant *volost* and clerical), landowner, and city elections special ethnic and religious subdivisions were established to separate "Russians and non-Russians," "Jews and non-Jews," "Poles and non-Poles," "Jews and Christians," "Russians and aliens."[22] And all divisions redounded to the benefit of the Russians and Ortho-dox, or were so intended.[23]

In the Pale of Settlement, Jews were frequently segregated within categories, particularly in cities where they were concentrated, and the Russians given equal strength if they were a minority or were granted as much as three times the voting strength of the Jewish populations.[24] Zealous officials sometimes overreached themselves as in Poltava and Kremenchug where Jews were assigned to a separate city division regardless of their qualifications for the first or second categories, and Stolypin declared the arrangement invalid.[25]

In Minsk *Guberniia* the Poles, holding 70 percent of the land, were outraged by the assignment of eighteen electors to the provincial assembly while the Russians, with some 30 percent of the land, were granted fifty-three places. One elector represented 154 Russians in the first city category while 240 Poles and 844 Jews voted likewise for a single elector. In the second category one elector represented 2895 Russians as against 5600 Poles and Jews. The Poles complained bitterly but fruitlessly about the violation of Article 29 of the Electoral Law which provided for divisions on the basis of "the total area of private property" held by persons of each nationality.[26] Then the annulment of Vitebsk and Dvinsk elections was reversed when the provincial election committee found that Bielorussians, whether Catholic or Orthodox, might vote with the Russian category.[27] And old wounds were opened in the Baltic Region when the German landowners were added to the Russian category in the counties.[28]

When the qualified voter finally entered the precincts to cast his ballot, irregularities at the polls and violations of polling procedures were immediately noticeable and endemic. They reflected both the parliamentary novitiate of the electorate and the incapacity or unwillingness of officialdom (with little experience in compromising with non-official pressures) to relinquish traditional patterns of action. Some irregularities committed by the voters were, at the same time, pathetic and comic. In St. Petersburg "direct elections" were interpreted as the right to vote at the most convenient polling place and voters frequently entered the wrong premises. Women were sent to vote for ailing spouses and busy employers dispatched their clerks to vote for them. Some voters came supplied with all vital documents including birth certificates. Others appeared with no acceptable identification.[29] Confused voters pleaded at the polls for some guidance in selecting candidates and some left in a huff when their queries were sidestepped discreetly or were rebuffed. Many were certain that they had to deposit their ballots in separate boxes for each party.[30] Some ballots were spoiled innocently, others with malice aforethought. Ballot boxes in St. Petersburg were stuffed with letters, and some, addressed directly to the Tsar, stated their choice of candidates. Passports were inserted, and even an insurance policy. Scrawled comments on the ballots offered write-in candidates and negative opinions on the electoral law and the elections. Some were covered with poetry declaiming a boycott. And there was the inevitable sarcasm in fictitious signatures and addresses: "zubr" (the European bison) and "Bieloviezh Forest" (the habitat of the bison in northeastern Poland), symbols of conservatism.[31]

Official violations of electoral regularities were transgressions of a more serious order. For they represented the less subtle manifestations of the administrative pattern that begot the new electoral law and its supplementary regulations. In scattered, significant centers (Kishinev, Minsk, Tula) the URP counted on bureaucratic forebearance to influence the ballot by a combination of wile and violence. They were allowed to agitate near the polling places and in Minsk actually occupied entrances and stairways to interrogate voters. Elsewhere they examined ballots on the pretext of providing information on candidates and exchanged their own for opposition lists. Or, as in Poland, they sequestered envelopes and destroyed their contents. "Defenders of the Jews" were beaten if they resisted interrogation.[32]

Correspondence from Iaroslavl to *Riech* reported brazen violations or ignorance of voting procedures by officialdom. Persons, other than observers, were admitted to the rooms where ballots were cast. *Uiezd* committees reviewed their own decisions, and the rightist mayor, Chestiakov, was simultaneously a member of the committee and an elector to the *guberniia* assembly from the first category. And the city administration begot considerable confusion by failing to inform voters in the second category that it had been divided into two sections.[33]

In Tiflis, administrative center for the Transcaucasus, some thirty opposition electors protested that in violation of Article 116 of the Electoral Law nine of their number had received neither lists of electors nor were they informed of the proper date for elections. They further observed that the chairman of the election meeting of the Russian curia had violated Article 79 of the Law by commenting on the undesirability and politics of peasant candidates. Finally, in Odessa, the huge election expenditures of former mayor Prostenko, a rightist candidate for the Duma, aroused considerable interest.[34]

Official harassment, sometimes grotesque and bordering on the illegal, offered still another obstacle to the apparently simple act of casting a ballot. But it was also more intensive and resourceful than in preceding elections. In the campaign and at the election meetings in the *volost* police officials were known to coax the peasantry, sometimes to their considerable annoyance, to vote with the right. In at least one instance a land captain sought to destroy the lists of rural delegates.[35] Other devices were somewhat less direct but as effective. Peasants and small landholders complained in some counties that the number of polling places were fewer than in previous elections and that voters consequently had to travel as much as eighty *versts* (about fifty-three miles) to reach some of them. Or officials were lax or tardy in informing the electorate of the place, date, and even purpose of peasant electoral meetings. Some *volost* meetings were burdened so heavily with matters not pertinent to elections that the naming of delegates was relegated to a comparatively unimportant position.[36] And there was always the temptation to inconvenience the voters by holding elections on weekdays with a minimum of publicity or to change the date without notice just before elections were to be held[37] Efforts were made at the *guberniia* meetings to isolate peasant electors or, as a last resort, to arrest them for petty violations of the criminal code.[38]

Workers were vulnerable on two counts. Their party adherence could be controlled in a real sense if they were employees of government-owned establishments, particularly railways. And they could be arrested and exiled for agitation on behalf of a non-legalized party or the right to agitate at all among the workers might be curbed.[39]

The power of the governors to assure the proper functioning of the election procedures could prove salutary. But it was likely to be conditioned by their commitment to assure the predominance of the wealthy and the Russians. Bureaucratic secretiveness and skill in manipulating the law were sometimes singularly effective in frustrating the intentions of the electorate. The public never knew in detail just what instructions on electoral procedures Stolypin had given the governors. It was known that he had publicly warned them not to violate the new law—after he had committed major legal mayhem against the old one. But the voters more or less expected local officialdom to take advantage of the senatorial interpretation which limited the Duma to the review of procedures involving only the elections of deputies in the *guberniia* assemblies and in larger cities.[40] And officials were not averse to intervening directly in the election campaign to influence the vote. Governor Rimskii-Korsakov of Iaroslav toured his province to urge his subordinates to vote for "true

Russians." And the Baku city administration, through its appointed electoral committee, issued ballots bearing the names of candidates it favored.[41]

The non-legal status of major parties was a basic irritant in public life—one that wisdom would seem to dictate that officialdom ignore except in cases of patent subversion. But in the excitement of the campaign, especially in the final stages, the practice of non-legalization served official purposes only too well. On the eve of elections the police in Moscow searched all premises where they might find the prepared ballots of the Kadet Party as indicated in the press: the homes of the secretary of the city organization and of all Party members distributing ballots. Few voters received prepared Kadet lists, and 11,000 were confiscated in the printshop of the *Kievskii Kurier*. In the order of things, the action was attended by numerous arrests.[42]

The non-Russian minorities were hampered in the proper realization of their meager suffrage rights by more or less open manipulation of the law. The Polish landowner category in Volyn, for example, was simply not allotted the number of delegates due them at the *guberniia* assembly. And the ballots of the Jewish electorate in Grodno were invalidated by inordinately strict interpretation of the law. Their votes were not counted in the final elections if they had not participated in the naming of candidates, or for misspellings and poor handwriting. The government would intervene only to the extent of requiring more liberal confirmation procedures. A finer touch was evident in the creation of two Jewish categories in the city of Chernigov—the cultured and others.[43]

The electoral law was evidence enough that the government desired and even promoted the victory of the legalized parties. And government officials, local and central, made their preferences clear beyond doubt in public utterances. Foreign Minister Alexander I. Izvolskii (a "liberal" by bureaucratic standards) informed the erstwhile French Foreign Minister S. Pichon that he was hopeful that a majority, governmental if not ministerial, would result from the elections. And among the congratulatory telegrams received by A. I. Guchkov was one from the Moscow city administration headed by his brother Nicholas, the mayor.[44]

For the reading public, the official St. Petersburg Telegraphic Agency reflected the eagerness of the authorities in promoting a moderate and right of center victory. There appeared to be no concern about its reportage of results. Its official correspondents collected and reported data in the localities by meetings and curias. Doubts were generated by its interpretation of the results. Throughout the campaign the Agency took advantage of the vague designations assumed by candidates at various levels to minimize the gains of the opposition and exaggerate the returns for legalized parties. "Non-Party" and "moderate" figures were invariably included among the supporters of the regime.[45]

While there were numerous "non-partisans" on the right in the campaign for the Third Duma, the liberal press was probably correct in assuming that the opposition also included some "non-partisans," "moderates," and those whose political affiliation was "unknown." The local press reported frequently that candidates known to be "progressive" were listed by the official agency as "moderates." The Tsaritsyn correspondent of *Riech* noted that the "non-party progressives and moderates" elected by small landholders were referred to as "monarchists" by the local police. And a comparison of reports from the St. Petersburg Telegraphic Agency and *Golos Moskvy*, the Octobrist Organ, revealed that the Agency referred to leftist peasant candidates as "moderates" when the opposition won an obvious victory. It emphasized current and past service in *volost* and village administration to underscore the moderate temper of peasant candidates. In the pattern of village life all capable adults were expected to serve at one time or other as *starost* or *desiatnik*.[46] The liberal press observed that peasant Social Revolutionaries were not likely to identify themselves to avoid repressive action by the rural police and land captains. *Riech* estimated that 65 percent of the peasant delegates were "progressive."[47] Victorious oppositional candidates from the national minorities were also likely to be classified as "moderates."[48]

The hierarchy of the Orthodox Church at the various levels believed that the cause of the official faith and its fold required them to interfere vigorously in the course of the elections. But official Church propaganda and preferred candidates frequently assumed a political position more rightist than the administration would habitually support. The extent of clerical intervention was bold indeed, and probably sprang from an exaggerated confidence in the influence of the Church over the rural population in political matters. A provincial archdeacon in the province of Kiev required his clergy to provide him with the secret questionnaire on electors prepared for the *guberniia* election committee. *Kievskii Viestnik* published a copy of the document which included information about each elector's faith, political convictions and affiliations, morality, and political trustworthiness.[49]

The archdeacon apparently hoped to cause sufficient mischief to terminate the candidacy, or at least inhibit support of, undesirable electors who might stand for the *guberniia* assembly and hence deputies for the Duma.

Peasant and small landholder electors were frequently corralled on their arrival in the provincial centers for the *guberniia* meeting. In Minsk and Vologda they were housed in the residences of the archbishops and bishops respectively to isolate them from contaminating oppositional influences. Just before elections prayer meetings were held and the electors were importuned to vote against "traitors" and "tsar killers," "flatterers and deceivers" bearing various names including the Party of Popular Liberation (Kadet). Their purposes, according to their reverences, was to divide the Russian land among their "alien" members and enslave the Russians even as did the Mongols.[50] In centers with a considerable religious tradition, like Kiev and Novgorod, prayers and sermons of a similar nature were heard in the imposing Cathedrals of St. Sophia. In some instances they were marched to the polls in serried ranks, "in new greatcoats and white lambskin caps." And occasionally they were adorned with the badge of the URP.[51]

The peasantry, insofar as they were interested in the campaign, had, in all probability, their own predetermined candidates. Since the small landowners tended to be conservative and were, in large measure, local clergymen, these efforts probably served, at the least, to diminish the oppositional vote among them.[52]

Unabashed support of rightist candidates by highly placed officials had become a commonplace political phenomenon by the summer of 1907. When they joined with like-minded elements among the clergy, a definite impression of their alienation from a considerable segment of the political scene was inevitable. Thus, the St. Petersburg electorate was both edified and bemused by a public utterance of Ioann Kronstadskii published by the City Prefect in his official journal. The churchman referred to the opposition as "contradictors of God's command" who were incapable of ruling but could only quarrel and do nothing really useful for Russia. And he called on those with a "scorched conscience," even the well-intentioned, like the "first minister-traitor [S. Iu. Witte]" to approach the Throne.[53]

IX
Elections

Provincial governors announced that primary elections in the *uiezds* for the various categories would take place on designated dates throughout the month of September.[1] Despite the uncertain impact of the new law on the prospects of the oppositional non-legalized parties, their respective press organs and those with some sympathy for them could not resist the temptation to prognosticate the outcome of the elections. Those willing to face realities could agree with *Iuzhnyi Krai* of Kharkov that "the new law places the country in an indefinite position" respecting the composition of the coming Duma.[2] And by the end of the campaign, just before elections, they were all prepared to admit their uncertainty.

The Kadets and their supporters could not but consider that the conservatives and rightists would have some kind of a majority, for that was the purpose of the law. The difficulty lay in predicting the size of the majority and the strength of the liberals. *Riech* acknowledged that a determination of "the numerical relationship of groups" in the future Duma was extremely risky. But it charged that the prophets were making purely logical deductions from the provisions of the new law without considering the mood of the population at election time in the various localities.[3] Yet, it proceeded to assign deputies to classes and areas of the Empire, as well as to parties. In September and October when the preliminary elections had ended, A. Smirnov, *Riech's* editor for electoral analyses, could foresee some 50 percent of the vote with the opposition, including the non-Russian parts of the Empire.[4]

In predicting the outcome of elections by parties, at the end of June *Rus* was willing to hazard a guess that the Kadets would hold some 175 seats because of Octobrist inertia, the general preference of the opposition for the Kadets as opposed to the leftists, and because of the Kadet reserve of oratorical skills.[5] As if to confirm this analysis, *Riech* noted that for the first time the Kadets were attracting peasant and worker votes. *Parus* added the thought that even the Kadet left wing would be diminished in favor of the center and right. And it was generally accepted that the chief source of Kadet strength lay in the second category of the city vote.[6]

Liberal claims for the opposition were by far less sanguine as the final elections approached. On October 14, the date set for most *guberniia* elections, their press would claim only ten provinces with seventy candidates as certain of victory. They indicated in detail where they expected to find the relative strength of the various hues of the political prism and concluded that the outcome of the elections depended on some twelve indefinite provinces with eighty-nine deputies. And they conjectured that in these areas the peasant and non-partisan votes would prove decisive.[7] The liberal analysts took full account of the circumstances favoring the legalized parties and could not find it in their hearts to allocate more than 30 percent of the Duma seats to the right and 35 percent to the Octobrists.[8]

The far right, perhaps for their own propaganda purposes or because they were unduly influenced by Kadet self-confidence, tended to exaggerate oppositional strength. Active rightist leadership in St. Petersburg was inclined to expect an "oppositional" Duma, or as Academician Sobolievskii expressed it, the Kadets would be able to hold the Third Duma, too, in their "velvet paws."[9]

At the other extreme the Social Democrats were resigned to their meager parliamentary ration. They expected few seats for the left and understood that some of the populists would be selected by the "bourgeoisie" and the landlord elements in the provincial meetings. Their opinion was supported by other oppositional elements.[10] Perhaps the most astute forcast of the campaign appeared in *Tovarishch* with the observation, just before the final elections, that relatively few extreme rightists (from the URP) and *zubry* (the more rightist gentry) were elected in the first stages. And it concluded that, sooner or later, given the predominantly moderate tenor of the Duma, it might be possible to form a constitutional center around the Octobrists and Kadets.[11]

Octobrist confidence stemmed from the realities of the electoral law. They did not find it advisable or useful to forecast their strength until late in the election period. Their chieftain, Alexander I. Guchkov, surmised, at the beginning of October, that of a total of 442 deputies the elections would yield some 288 Octobrists and rightists as against 154 Kadets and leftists. This would represent approximately a majority of two-thirds of the seats for the "moderates" and rightists. That majority, he asserted, would examine the budget, control the abuses and sins of the bureaucracy, and would resolve basic problems demanding immediate attention.[12] Professor Miliukov, the Kadet leader, was inclined to agree with Guchkov's arithmetic. But he believed that moderate and rightist power would be restricted by the great body of non-partisan deputies. He held that the experience of the first two Dumas had demonstrated that these elements would follow the opposition and put a rein on the Octobrist tendency to go along with the *zubry*.[13]

The Kadets, held by the Law in an unfavorable position which could hardly reflect their potential strength, might well wager on the undecided—or at least hope that the non-party deputies would favor their cause. This was an elusive element that could filter through the elaborate system of artificial allocation of votes and categories, and would not organize until the Duma was in session. In the First and Second Dumas, elected under more favorable auspices, they represented roughly 23 percent and 10 percent of the membership, respectively. In the First Duma they tended to be oppositional in the spirit of that body, and in the Second they voted as often with the center as with groupings to the right. Much depended on whether they represented a truly independent stratum of the electorate or an element that assumed a protective coloration.[14]

When the peasant voters met in "preliminary" gatherings to select delegates from each *volost* to *uiezd* meetings, they continued to demonstrate their cautiousness and a significant current of apathy. The non-party designation was popular, and it emerged largely as a device to avoid labels to the right and left which might prove distasteful to local opinion or the authorities. It might also conceal political indecision.[15] As significant were the reluctance of the peasantry to enter the lists and its general, political indifference. Some candidates from the *volosts* declined nomination as delegates to the *uiezd* assemblies. The Peaceful Renovationist leader, M. Stakhovich, noted a tendency to designate candidates by unofficial lot—after a proper prayer. And absenteeism in the *volost* meetings, a factor in preceding elections, assumed embarrassing proportions.[16] The villager easily gauged his weakened political position and it was no great feat for the populists to convince him that he would sit in a conservative and rightist Duma. And the dissolution of two Dumas with impunity could not but impress him.[17] In some instances repeated calls were needed to assemble the peasantry, and some meetings were not held at all because of poor communications and sheer apathy.[18] The number of meetings which never materialized ranged from 5 percent to almost 50 percent in the various localities. And there were frequent reports of a weak response in European Russia and Poland when they were held.[19]

These circumstances seem to offer a reasonable reflection of peasant attitudes toward the Duma. It is quite impossible to determine with any exactitude the political mind of the intensely parochial, heterogeneous, and inarticulate mass of the peasantry still hobbled by a considerable leaven of illiteracy. And those who would determine peasant attitudes were frequently not without their purposes. But the nature of some official reports would seem to indicate a commendable effort to ascertain the views of the local population with some degree of objectivity. The Kharkov Provincial Okhrana Department, reporting for both Kharkov and Ekaterinoslav *Gubernii*, indicated that the peasantry were interested almost exclusively in the acquisition of land and this concern conditioned practically all of their considerations.[20] By the summer and fall of 1907 the Duma seems to have lost its attraction for them and they were little concerned about its survival or activity. Some felt that it might prove useful if it desisted from interfering with the "tsar's work." Others saw it as superfluous because it yielded no land and could not be interested in popular needs because it was elected by the *pomiestchiki* and the police. They regarded the preceding Dumas as more popular and better intentioned but weak in the face of bureaucratic power and hence able to accomplish little for the peasantry. The First was dissolved because it wanted to give land to the peasant, and the Second because it was socialist and a mortal danger to the Tsar. The main impact of both bodies on the peasant mind seemed to have been the leftist propaganda on repression and heavy taxation and the calls to the communes to settle matters themselves. Otherwise the peasantry hardly comprehended the political programs of the deputies, parties, or newspapers and reacted perceptibly only to those who would promise them land.

The combination of indifference, apathy, absenteeism, political circumspection, and some clerical and official pressure were apparently effective in reducing the oppositional element among the peasantry. This is apparent in the strong showing of the conservative and rightists rural electorate in the wake of the predominantly oppositional bias of the first two elections in the communes. Official reports probably exaggerated the supporting vote from the villages, but the liberal analysis concurred in the victory of the right and center among the *volost* voters.

According to the most complete figures available on local elections, those issued by the St. Petersburg Telegraphic Agency (PTA), the *volost* peasant householders elected 4092 rightist delegates, 6142 conservatives, and 1616 "progressives" and Kadets, while the leftist peasants elected 371 delegates. The liberals attributed greater strength to the right in the *volost* elections than the official figures indicated and accorded considerably greater voting power to the left—over three times in *volost* and six times in the preliminary small landowner elections.[21]

The same factors, apathy and poor communications, affected the election of delegates from the generality of small landowners (with one-fifth of a qualification) to the *uiezd* assembly. In many counties a number of preliminary election meetings were not held as too few small landowners appeared. This reduced the number of delegates to the *uiezd* assemblies.[22] In this category the clergy reacted vigorously but here, too, there were symptoms of political lethargy. Some voted under orders from their superiors while others responded under a barrage of agitation by lay and clerical officials.[23]

The lower clergy, along with other small landowners, sent a preponderance of conservative and rightist delegates to the *uiezd* assemblies. In the central and eastern regions of European Russia, where the landholdings were smaller, the clergy tended to name "progressives" at elections sandwiched between prayers and chantings of "God Save the Tsar." In the south, with the larger holdings, they voted for conservatives. In the western borderlands their votes for conservatives and monarchists were carefully calculated. They were concerned that the Duma pay proper attention to the Church and religious affairs and to religious education. The left, threatening socialism, would certainly generate some anxiety among them and they feared that a leftist Third Duma would fare no better than the first two.[24] The PTA reported that the small landowners, including the clergy, named 2752 rightists delegates and 2766 conservative. Those classified as liberals numbered 675 and the leftists some 250. There was a significant number of delegates among both the small landowners (1070) and the *volost* peasantry (1838) whose political affiliation could not be identified. Unless they were affected by special local circumstances, they were not likely to change materially the relative strengths of the political groupings of these broad segments of the electorate.[25]

The oppositional press frequently indicated that it was inclined to list most of the non-party element (which probably included some of the "unknowns") with the left and complained that the government underestimated the oppositional vote. It is certain that by the reckoning of the most conservative estimates, these of the PTA, the moderate and oppositional peasant, non-party delegates were more than twice as numerous as the listed rightist non-partisans (6312 against 3025). And the moderate and oppositional non-party delegates among the landowners somewhat outnumbered the rightist non-partisans in that category (2012 against 2469).[26]

The new working class had always been designated as a separate curia which sent delegates to *uiezd* or intermediate city meetings from shops and factories. Absenteeism was rife, as in all other strata, exacerbated by the Social Revolutionary insistence on the boycott of elections. In some localities from one-third to almost one-half of the constituencies did not participate in the primary elections.[27] Here too, official and liberal reportage differed considerably. They agreed in assigning the largest bloc of workers' delegates to the left (45 percent according to PTA, and 24 percent according to *Riech*). But within the left, official returns allowed a considerably larger percentage than the liberal press to the Social Democrats (PTA 68 percent, *Riech* correspondents 40 percent). The Kadets were likely to be less charitable towards their arch rivals in the opposition. Both counts assigned a surprising percentage of worker delegates to the conservatives, moderates, and reactionaries. But the liberals would allow themselves only five percent of the worker vote as against the official figure of 10 percent. While they welcomed the labor vote and hoped to influence it, the Kadets never seemed to have regarded direct support from the workers as an immediate possibility. And, as usual, the Kadets were willing to allow the rightists some 30 percent of the labor delegates and the PTA but 10 percent. Even so, a median figure of 20 percent for labor in the right was somewhat startling.[28]

The peasant and small landowner delegate meetings at *uiezd* centers and the large landowner, provincial townsman, and worker electorates voted for electors to the *guberniia* assemblies who would, in turn, select deputies for the Third Duma. The elections to the *guberniia* assemblies offered a significant reflection of the electorate and at the same time indicated rather clearly the ultimate purposes of the regime. The landowners were endowed with a preponderance of places—50.4 percent as against 31 percent under the law of December 11, 1905. They were assigned a majority in twenty-seven of fifty-one provincial assemblies and lacked a majority of one vote in the other twenty-four. This was easily remedied with the division of the city voters into two categories according to wealth and the certain coalition of the landlordry with the wealthy electors of the first category. Worker electors were reduced from four percent of the electors at the provincial assemblies to two percent (229 to 164), and the peasantry were cut from 34 percent to 22 percent of the *guberniia* electors.[29]

With Kryzahnovskii's astute excisions and modifications, the results of the elections to the *guberniia* assemblies were pre-ordained.[30] It was no surprise for the electorate that the number of opposition electors (progressive, liberal and leftist), fell from 54 percent in the second elections to 28 percent in the third. The significance of the vote from the *uiezdi* lay in the complexion of the delegations from the various categories. For it was only in the final vote from the *guberniia* assemblies that the electoral law could fully control the balloting for the Duma.

Approximately the same differences observed in the preliminary elections were apparent in the official and liberal reportage on the results of the vote to the provincial assemblies.[31] The stolidly conservative mood of the country gentlemen, reflected at the Fifth Zemstvo Congress, changed hardly at all, and the PTA reports counted the opposition in the entire landowner curia as 17 percent as opposed to 24 percent in the second elections. *Riech*, agreeing substantially, would allow the opposition landowners 20 percent in the third elections. Yet, even this favored category suffered from the general political malaise. A considerable portion of the eligible voters failed to appear at the polls and thus frustrated some of the basic purposes of the electoral law. In about a quarter of the *uiezdi* some 30 to 35 percent of the landowners had not voted. Apathy and a sense of political security were probably the determining factors. In provinces where there were few landlords—Viatka, Olonets, Perm—voting was unusually light. In Olonets, for example, only fourteen of twenty-six electors were named.[32]

The drastic reduction in the vote of the small landowner element (by one-third as compared with the second elections) was largely achieved, as noted, by the elimination from the land-

owner category[33] of commune peasants with private holdings
and burghers with rural holdings. The decline might have been
considerably larger had the clergy not participated heavily. The
impact of the significant clerical vote in the preliminary and
uiezd elections was evident in the presence of their electors in all
categories of the *guberniia* assemblies. In eight provinces they
numbered at least one-half of the landowner electors (Astrakhan,
Vologda, Vladimir, Viatka, Grodno, Kiev, Podolsk, and Perm)
and one-third in Minsk and Tver. They were at least 25 percent
of the landowners in Vitebsk, Kostroma, and Iaroslavl and some
20 percent in Moscow, Mogilev, Riazan, Saratov, Volyn, and
Kazan *gubernii*.[34] Only in Arkhangel, Kaluga, Tomsk, Kursk,
St. Petersburg, Smolensk, Ekaterinoslav, Vilno and Tula
gubernii and in the Oblast of the Don Army did they fail to seat
a single elector in the *guberniia* assemblies.[35] Thus they had
considerable leverage at the provincial level, and the moderately
liberal *Viestnik Evropy* considered that they were about equally
divided between the "right" (the Octobrists and the parties to
their right) and the left (the moderate liberals and those to their
left) with a slight edge for the right.[36] The weight of this element,
moderate and conservative, but with its peculiar interests and its
proximity to the peasantry could not but concern the administration. It was apparently one of those factors which the engi-
neers of the "governmental revolution" could not foresee and
whose impact it could not foretell.

Correspondents reporting to *Riech* conceded the conservative
trend among the peasants at the provincial level. But they judged
that 47 percent named as electors to the *guberniia* assemblies
adhered to the opposition. The official PTA calculated peasant
opposition as more nearly 25 percent.[37] Given the composition
of the peasant representation in the *uiezd* meetings a majority
to the right of center was inevitable at the provincial level. But
the record of peasant voting at the first two elections would
seem to warrant a somewhat greater percentage for the opposition
than the official figures indicated.

In the city vote, as in the countryside, the wealthier and presumably more conservative elements were given an artificial
proponderance of strength. In this connection, the generally
oppositional bias of the towns was further circumscribed by the
limitation of direct elections to the Duma to seven cities (St.
Petersburg, Moscow, Kiev, Odessa, Warsaw, and Riga) with a
population of 250,000 or more. And the suffrage of nineteen large
cities was merged with that of the *gubernii* where the rural
elements predominated. The strength of the towns in the pro-

vincial assemblies was actually raised from 22 percent to 25.3 percent of all electors, but the first category named 56 percent of the city electors.[38] It was assigned 738 electoral seats as opposed to 570 for the second category.[39] In 199 *uiezdi*, 27,690 voters in the first category named 341 electors while in the second curia, 176 *uiezdi* with 126,460 voters elected 225 electors. Thus, in the localities indicated each elector in the first category was named by 81 voters and in the second by 560.[40]

Reports on city elections did not differ markedly in official and liberal tallies. But the PTA reported only on the city vote as a whole without analyzing results in each category.[41] Both sources indicated a considerable victory for the opposition. The official tally alloted 62 percent of the electoral seats to the non-legalized parties; the liberal analysts claimed 66 percent. *Riech's* correspondents would admit only of 33 percent for the "right" (including the conservatives). The remainder (1 percent) was designated as "unknown" or "non-party." *Riech* allowed the rightists and conservatives 43 percent of the electors from the first category, and in cities with a direct vote the liberals were accorded 45 percent and the leftists 7 percent, respectively. In the second category the liberal count conceded only 17 percent of the seats to the right of the Kadets and assigned 56 percent to the liberals and 18 percent to the leftists.[42]

In effect the division of the towns into two categories did not weaken the opposition to the extent that the government had anticipated. In the assemblies of four *gubernii* the strength of the opposition in the towns had increased somewhat (Moscow, Vologda, Kiev, Stavropol), and no appreciable change had occurred in the representation from the cities of eleven, largely northern, provinces (Vitebsk, Vladimir, Viatka, Ekaterinburg, Nizhegorod, Kovno, Olonets, St. Petersburg, Smolensk, Tver, Chernigov).[43] But the general rightward trend of the cities was unmistakable and was due largely to the artificial division of voters by income. In the second elections to the provincial assemblies the oppositional elements in the cities named 86 percent of the electors. And in the third elections the opposition in the second category, with its "democratic strata," was able to name 79 percent of the electors. In the second elections leftists seated 25 percent of the electors, and in the third the second category yielded only 18 percent. The Kadets dropped from 37 percent of the electoral seats from the cities in the *guberniia* assemblies to 34 percent.[44]

The PTA reported that the leftist parties had elected 85 percent of the workers' electors to the *guberniia* assemblies and with the liberals the opposition held 93 percent of the workers' seats.

Riech's correspondents allowed the left 90 percent of the proletarian electors with only one place for the liberals and nationalities. There was no doubt about the resounding leftist victory in the worker category, especially since the official tally admitted that only three electors could be classified as "unknown" and as "non-party." All of the Moscow *Guberniia* electors were Social Revolutionaries which would indicate considerable local defection from the boycott. Almost all of the St. Petersburg worker electors were Social Democrats. They captured the large Putilov and Tellman plants aided by the Social Revolutionaries who did not vote or named Social Democrats.[45]

Yet, in the worker elections to the *guberniia* assemblies, the impact of the Social Revolutionary boycott campaign was widespread. There were few or no elections at all in significant factory and railway centers (Nizhi-Novgorod, Iaroslavl, Voronezh, Lodz), and the boycottist mood was strong in the industrial wards of St. Petersburg (Narva, Vyborg). The Moscow workers, on the other hand, showed considerable interest in naming electors to the *guberniia* assembly.[46]

A basic purpose of the electoral revision of June 3, 1907, was the limitation of the influence of the non-Russian and non-Orthodox electorate. Yet the relative strength of the ethnic and religious minorities in the provincial assemblies offers an intriguing index of their persistent interest in the Duma.[47] Largely because of the action of the new law only a small percentage of the overall number of electors were from the non-Russian peoples, some 604 to 622 of 5,030 electors, or 12 to 12.4 percent.[48] And an indeterminable number of each ethnic or religious group, a small number in the case of the larger groups, were sent as Kadets or Social Democrats rather than as representatives of specific minorities.

The Germans were the largest, single "national" group listed in the *guberniia* electoral assemblies, numbering 232 to 238, or a maximum strength of 37.5 percent to 39.4 percent of the minority delegations.[49] They represented primarily German interests and some 54 percent of them came from the Baltic provinces of Kurliand, Lifliand, and Estliand. But they were scattered throughout European Russia with sizeable enclaves sending seven to fourteen electors each from the Territory of the Army of the Don Oblast, St. Petersburg, Samara, and Taurida, Kharkov, and Kherson provinces. As the aristocracy of the Baltic Region they were naturally best represented in the landowner curia where they seated 176 to 182 electors or 61.2 percent to 62.5 percent of the minority electors in the curia at *guberniia* assemblies.

They represented 75.8 percent to 76.4 percent of the German delegation. The *volost* delegates to the *uiezd* assemblies sent nineteen Germans to the *guberniia* assemblies. The provincial city categories listed thirty-four (sixteen from the first category, fifteen from the second, and three identified only as city electors) or, at most, 14.7 percent of the German delegation at the provincial assemblies. Three electors represented the workers—under one percent of the German electors.

The Jews, with 154 to 161 electors, were the second largest ethnic minority in the *guberniia* assemblies—some 25.8 to 26.6 percent of all minority electors. By cultural pattern and because of legal disabilities they were not represented in the rural categories. They numbered seventy in the first category, 71 percent to 75.2 percent of all minority elements from the wealthy city curia. They were fifty-nine to sixty electors strong in the second city category—a maximum of 61.4 percent to 62.7 percent of all minority delegates in the category. Some twenty-four were listed only as city electors, being over 85 percent of all minority electors so classified. They had only one identifiable elector from the workers' curia.

The Poles, though badly underrepresented, sent an impressive delegation of ninety-five chiefly from the "Vistual Provinces" (the Kingdom of Poland), with some scattered elements representing landlord interests from the Lithuanian and Bielorussian provinces. In toto they represented 15.2 to 15.7 percent of the minority electors and only three of them came officially from the city delegations and two from the workers' curia.

The Moslems were the fourth largest minority delegation with sixty to sixty-two representatives at the *guberniia* assemblies. These were 10.6 to 15.7 percent of the national and religious representation at the provincial stage of the elections. Their essentially rural character is reflected in the twenty-nine Moslems elected from the *volost* delegates and sixteen from the landowner curia as against ten from the first and seven from the second town category. And they sent no one from the workers' meetings. They came chiefly from the traditional Moslem areas of European Russia: the Crimea and the middle and south Volga regions.

Other national delegations were quite small. The Lithuanians sent about sixteen electors, the Letts a dozen, and the Georgians, the Rumanians (from Bessarabia), and the Finns (from Arkhangelsk and St. Petersburg *gubernii*) sent two each.

Taken in their broad perspective, the relatively complete official data on the elections to the *guberniia* assemblies represent something more than statistical interest. For they offer some measure of how the "grass roots" reacted after the changes rendered in the Electoral Law of June 3, 1907, so disheartening for the great majority of the voters. They reflect a conservative trend which could only support official purposes to a greater or lesser degree. Arising from a melange of apathy, artificial groupings and restrictions, and a sense of weariness and perhaps even satiation with a receding revolutionary effort, the elements to the right of the Kadets demonstrated significant strength in all categories. The electorate seemed to be groping toward some kind of stability—even in terms that were unpalatable for the great majority. And herein lay, perhaps, the deceptive nature of the calm which followed. But at the same time, the popular mood might provide the opportunity for a more meticulous, effective construction of parliamentary foundations—under relatively stable circumstances.

The vote for electors to the *guberniia* assemblies rather clearly indicates the persistence of a substantial, sustained interest in the Duma by various socioeconomic segments of the population of the Empire. Though beset by a lethargy that, to a degree, dogged the electorate of the preceding campaigns marked by a more revolutionary and expansive mood, they reflect a continued attraction to the polls by the significant landlord and clerical elements and among the important German, Jewish, Polish, and Moslem minorities. The Germans were largely from the favored large landowner category and might be expected to react positively. But the lively response of other considerable ethnic groups in the face of vigorous, curial gerrymandering would seem to connote an absorption in organized political action as an avenue for ameliorating their deteriorating political leverage. Somewhat like the Social Democrats they concluded that the Duma might be just the place to maintain a noisy fire on the regime to publicize its sins against society and also to bring increasing pressure on it for change.

The elections from the *uiezd* centers brings into sharpest relief the wide participation of the generally conservative clerical electorate through its small landowning qualifications. Some of this activity may have resulted from considerable hierarchical pressure but the priest-landowners quickly sensed their strength and their capacity to act on their living standards and religious concerns. And this was not entirely acceptable to the bureaucracy. It had never relished the pressure of the lower clergy as it contrasted its position and way of life with that of the upper hierarchy. It held the clergy's political capacities and attitudes in some contempt. And it was concerned that the representatives of the local priesthood could not generate any considerable excitement over nonclerical issues.

Among the other strata, the peasantry were the most laggard in the *guberniia* electorate (except, perhaps, the low-income groups in the towns). Normal apathy and political illiteracy was reinforced by the failure of the preceding Dumas to meet their craving for land and by their reduced electoral power. The propertied burghers, the intellectuals, and the literate clerical elements in the cities could be expected to maintain a lively interest in their new-found suffrage. And the general trend of the labor vote held no surprises. But considering the apathetic and pessimistic mood of the greater part of the electorate, the workers made an impressive showing in naming all of their electors. The boycott movement took its toll but they were accessible to the Marxist propagandists, and they were accustomed to demonstrating their economic and political power.

Elections for deputies to the Duma in the *guberniia* assemblies were scheduled for October 14, 1907, in forty-one of the fifty-one provinces of European Russia, and were to last for three days. The remaining elections were to be held by the end of October.[50] The balloting was preceded by complex negotiations to name specific individuals, allot a ratio between large and small landowners and the peasantry and, above all, the discussions were to assure the selection of proper candidates for the peasantry.[51] The first two elections had demonstrated decisively that the populist programs held greater appeal for the countryside than official nationalism. The peasant would respond to promises of a higher, more stable income, based on a broader acreage. These aspirations, an active threat in the revolutionary period, remained to haunt the landed gentry and disturbed the clergy with small private plots.

The provincial gentry, endowed with considerable, effective control and influence in the *guberniia* assemblies, were most direct in their quest for the peasant deputies who resembled the political stereotype most attractive to the authors of the electoral law. At the assembly sessions the landlord majorities assigned the peasant electors any number of deputies they considered suitable, within the limits of the law, according to the mood and number of peasants present and voting. Their hands might be tied in the borderlands where the politically astute peasants could manipulate a choice of non-Russian allies—at least for bargaining purposes.[52] While most of the peasant electors who might be selected for deputy seats were probably authentic commune peasants, they certainly bore a more conservative political hue than the noisy populists and Trudoviki predominant among them in the first two elections. And some selected were, in fact, rural bourgeoisie—traders and shopkeepers.[53]

In major urban centers participation in elections appeared to run rather high, but official figures apparently account only for those permitted to vote. In St. Petersburg some 50 percent of the voters in the first category participated in the basic elections (but 20 percent of these failed to appear for the runoffs), and some 70 percent voted in the second category. In Moscow 68.5 percent of the electorate participated and in Riga about 70 percent.[54]

Characteristics of voting in the large cities would vary widely given the complexities of Russian society. Yet the deligence of the Moscow election officials provided the clearest and most comprehensive study available of urban participation. Hence it offers the salient features of city voting and delineates in considerable detail the nature of the urban electorate.[55] For the complex qualifications for urban voters defined in the electoral law provided a remarkably complete record of the socioeconomic strata of the towns. And the nature of their participation in the balloting reflected a prism of political attitudes somewhat broader than ideologically oriented parties. In Moscow the largest segments of the electorate voting on the basis of property or tax qualifications in both categories were those who paid a professional tax (26.5 percent) and those who rented large apartments for which they were taxed (24.7 percent). Owners of industrial and commercial enterprises (14.7 percent), real estate owners (14 percent), white-collar workers in private service (17.6 percent), those who paid no taxes on small apartments (1.8 percent), and pensioners (0.03 percent) completed the list of registered voters. The untaxed apartment renters, a significant sector of the city's population, obviously made no special effort to register personally as required by law. Those who paid taxes could be identified from the tax lists as registered automatically for voting.[56]

In the first city category in Moscow nearly all the voters could be qualified as property owners (97.6 percent), and of those 95 percent were homeowners. White-collar employees and all apartment renters (taxpaying and non-taxpaying) together comprised three-quarters of the voters in the second city category. Employees of commercial establishments, almost all in the second category, represented the largest occupational group in the electorate (20.6 percent of all Moscow city voters). The second curia included most businessmen since their qualifications were smaller than those of the homeowners (17.9 percent of the second category).[57] Given a sense of status, relative well-being and sophistication, and with a considerable leaven of property consciousness, these elements in the second category, while not entirely satisfied with their lot, were not likely to combine in a revolutionary wedge.

Contemporary local officialdom, unlike the revolutionary opposition, differentiated the liberal professions from the middle class and designated them as 12.4 percent of all Moscow voters.[58] They comprised about 13 percent of the second category and but 7.5 percent of the first.[59]

An impressive 68.5 percent of all eligible voters (those allowed to vote) balloted in Moscow, but they represented only a meager 11.3 percent of the voters with a right to vote. Yet this compares with 14.2 percent of those with a right to vote in the second elections and 14.8 percent in the first. Indifference, interpretations, failure to meet residence qualifications or to present proper documents accounts for the relatively small turnout in the third elections.[60]

The greater part of the voters who participated in the elections in Moscow was relatively young. The largest segments were those aged thirty to forty (34.1 percent) and forty to fifty (29.4 percent). And within these age groups the rate of participation was the highest: 69.8 percent of those in their thirties and 70 percent of those in their forties.[61] Yet, fewer voters in these age groups participated than in preceding elections.[62]

The sharp rise in absenteeism among the various categories was starkly revealed in the dry statistical record of the Moscow elections. The lower income groups, particularly the workers, were influenced by the boycott campaign and the frustrations generated by the election law, and they ignored the polls in considerable numbers. Some 46 percent of the workers failed to vote.[63] But even among the liberal professions, which encompassed the greater part of the intelligentsia, from half to a quarter of the eligible voters did not cast a ballot. The element of indifference evident to some degree in preceding elections was now reinforced by a sense of frustration stemming from repression, the conditions of the election law, and a realization that the regime would not adhere to its own rules or would interpret them narrowly when its fundamental interests were challenged.[64] Only the clergy in Moscow, as elsewhere, showed a lively and continuing interest in the elections and 82 percent of their number participated.[65]

The statistical summary of Moscow's elections bore out the harsh realities emanating from the Law of June 3, 1907. Only 14.4 percent of all votes were cast in the first category and 85.6 percent in the second.[66] In the preceding elections Moscow's direct representation was elected largely by the employees of public and state institutions and private enterprises. In the current balloting, although they comprised a third of the voters, they elected only two of the four deputies, those alloted the second category.[6] The confidence of the more substantial elements is reflected, to a degree, in the voting pattern of the first category. They were more intensively interested in the runoff elections than in the "basic" voting. The reverse was true of the second category.[68]

The final elections were carried off quietly, if those more fully reported in the cities can serve as an index of public attitudes and behavior. A considerably stricter control was instituted in the main centers and voters with doubtful credentials were questioned more thoroughly. And the runoffs were less lively than the first balloting.[69] The varied, harried, and restricted electorate of the Russian Empire produced a remarkably moderate representative body, considering that the electoral law offered every possible advantage for the election of elements to the right of center. Only fifty-one extreme rightists were named, some 11.4 percent of the deputies to be elected to the Third Duma. Together with the committed, but not fanatical, Nationalist group of twenty-six (5.8 percent of the Duma) and the seventy Moderate Rightists (15.6 percent), the right wing of the Duma counted 147 deputies (32.8 percent). This was somewhat smaller than the representation of the moderate constitutionalist Union of October 17 with 154 seats (34.5 percent of the Duma). The Kadets emerged with a fraction of fifty-four members (11.2 percent), including some imposing figures, and they continued to maintain a "hegemony" of sorts over the shrunken, if unchastized, nonrevolutionary opposition. They were familiar enough with the program, temperament, and mood of the newly formed Progressive fraction of twenty-eight deputies (6.3 percent of the Duma) to count on it for considerable support even though it represented a somewhat more moderate strain of liberalism. For the most part, moreover, the national minorities had voted with the Kadets. And there was, in fact, a potentially considerable constitutional center if the Octobrists found it useful, or necessary, to behave like constitutionalists. Two cohesive, if undersized, groups from the western borderlands would have their day in the Third Duma: the Polish Kolo of eleven deputies (2.4 percent) which had captured all of the seats not assigned specifically to Russians in the Vistula Provinces (the former Kingdom of Poland) and the Polish-Lithuanian-Bielorussian Group with seven deputies (1.5 percent). The Moslem Group of eight deputies (1.7 percent), representing the same religio-political electorate that had sent thirty deputies to the Second Duma in the preceding February, painfully dramatized the plight of this considerable minority element. The remainder of the opposition, the Trudoviki with fourteen members (3.1 percent) and the nineteen Social Democrats (4.2 percent) were but wraiths of their former potent delegations. The electorate would undoubtedly continue to hear their shrill voices, but they could have no substantial affect on the Duma's decisions.[70]

The elections yielded the administration approximately what it wanted, with perhaps a larger body of intellectuals of liberal persuasion than it anticipated, and a considerable clerical delegation which was likely to be conservative but not entirely controllable. It won supporting delegations from provinces in which the liberals expected an oppositional victory (Vitebsk, Grodno, part of Olonets, and Taurida). But this windfall was offset by mixed supportive and oppositional representations from provinces (such as Simbirsk and Orenburg) where the conservatives and rightists had expected a clear sweep. And there were "brilliant" oppositional victories in some doubtful *gubernii*—as in Kazan.[71]

X
The Complex of Fractions

The Russian multiparty system, like the groupings in other continental parliamentary structures, generated a significant quality of political instability which at moments of intra-party crises verged on volatility. In the course of the five years spanned by the Third Duma the membership of the groups and fractions altered with kaliedescopic abruptness as members passed from one to another and new agglomerations emerged as fractions and groups merged with each other. And the elections provided considerable and varied data reflecting the political, social, economic, and cultural realities of broad segments of the society of the Russian Empire—even with the distortions determined by the revised electoral law.[1]

As organized shortly before the opening of the Duma in November, 1907, the Rightist Fraction included all of the extreme rightist deputies.[2] The Union of the Russian People was as yet undivided and by unofficial count numbered at least thirty-two of the fifty-one Rightist deputies. The secession of the Archangel Michael hardly affected the fraction which changed little since Purishkevich and his cohorts favored participation in the Duma.[3] Although twenty-three noblemen were elected (45 percent of the fraction), a strong contingent of eighteen clergymen (35 percent) would have considerable influence on Rightist attitudes in the Duma. And there were eight peasants (16 percent) named, in all probability on the initiative of the strong noble representation at the *guberniia* assemblies.[4] While an extreme and politically vulgarized Slavophile ideology was the binding factor in the Rightist Fraction, there were among the nobility some 20 percent who were primarily bureaucrats or intellectuals, and these informed the back country *pomiestchiki*, deeply agitated over their economic and political position, with a broader perspective of possibilities and tactics.

Given the nature of their ideology, the Rightist Fraction was overwhelmingly Russian (82 percent) and Orthodox—there being only one non-Orthodox, an Old Believer. Other nationalities included five Bielorussians (10 percent), two Ukrainians (4 percent) and one Zyrian. One deputy differentiated himself as a

Cossack.[5] The single largest contingent came from the broad west and Southwest Border area, twenty-one in number (some 40 percent of the fraction). Six more came from the Dnieper provinces (12 percent), two from Vilna, three from Kherson and one each from Ekaterinoslav and the Caucasus, representing the Russian population where its number and interests might not predominate. Yet the second largest group of twelve (24 percent) came from the Central provinces, and four more (8 percent) were sent from the Russian North.[6]

The large noble representation placed the Rightists among the best educated groups in the Third Duma. Twenty-four (45 percent) of their number had a higher education while eighteen (35 percent) enjoyed an intermediate or military training and only nine (18 percent) had a "home" education. In this respect they were outranked only by the Octobrists and Kadets with their strong contingents of intelligentsia, and by the predominantly noble Nationalists.[7]

The Rightists represented a vested element of the Russian economic and social structure. Twelve of the nobles derived their income primarily from agriculture with an average holding of 2,335 *desiatiny*.[8] The nine nobles whose income was non-agricultural were bureaucrats or practiced the liberal professions. The clerical Rightists had an average holding of forty-four *desiatiny* as against seven *desiatiny* for the peasants in the Fraction. Seventy-five percent of the Rightist deputies with a non-agricultural income earned over 1,000 rubles annually.[9]

The Rightist Fraction enjoyed a relatively stable membership, fluctuating from a low of 11.5 percent of the membership of the Third Duma in the second session to a high of 12 percent in the fourth.[10]

Two bodies of deputies in the Third Duma were elected originally as a part of the rightist bloc but soon found their association with the extremists ideologically and politically unpalatable. They were the Moderate Rightist Fraction and the Nationalist Group. In the negotiations for Duma officials between the Octobrists and the Rightists, the Moderate Rightists were regarded as an informal subdivision of the latter.[11] Some friction developed between them over the nominee for vice president and assistant secretary of the Duma.[12] But their chief differences were those of ideology and temperament, and by the second week in November, 1907, their separation into distinct and separate parliamentary groups was an accomplished fact.[13] The moderates, headed by Count V. A. Bobrinskii, P. N. Krupenskii, and

A. K. Demianovich were scandalized by the calculated, disruptive behavior of the Rightists aimed at discrediting the Duma. They were disgusted by S. I. Kelepovskii's outbursts in his second appearance in the Third Duma calling for the expulsion of the opposition from the Presidium—as it had excluded the Right in the Second. And they noted A. N. Tkachev's assertion that the Duma could not create committees because they existed in the republican French parliament. How, they asked, was it possible to work with people of that cultural level? Early in the Duma's activities they opposed the resurrection of the campaign against terror since it could cleave the conservative rightist majority and only make difficulties for the government in combatting it. And judging from past experience they felt that it would give substance to the charges that the Duma was most adept at acrimonious argument.[14]

The Moderates contended that their action in separating from the extremists would strengthen the ranks of the constitutionalists. Krupenskii explained to the press that the Moderate Right was more liberal than people imagined, and they would surely enact reforms that would satisfy popular needs. They supported broad reforms as necessary for progress and well being but they opposed revolution which could burst forth at any time if only given some leeway.[15]

The essence of the program of the Moderate Rightist Fraction consisted of three points: the indivisibility of the Empire, a legislative Duma, and a point which identified them typically with the right wing of the Duma—the inadmissibility of equal rights for the Jews. On November 14, 1907, their complete program appeared in the capital press.[16] The Fraction recognized the institution of representative government as irrevocable and considered it necessary to establish a Duma fraction with the purpose of defending the interests of all parts of the Empire by legal legislative means established by the "autocratic tsar." The program called for complete pacification by a strong state authority. It sought state support for the development of Church life at all levels and within canon law. It would especially secure the parish clergy materially. The Moderate Rightists would equalize the peasantry juridically and improve their condition by pursuing Premier P. A. Stolypin's program of enclosure and resettlement, and they would find sources of credit for the villagers. They would promote a program of social insurance and security for labor and labor organizations. But they would insist on the inviolability of private property. They would strengthen local self government to promote the cultural and economic needs of the population, and they would include border areas where national minorities predominated; but here the interests of the Russian population had, by all means, to be protected—"locally, as well as nationwide." They would exclude only the Jews from these provisions but, with a shade moderation, they would eliminate "their senseless repression." It is not entirely clear whether they would oppose all economic and residence disabilities or only unsettling pogromist activity. The dissemination of public education, with a technological emphasis, was imperative, but so was the elimination of political activism in it. Radical court reforms were needed to protect state and individual rights in order to realize accessible, speedy, and independent justice. They called for the review of law governing the press so that it might serve justice and the commonweal and repress calumny and immorality.

Some sixty-nine deputies withdrew from the Rightist Bloc to join the Moderate Rightist Fraction. But by the end of November they were having second thoughts and proposed a meeting to patch up differences. They were concerned that bifurcation could only weaken the far right. And they hoped to dominate or, perhaps, control the extremists through their numerical predominance in a rightist fraction. Efforts were made to work out a general program acceptable to all rightist elements, but at a conference on January 22, 1908, it was apparent that the Moderates would insist on the complete acceptance of their views and efforts at reunification collapsed.[17]

The Moderate Rightist Fraction was a stereotype of the deputations to the right of center except for its unusually large peasant contingent.[18] It was dominated by a strong, landed, noble delegation, largely from the central, Dnieper, and southwest border regions. The nobility numbered some twenty-two deputies (31.8 percent of the fraction) only three of whom derived their income primarily from private practice in the liberal professions. Twenty-three (33.3 percent) were peasants and fourteen were clergy (20.2 percent). The clerical contingent included an archbishop, Evlogii, famed for his intensive effort to create the "Russian" province of Kholm from portions of Vistula provinces. Some twenty-nine deputies (42 percent) held under 100 *desiatiny* of farm land while twelve (18.3 percent) held over 7,000 *desiatiny* and five more (7 percent) owned between one and two thousand *desiatiny*. Eleven deputies (16 percent) with non-agricultural incomes earned more than 1,000 rubles annually, and two made over 5,000. Forty-nine (71 percent) were Great Russian, nine (13

percent) were Ukraninian and six (8.6 percent), Bielorussian.
Thirty-six deputies in their thirties and the same number in their
forties were each 37.6 percent of their fraction respectively, and
eleven (16 percent) were in their fifties. Twenty-five (36.2 percent)
enjoyed a higher education and twenty (27.5 percent) an intermediate, usually clerical, training. Most of the peasants had a
lower education. The largest contingent of Moderate Rightist
deputies numbering twenty (29 percent) was sent from the Southwest, beyond the predominantly Great Russian *gubernii*, while
seventeen (24.6 percent) had experienced zemstvo service and five
(7 percent) had served in the First and Second Dumas while six
(8.6 percent) had been justices of the peace.

The Moderate Rightist Fraction was relatively stable in the
two years of its independent existence, losing five of its members
(three to the Progressive group) and gaining seven (four from the
National Group). All but one of the six lost by death and resignation were replaced. The Fraction was absorbed by the comprehensive Russian National Fraction in the third session. Thus, as an
independent fraction it gained slightly in membership (from 15.8
percent to 17.2 percent).

Early in December, 1907, another element of the Rightist Fraction led by Prince A. P. Urusov, V. G. Vetchinin, and I. K. Giubernet separated to form the National Group. The same fear of losing influence inhibited both the Moderates and the Nationalists
from organizing as separate bodies. And the same distaste for the
extremism of program and tactics of those deputies who belonged
to or sympathized with the URP motivated their ultimate separation. An effort to join with the Moderate Rightists at the Conference of January 22, 1908, failed as that large group insisted on
acceptance of its program.[19] But their own program, issued
shortly thereafter, bore a striking resemblance to the Moderate
credo. It was noticeably less specific and several shades more
nationalistic with its emphasis on the slogan "Russia for the
Russians."[20] Somewhat earlier their spokesmen had indicated
that they would place all primary education in the hands of the
Church and allow those who qualified to enter two-years, state-
operated grammar and secondary schools. Like the Moderates
they emphasized a technological, intermediate education, reflecting the same class-economic considerations.[21] Yet their negative
reaction to the furore raised by the Rightists over P. N. Miliukov's
assault on official policy in a speech delivered in New York City
in January, 1908, and their willingness to support an Octobrist as
Vice President of the Duma, portended a generally moderate
course.[22]

Fifteen Nationalists were elected to the Third Duma, but some eleven deputies soon joined them after the first session opened to form a Group of twenty-six. This was indeed a haven for the conservative, Russian, Orthodox, moderately wealthy nobility hailing from about the same areas as the Moderate Rightists. The Nationalists were somewhat older, on the average, than the Moderates and not as well educated. But they had garnered considerable experience in public office—in local, class and representative institutions.[25]

A closer examination of the National Group reveals that it included thirteen landed and seven non-landed titles (77 percent of the Group). The non-landed nobility numbered three bureaucrats, a teacher and two retired military officers. The remainder of the Group consisted of two clerics, two peasants, a railway worker and a physician. The Group was entirely Orthodox with twenty-three Great Russians (84.5 percent) and three Ukrainians. Twelve deputies were in their forties (46 percent) and seven (27 percent) in their fifties. None was younger than thirty-one. Half of the Group, mostly from the rural nobility, had a secondary education, and eight deputies (30.3 percent) had completed courses of study in higher institutions of learning. Nine of the landowners owned between 400 and 2,000 *desiatiny,* and five (19.2 percent) held under 100. The same number held between 100 and 400 *desiatiny.* Five of the eight deputies with primarily non-agricultural income earned between 1,500 and 6,500 rubles annually. Over half of the Group had some experience in public office. Eight had seen service as Marshals of the Nobility, six (23 percent) had been in zemstvo service, three had served as justices of the peace, and one had been elected to a previous Duma. As with the Moderates, the largest delegations stemmed from the Central and Dnieper regions with six deputies from each and the Southwest with five.

During its independent existence for two sessions of the Third Duma, the National Group saw a change in about 20 percent of its membership. It lost five deputies—three returned to the Rightists —and gained two. In addition, one deputy died and one resigned. In its brief flare of glory in the second session the Group represented 4.75 percent of the Duma's strength.

In October of 1909, early in the third session of the Third Duma, the two aforementioned bodies, the Moderate Rightist Fraction and the National Group, ultimately found it feasible and purposeful to join forces and merge into a single Russian National Fraction. Their chief goal was to form into a "solid right center" between the Rightists and the Octobrists which would be rendered independent of both but might enter into agreements with either or both of their neighboring fractions. They reckoned that with the Octobrists and others who might join them they would have an absolute majority in the Duma.[24] The consistent nationalism of the Fraction was guaranteed by the leadership of the Moderate Rightist elements which sprang from the Great Russian landed minority in the southwest borderlands: the *plus royaliste que.* . . .[25]

The merger was executed with remarkable agility within a period of two weeks, for there were truly no basic programmatic differences. Preliminary talks were concluded by October 20, 1909, when the Moderate Rightist Fraction reluctantly accommodated the smaller Nationalists in accepting their more inflexible stand on the position of the Jews.[26] The final union took place on the premises of the Moderates on October 25, when the National Group appeared dramatically in a body. And the combined meeting proceeded under the chairmanship of P. N. Balashov, the Moderate leader, to name the fraction and confirm the program agreed on in the preliminary conferences. The meeting permitted only one last significant change when it agreed to exclude the final point of the draft program. This would require an improvement in the life of the lower bureaucracy and a safeguarding of its legal position. There was apparently no strong desire among the nationalists to challenge or embarrass the government in the matter of the traditionally small pittance allotted the army of clerks in the lower ranks of the bureaucracy.[27] The bureaus of the component parties resigned at once but continued to function until October 29, when the Fraction elected Balashov as President and another Moderate Rightist, D. N. Chikhachev, as Secretary.[28]

The program of the Russian National Fraction rang the changes on the trefoil slogan of official nationalism, under the modified conditions of parliamentary government. It demanded the preservation of the "unity and indivisibility" of the Russian Empire and the protection of Russian interests in all of its parts. It called on the "autocratic Tsar," together with the Imperial Duma "established by him" to promote the realization of legislative authority. It demanded the "broad promotion of the development of the predominant Orthodox Church," its eparchial parish life, and the material conditions, especially of the rural parish clergy.

Like most conservative deputations, the Russian Nationalists voiced a concern for the welfare of the toiling masses—with certain benevolent conditions. Their program demanded the equalization of peasant rights and an improvement in the economic condition of the peasantry through enclosure—a more "cultured" form of landownership—and resettlement, along with cheap credit: the basic Stolypin formula. And in full accord with the Premier-President, they insisted on the security of private property. With this condition, labor, too, was to enjoy broad freedom and the added boon of social insurance.

Then, the Russian Nationalists were interested in local government free of bureaucratic tutelage but guaranteeing the rights of Russian minorities in the borderlands. The non-Russian minority peoples, with the exception of the Jews, were also to enjoy economic self government but, again, with the assurance of the protection of Russian interests. And the government was to support the economic foundations of the country—agriculture and agricultural industry.

Education was to be universal but it was to serve nationalist concepts. For the schools were to stimulate Russian national consciousness through a program that smacked of the Nicolaitan system, based on the principles of faith, love of fatherland, and the development of a sense of duty and legality. Technological education was to be emphasized and politics rigorously excluded. The Russian Nationalist program, in a word, sought safe educational channels and an official counterreaction to student activism. The press, too, had to be controlled by law to perform its proper function by serving "truth, justice, and the general good on one hand" and to suppress revolutionary, slanderous, and immoral (pornographic) activities on the other.

Like their political antecedents, the Russian Nationalists consisted of highly limited constitutionalists and decisive Russian patriots. Their leadership proclaimed that their nationalism was not "cannibalistic"; that it was better to assure that people would be satisfied with their life and fate. Their principle was "live and let live." Only harmful, antagonistic tendencies directed against the Russian state system would bring out their opposition. Yet they identified those tendencies with some of the major non-Russian elements. For the Finns were to be "equalized" with the Russians, a euphemism for the limitation of their autonomy, and Finnish Vyborg and Polish Kholm were to be "returned" to the Russians. And the Jews, the prime target of all nationalists, from the Octobrists rightward, were to be ascribed to the Pale of Settlement by a "final" law and they were to be removed completely from the schools, courts, and press.[29]

The constitutionalism defined by the Russian Nationalists reveals that they were as little aware of the factors that made for acute popular frustration (even while sharing some measure of them) as were the extreme rightists. Anticipating the possibility of Stolypin's resignation, they feared that the Premier would thereby promote "parliamentarism." And they called for further basic change in the electoral system for a new Duma. For they expected the Law of June 3 to produce only a Duma worse than its predecessors, and that its dissolution would bring a reversion to the bureaucratic regime which almost ruined the country. Better that Stolypin first dissolve the Duma with a new electoral law which would assure a majority that would share his nationalism and his policies for the various national minorities. "The opposition forgets that you [Stolypin] are the appointee of the Tsar and not parliament and that you behaved according to the Tsar's will based on factual and juridical state law which no law allows parliament to interpret."[30]

For the moment, the Octobrists welcomed the new political aggregation. Guchkov regarded it as a "natural union" which would stabilize the unsteady elements of the center, counter their fractionalization, and thereby increase their influence in the Duma.[31] Yet there were differences of temperament and perspective to counter any nationalist-conservative union between the main body of the Octobrists and a putative right-wing of the center in the new Duma. And the far right paranoically regarded the merger of the moderately rightist elements as a "conscienceless conspiracy with the Octobrists."[32]

The Russian National fraction was among the larger units in the Third Duma, numbering ninety-one members when it was formed (18.8 percent of the total membership of the Duma). And its composition naturally reflected the social, ethnic, religious, and cultural texture of its component groups.[33] Some fifty-three deputies (58.2 percent of the fraction) stemmed from the nobility. Thirty-four of this noble contingent were landed, seventeen were bureaucrats, and seven of the nobles derived their incomes from the liberal professions. The next largest groups in the Russian National Fraction were seventeen peasants (18.6 percent) and twelve clergymen (13 percent). The latter included the Archbishop Evlogii of Kholm and Liublin.

By far the largest occupational segment of the fraction consisted of forty-nine landowners (51.7 percent). Thirteen of these listed themselves as farmers, that is, small landowners. Among the sixty-one deputies in the Fraction engaged in agriculture (67 percent), sixteen (26.2 percent of those engaged in agriculture) held under 100 *desiatiny*, twenty-eight (45.8 percent of those in agriculture) held between 100 and 1,000 *desiatiny,* while thirteen land-owners (21.3 percent) held over 2,000. By Russian standards this was a well-to-do representation. Of the seventeen deputies who derived their income from non-agricultural sources, twelve (70.5 percent of this category) earned 500 to 5,000 rubles annually and seven (40 percent) had an income of over 5,000 rubles.

The southwest borderlands and central European Russia provided most of the Russian National deputies. Those stemming from the Southwest numbered twenty-one (23 percent) and included much of its leadership. Some sixteen (17.5 percent) hailed from the Dnieper, fifteen from the North Central and fourteen (15.3 percent) from the Central provinces.

Like other fractions with a large aristocratic contingent, the educational level of the Russian Nationalists was high and their public service record impressive. Thirty-seven deputies (40.6 percent of the Fraction) had a higher education and thirty-two (35 percent) an intermediate schooling. Thirteen had considerable experience in local administrative service on the zemstvo boards and five in the city dumas. Twelve had been justices of the peace and seven were deputies to the Second Duma.

Throughout the three sessions of the Duma in which it functioned, the Russian National Fraction remained remarkably stable—up to a point. Only two of its members died and three resigned, and only one of these was not replaced. But the solid record was marred at the end of the fourth session (April, 1911) by the defection of sixteen members, all former Moderate Rightist, to form the Independent Nationalist Fraction. Thus its forces fell from 20.6 percent of the Duma in the third session to 17.4 in the last.[34]

The small Independent Nationalist Fraction was formed largely under the aegis of its two most active members, old Duma hands P. N. Krupenskii and P. V. Sinadino. They had been among the most ardent nationalists in the Second Duma and, with their followers, sharply reflected a broad current common to all nationalist elements to the right of center. For in each of these groupings there were numberous Russians who stemmed largely from the border, non-Great Russian Areas. They felt a compulsion to emphasize the interests of this minority in areas strategic for the security and cohesiveness of the Empire. And their emotional involvement was heightened by the consciousness of their situation as an outlying but integral part of the majority, subsumed in the concept of "nationality." Hence the Fraction announced as its chief principles the "Imperial idea and the need to bind the center with the borderlands" and to attract those groups of the population "which have long been dependably conservative."[35]

In a word, the "Independents" were concerned with any degree of sympathy which the population and the administration held for the European minorities. They were adamant in their unwillingness to allow for any significant political influence on the part of the "alien" elements in the borderlands. And they proposed that the non-Russians in these sensitive areas leave or become assimilated. How they expected to realize this in regions where the indigenous peoples were the vast majority or a considerable segment of the population is not clear—unless they were referring only to the urban Jewish aggregations. And the programs of the Government and the rightists were certainly innocent of sympathetic sentiments for the denizens of the Pale.[36]

The sixteen deputies in the Independent Nationalist Fraction were relatively homogeneous in almost every respect. They were predominantly noble landowners in the higher, rural, economic strata. They were Great Russian, Orthodox, well educated, middle aged, and steeped in public experience. And most of them came, of course, from the western border areas of the Empire.[37] The Independents were nobles except for a parish priest and three deputies from the urban categories. And the nobles were all landowners except for a physician who, with two others, were in government service. Five (31.2 percent) had holdings of over 3,000 desiatin and none held under 100. Information on the salaried element is meager, but it appears to be more than economically comfortable. The non-agrarian Independent Nationalist deputies were remarkably shy about divulging information on their incomes. Only State Secretary V. N. Protsenko listed a home valued at 25,000 rubles, Sinadino a salary of 6,000 rubles, and N. M. Soltuz noted that he held some real estate. There were only three non-Russians among the Independent sixteen: a Moldavian, a Greek, and an Armenian and only the last was non-Orthodox. Nine (56.2 percent) had a higher education, six (37.5 percent) an intermediate training, and only one a lower. Six deputies were in their forties and four in their fifties while those in their thirties and sixties numbered three each—a vigorous, seasoned fraction, yet surprisingly placid.[38]

This small fraction was indeed rich in public experience. One deputy had served in both preceding Dumas and three held seats in the Second. Six had served on zemstvo boards; two had been mayors; four, justices of the peace; and one, a county marshal of the nobility. The salient "border Russian" character of the Fraction was underscored by the ten deputies (62.5 percent) who hailed from the Southwest and Dnieper areas while the next largest group of four represented the Volga provinces. No member of the Fraction shifted allegiance during the course of the fifth session of the Third Duma.

In the course of the second session an anomalous group congealed into the nucleus of a body which was to gather during the remaining three sessions. This was the Non-party Group, peculiar to the infant Russian parliamentary scene.[39] Apparently organized, at the start, as a combination of rightists of various class origins, the movement developed in the third session as an essentially peasant effort.[40] The priests and peasants who joined the new Group regarded themselves as a segment of the moderate right—somewhat to the right of the Octobrists. And like the latter they rested their position on the Manifesto of October 17, but placed a special emphasis on Orthodoxy. They represented something of a new hope for moderate elements on their right, but the Octobrists leaders were concerned that they might further splinter the moderate vote.[41] Yet, when the Duma was notified officially of their incorporation on October 21, 1909, the Non-partisans protested that they would vote together only on matters pertaining to peasant concerns and otherwise would hold to the views of the parties of their origin. They would have, as it were, a dual allegiance—party and peasant.[42]

But an examination of the personnel of the Non-party Group would indicate that while it had a peasant majority, it attracted landowner, clerical, and even burgher representatives. It is likely, moreover, that some of the peasants in moderate economic circumstances were carefully culled by the provincial electoral assemblies, dominated by the local nobility. This would indicate that the Group's interests ranged considerably wider than those of the allotment peasantry.[43]

The Non-party Group began its life modestly with only six registered adherents, but sprouted marvellously, especially in the third session when its existence and operations attracted wider attention. And in the fifth session it reached a total of twenty-nine at its largest. The fifteen peasant deputies were 51.7 percent of the Group and the five nobles over 17 percent. There were also four burghers, three clerics, a Cossack, and an unclassified deputy.

The noble landowners and the burghers had substantial incomes but were not among the wealthiest in their classes. And the clerics were, as usual, more affluent than the peasant majority.

Most of the nobles were landowners in relatively moderate circumstances, holding under 1,000 desiatiny while one was a government official earning under 3,000 rubles annually. The majority of the peasants (eleven) were quite typical, holding under fifty *deiatiny*. The town deputies earned up to 3,000 rubles and the income of the clergy ranged between 400 and 1,000 rubles.

Ethnically, the Group was over 70 percent Russian and there were twenty-five (86.2 percent) who were Orthodox. Twenty-one were Great Russian, four were Ukrainian, and two, Bielorussian. The two non-Russians were Lithuanian and Armenian. The non-Orthodox included two Old Believers, a Roman Catholic, and a Gregorian. All but six of the Group came from European Russia (four from Asiatic Russia and two from the Caucasus) and of these the Central and Volga Regions each sent five deputies, and the Dnieper provinces sent four.

The Group's emphasis was on youth, and while it was poorly educated its record of public service was not mediocre. Nine Non-partisans were in their thirties (31 percent of the Group) and eleven in their forties (38 percent). Six were in their fifties and three in their twenties. Reflecting the predominantly peasant coloration of the Group, 51 percent had a lower or "home" education (lower—31 percent, home—20 percent). Those with a higher and secondary education represented about 20 percent of the Group respectively. Yet, seven Non-partisans had held public office, including two who had served in past Dumas, two in the zemstvos, and one as a mayor. Two had been justices of the peace.

As a Group that attracted accretions in every session of the Duma, it was naturally in a state of constant flux, yet it lost only four adherents: one each to the Progressives, Octobrists, Russian Nationalists and Rightists—all in the fourth session. The greatest gains were six from the Moderate Right, a like number of Octobrists, and five from the Progressives. They also attracted three Kadets, four Trudoviki, and the same number of Social Democrats. Their predominantly small-unit agricultural interest and their loose party allegiance in the young parliamentary structure would explain these accretions which raised their "power" from something over one percent of the Duma in the second session to over five percent in the third. None of these adherents ever considered himself a defector from his original fraction or group —as reflected in their easy movement away from the Non-partisans.

The Fraction of the Party of the Union of October 17 with its original contingent of 154 members was the largest in the Duma.

Given its size, central position, and heterogeneous, class texture, it proved to be one of the more restless bodies in the Russian parliament.[44] As in other conservative and rightist representations, the nobility predominated. They were some 60 percent of the Fraction and included a goodly leaven of professional and bureaucratic elements. The Octobrist Party was popularly characterized from its inception as that of the greater bourgeoisie. While it attracted the votes and support of the financially more substantial, commercial-industrial businessmen and numbered most of the deputies who were businessmen (about two-thirds) including some of their most outstanding representatives, the entrepreneur element was not an unduly large part of the Octobrist electorate if the Fraction properly reflected their vote.[45] They were at most one-third of the Fraction and only about an eighth of these might be considered substantially wealthy. Their position was most significant as the moving force of the large left wing of the Octobrist Party and its Duma representation.

From a closer examination of the Fraction it is apparent that the nobility numbered ninety-one deputies in all, and some forty of their number (44 percent of the nobility) held a significant amount of land (over 1,000 *desiatiny*) but eight of these might equally be classified with the eighteen (12 percent) who enjoyed incomes from non-agrarian sources. The peasantry and the clergy (26 percent of all landholders in the Fraction) held most of the "economies" under 400 *desiatiny*. Some twenty-five landholders (24 percent of the landholders) held 400 to 1,000 *desiatiny*; nineteen (18 percent) held 1,000 to 2,000 *desiatiny*; and twenty-one (20 percent) held over 2,000. No more than forty-four deputies (29.7 percent of the Fraction) had incomes from non-agrarian sources. Of these, twenty (13.5 percent) earned more than 5,000 rubles annually.

The Octobrist Fraction was predominantly Great Russian and Orthodox from every part of European Russia except Poland and the Ural Region; it enjoyed a high educational level which might well be expected of a group of this order, and as a seasoned aggregation it had accumulated the broadest political experience in the Duma. Some 125 deputies (84.5 percent) identified themselves as Great Russians. There were ten Ukraninians (6.7 percent), and the German subgroup largely from the Baltic Region consisted of eleven deputies (7.5 percent). The Fraction also included a Bielorussian and a Tartar. The ethnic structure of the Fraction more or less determined its religious composition. The Orthodox counted 131 members (88.5 percent) and thirteen were Lutherans (8.7 percent). Two Old Believers, a Mennonite, and a Moslem completed the religious roster. The largest Octobrist delegation, forty-eight deputies (32.4 percent), came from the Central Region. The North Central Region sent 27 (18.2 percent); the Dnieper, twenty-five (16.8 percent); and the Volga, twenty-three (15.5 percent). The Baltic sent seven Octobrists; the Northwest, Southwest and Crimea four each. Three came from the northern provinces, two from the Don *Oblast*, and one from the Caucasus. Asia sent none.

The educational level and the public service record of the chief conservative fraction were predictably high and reflected its maturity. Eighty-one deputies (54.7 percent) enjoyed a higher education, and thirty-six (34.3 percent) an intermediate. Yet, a fifth of the Fraction had only village tutelage. Forty-four members (29.7 percent) had served in the zemstvos, the seed bed of conservative constitutionalism, and nine deputies (6 percent) had seen service in previous Dumas. Nine had served in city councils, five had been mayors, and nine had been elected marshals of the nobility. Twenty Octobrists (13.5 percent) had been justices of the peace. The range of the Fraction's age groupings was felicitous, almost ideal, for a political body, with 127 (85 percent) of its members between the ages of thirty and sixty, and fifty-two of these (35 percent) were in their forties. Only three were less than thirty years of age.

Like other large, ideologically composite political groupings, temperamental, doctrinal, and socioeconomic differences tended to bifurcate, then splinter, the main body of the Octobrist Fraction. At the very least, its membership shifted restlessly in all sessions. In the course of the five sessions of the Third Duma it attracted only two deputies, a Moderate Rightist and an unattached deputy, and the majority of its losses by death and resignation were not restored as their replacements were elected to other fractions and groups. Six deputies who resigned were replaced by only three who were newly elected, and twelve who died in the five years of the Third Duma were succeeded by only half that number of Octobrists. But the Fraction's greatest losses stemmed from shifts to other parties and the formation of a significant splinter unit. In all five sessions the Octobrists lost some thirty-one deputies, chiefly to the Progressive and Russian National Fractions, that is, to elements somewhat to the left and right of the Union of October 17. Each gained seven deputies from the Octobrists, four centered their attention on the Non-party Group, and the Moderate Rightists, Kadets, and National Group each attracted an Octobrist. The loose structure of the Octobrist Party and the hardening attitudes of its major components, both in support of and in opposition to official policy, were bound to bring serious defections on both flanks, especially on the right.

The single largest depletion of the ranks of the Octobrists in the Duma came with the formation of the Right Octobrist Fraction. Differences between the bulk of the membership and the rightist minority were noticeable from the beginning of the Duma sessions. The "rightists" stemmed largely from the central and Volga provinces which had felt the impact of peasant disturbances and where some local Octobrist organizations, as already noted, had joined with rightist and nationalist elements during the election campaign in violation of Party discipline.[46] The Fraction did, in fact, recognize this clash of attitudes by allowing representation on its bureau by "tens," that is, from groupings rather than from the membership as a whole. Thus, the right wing was able to name four members to the bureau.[47]

Differences were brought into the open when Ia. G. Gololobov of Ekaterinaburg, an outspoken "rightist," challenged the decisions of the Fraction in debates on an interpellation to the Ministers of the Interior and Justice charging repression of local trade unions.[48] Gololobov, as reporter for the Committee on Interpellations, observed on February 25, 1909, that he was hopelessly opposed to the Octobrist stand which recommended the acceptance of the interpellation. He proposed its rejection on grounds that it was merely a complaint to a provincial Office of Societies and Unions and had demonstrated no illegal actions on the part of the central government. He maintained that the Ministry of Justice had no jurisdiction in the matter of closing provincial offices; hence, the interpellation was requesting that a Ministry take over judicial appellate functions. He expressed surprise that the Octobrist Fraction, so well endowed with judicial expertise, was guided by the use of its discretion (usmotrenie) rather than by the law.

The statement begot something of a sensation in Duma circles and was immediately elevated to the status of an "affair," the "Gololobov Affair." The Octobrist Fraction and Party, constantly under attack for political flacidity, felt impelled to demonstrate its cohesiveness. A Fraction meeting on March 11 denounced Gololobov's deviationist speech as impermissible, as an impossible barrier to the future conduct of the Fraction's activities. Guchkov demanded an end to these "anarchistic" statements discrediting a serious political party, and the left wing of the Fraction challenged Gololobov's right to retain his seat in it.[49]

Gololobov himself exacerbated matters by submitting a letter to *Novoe Vremia* requesting that it publish his speech verbatim, since it had already disclosed the opinions of the Fraction's majority.[50]

The Central Committee of the Octobrist Party examined Gololobov's public statements in mid May and resolved that since he had committed a serious infraction of Party discipline, and had slandered the Party in his statement of February 25, it was difficult to reconcile these utterances with membership in the Party.[51] Shortly thereafter the Fraction defeated Gololobov's bid to represent it in the Committee on City Self Government and was shocked to learn that he was selected for that position by rightist fractions. Gololobov maintained that this was done without his knowledge.[52]

At a meeting of the Fraction on May 18, 1909, E. M. Sheidemann and Baron N. G. Cherkasov, both "rightists," were accused of visiting Stolypin to complain that the Fraction was moving leftward. And it was charged that they had presented the Premier with a list of Octobrist deputies who would support a bill (to be voted on shortly) which would ameliorate the position of the Old Believers.[53] Baron Cherkassov had recently distinguished himself by voting against his Party on the bill, but the accused stoutly protested their innocence, holding that the Moderate Rightists had collected signatures of the opponents of the bill. The Fraction reacted by establishing a procedure to oust recalcitrant members.[54] Four days later N. N. Lvov and Gololobov submitted official notice of their intention to leave the Octobrist Fraction.[55] And a meeting of May 24 expelled Cherkasov and L. V. Polovtsov, who was immediately welcomed into the Moderate Rightist Fraction.[56]

Concern over the division deepened with the approach of the Third Congress of the Octobrist Party. Some branches even refused to send delegations.[57] Statements at the Congress reflected the disorganizing effects of indiscipline. Some speakers, representing the majority, were of the opinion that the Party would be strengthened if the recalcitrants departed and brought an end to the divisive conflicts. It was noted that in an important central province, personal sympathy and close friendship had moved the local Octobrists to send a rightist to the Imperial Council. The rightist delegates attacked the Party for its tepid nationalism and loss of support among "true Russians." The Party bureau disputed all aspersions cast on its national ardor and a newly elected bureau included no right-wing members.[58] *Golos Moskvy* observed wistfully that at least there were no walkouts, demonstrations, or "despotic denunciations" at the Congress.[59]

In mid October Baron Cherkasov and M. A. Novitskii pressed for the formation of a non-party center group but the Octobrist separatists hesitated, apparently because of the unduly large number of clergy, the small landowners with their special Church orientation, who showed an interest in joining.[60] But with the exodus of the rightists impending, they publicized a project of a statement motivating their actions.[61] They represented themselves as a weary minority harried by constant arguments on principle involving almost every question that arose during the past two sessions. They deplored the leftward tendencies of the majority and the necessity to vote for what they regarded as a "Kadet" course. They felt that a quiet, official separation would benefit both elements of the Fraction and promote the effective operation of each faction. They saw no reason why the rightist Octobrists should expose themselves to the censure of their constituents for decisions with which they could not, in all good conscience, agree.

From the end of October, 1909, it was apparent that a splinter Octobrist group was aborning and in mid November Baron Cherkasov announced that at least ten Octobrists had decided to create a Right Octobrist Fraction. They apparently sought to avoid a clerical preponderance by limiting their number to Octobrist defectors, and by November 23, a small Fraction was in existence.[62] The new body was in no hurry to promulgate its program. A hidebound statement of purposes might limit its growth. Besides, as Baron Cherkasov observed, they attributed no great significance to a theoretical program and were focusing their attention on questions of tactics in matters concerning official policy.[63]

The eleven deputies in the Right Octobrist Fraction were all landowners—seven noblemen and four clergymen. But two of the nobles derived their incomes primarily from their salaried positions in the bureaucracy.[64] Three of the four nobles who reported their holdings owned between 100 and 1,000 *desiatiny* and one over 1,000. Baron Cherkasov listed his income at 15,000 rubles while the *chinovniki* earned between 2,000 and 3,000 rubles annually. The four clergymen held from 50 to 100 *desiatiny*. It is not particularly surprising that there were only Russians and Orthodox in the Fraction and that their educational level was relatively high. Four of their number had a higher education, and seven an intermediate. They were a youngish group with six deputies in their thirties and forties, and four were in their fifties. None had any previous Duma experience, but three had served in zemstvos and four in city dumas. The Central and Volga provinces sent four deputies, the largest contingent, and three came from the Dnieper *gubernii.* After its formation the Right Octobrist Fraction neither gained nor lost membership in the Third Duma.

The Peaceful Renovationists *(Mirnoe Obnovlentsy)* who entered the Duma continued their Party's strenuous efforts to strengthen those elements which they regarded as truly constitutionalist (the left Octobrists, the Kadets, and the moderate populists) by forming them into a coalition.[65] They had received little encouragement from any quarter during the election campaign. But when they analyzed the results of the elections, their concern for their own weakness in the Duma, as well as that of the entire "progressive" representation, begot a movement to unite and organize the independent constitutionalist deputies as a nucleus for a broader parliamentary union.

The guiding spirit of the unification effort was I. N. Efremov, chairman of the "M.O." Fraction. He estimated that there were thirty unattached constitutionalist deputies and invited them to a Peaceful Renovationist meeting at his apartment to organize for work in the Duma. He observed that their common grounds would be constitutionalism and progressivism. He defined the latter as the realization of reform in a democratic spirit to raise the well-being of the popular masses, a purpose which could be realized only in a reformed state structure. The parliamentary coalition would serve chiefly as a link between their close ideological associates, the Octobrists on the right and the Kadets on the left.[66]

Fourteen deputies in all met on November 1, 1907, to organize what was informally known as the "Progressive Group." Their number expanded to forty at the second meeting on November 7, but only twenty-five joined a "Fraction of the Progressists and Peaceful Renovationists" with Efremov as its chairman. Efremov explained to the large meeting of November 7 that since the nonparty progressives were the only unorganized group in the Duma they could not be expected to act together. And as a practical matter they could not expect appointments to the Duma committees.[67] Efremov observed that those in attendance were independent because they valued their freedom of action and because they were not able to accept the various party programs in their entirety. They feared depersonalization and subordination to party

regulations, and they were suspicious even of the Peaceful Renovationists to whom they were attracted.[68]

Since these individualists of moderate liberal persuasion had
only the loosest ideological bonds, to maintain the cohesiveness
of the Fraction as well as its political effectiveness the component
elements decided that it was superfluous to elaborate a detailed
program of action.[69] They would continue to examine their tasks
dispassionately, undogmatically, independently, now that the
"period of attraction to party programs and fashionable slogans
has passed."[70] They could not predict what positions the various
fractions would take and how they would differ from each other.
Hence the "Progressives" would make their decisions on each
question separately, accepting invitations to both Kadet and
Octobrist meetings, and would maintain connections with extreme groups only for informational purposes.[71] The "Progressives" were unusually sensitive to any whisper of a suggestion
that they were considering any sort of program and were especially horrified by insinuations that the Peaceful Renovationists
in the Fraction were insistent on the acceptance of their special
Party program.[72]

The combined Progressive and Peaceful Renovationist Fraction officially numbered twenty-eight deputies at the beginning
of the first session of the Third Duma but lost three deputies by
the time the session adjourned. Of these, only five were former
Peaceful Renovationists.[73] Ten were nobles, six were peasants,
and four were men of the cloth. Two burghers, two practicing
the liberal professions, a manufacturer, and a Cossack completed
the Fraction's occupational roster. Two deputies apparently
proffered no data. Obviously, the Progressives enjoyed a relatively
high income. Nine deputies held over 400 *desiatiny* and one over
1,000. The non-agricultural element was also fairly well-to-do.
Nine earned under 500 rubles annually, five, between 500 rubles
and 5,000 rubles, and one over 5,000 rubles. There were but two
non-Russians, a Lett and Abkhaz, in the Fraction, and the lone
Lutheran was the only non-Orthodox member. Most of the deputies, seventeen, were in their thirties and forties, two were in their
twenties. The six peasants with a primary education lowered the
overall level of the Fraction somewhat, but nine had secondary
schooling and ten a higher education. The Fraction's service level
was quite respectable. Five had served in the zemstvos, three had
been marshals of the nobility, and two were veterans of the first
and second Dumas. Except for two deputies from the Baltic, the

Progressive and Peaceful Renovationist Fraction stemmed from the "basic" Russian areas. The Central provinces with six and the Volga with seven deputies sent most of the Fraction; the Ural Region sent four, three came from the North Central *gubernii*, and two from the Don Oblast.

As a fraction, the Progressives were relatively homogeneous ideologically. Hence, it was a generally stable element in the Third Duma. In all five sessions it gained twelve adherents, chiefly in the first (nine, including six Octobrists), and lost seven—all to the Non-Party deputies, except one to the Kadets. Only one of the six lost through deaths and resignations was not replaced in the by-elections. Their strength rose from 6.33 percent of the Duma in 1907 to 8.37 in the fifth, but something of a decline from 9 percent in the third and fourth sessions. Not a large Fraction, it was able to reinforce the intellectual expertise of the Duma and add an energetic fistful to the liberal opposition.

The Constitutional Democrats were in the psychologically comfortable, but politically frustrating, position of being able to assume that their representation in the Duma could not achieve its full potential strength under the revised electoral law. And they hovered steadily around 12 percent of the Duma (from fifty-two to fifty-four deputies) in all five sessions.[74] The Bolsheviks, paced by V. I. Lenin, were ever ready to point to the class structure of the Kadet Party as proof that it was essentially a middle class party; typical in that it was ready and willing to strike a bargain with the government. Aside from a strong strand of anti-intellectualism, or more accurately mistrust of intellectualism, apparent in Lenin's attitudes, he was deeply concerned by the attraction of the Kadets for the leadership of the parties to which the peasants subscribed. For they were petty bourgeiosie who might be convinced of the efficacy of parliamentary, as opposed to revolutionary, responses. A considerable portion of Lenin's writings in the Duma period and his capacities for sarcasm and vituperation were dedicated to countering Kadet influences.

Lenin's concerns were grounded well enough, but he proceeded from the wrong assumptions. The Kadets were not primarily informed in pursuing their political purposes by the interests and attitudes of an industrial, rentier, or landed stratum. They reflected, rather, the attitudes of the political liberalism of the European intellectual in the decades of the late nineteenth and early twentieth centuries. They would realize the freest possible status of the individual in society and his economic well-being, through parliamentary procedures. Their landed element was willing to endure the expropriation of a part of its holdings. And the basic philosophy and prejudices of the Kadets regarding the peasant commune resembled those of the populists and marxists, except for their programs of land nationalization.

The cold data on class composition hardly reflected the political philosophy and motivation of the liberals. Their majority would have no truck with a conservative-reactionary cabinet and for this they were severely excoriated by their conservative, landlord, and industrialist competitors in the political arena and by their own small but articulate right wing. And their strenuous efforts to deflect the Duma from an illegal course was motivated not by a "pursuit of ministerial armchairs" or a bourgeois attraction for acceptance in the "higher spheres," but by a concern for the preservation of the infant parliamentary institution. If they sinned in this connection it was rather in a "revolutionary" (as opposed to "responsible oppositional") direction as at Vyborg in July, 1906, following their public appeal for their agricultural bill in the First Duma. The more cautious liberals and conservative constitutionalists were always concerned with a persistent tendency to see "no enemies on the left."

Reckoning on the basis of legally defined class lines, almost half of the Kadet deputies who sat in the first two sessions of the Third duma (fifty-two deputies, or 49 percent) were of noble origin. But over half of these (fourteen, or 53.8 percent) gained their incomes from sources other than land. Forty-five percent of the Kadet Fraction (twenty-four members) practiced in the liberal professions; five were government officials, and two claimed to be industrialists. Only fifteen identified themselves as burghers. There were also six peasants and five Cossacks in the Kadet delegation. One deputy offered no data on his official class status.

Most of the Kadets were economically quite comfortable by Russian standards. Of the landholding elements, seven deputies owned or held under 1,000 *desiatiny*, four between 2,500 and 5,000 *desiatiny*, and one evaluated his orchards at 17,000 rubles. Nineteen Kadet deputies (35.8 percent) with incomes from non-agricultural sources earned between 500 and 5,000 rubles annually and nine (16.9 percent) had an annual income of over 5,000 rubles. Only one earned less than 500 rubles and seven were shy about submitting data on their incomes. Lawyers reported only property or home values.

The rightist and conservative parties were wont to charge the Kadets with a strong minority, particularly Jewish, influence and sympathies. As a party which rested on a strong city electorate it included in its leadership some Jews who held a significant position in intellectual circles. But given its basic ethnic composition and constituency, the Kadet Party was predominantly Great Russian. And this is reflected in the profile of its Fraction. Forty-four members (83 percent) were Great Russian and the remainder were a scattering of Ukrainians, Poles, Estonians, and Armenians with two each, and one German and one Jew. Fifty-three deputies (81.8 percent), including the Great Russians and Ukrainians and one of ethnically Jewish origin, were Orthodox. The two Poles were Roman Catholic while the two Estonians and the German and a Volga Russian were Lutheran. This melange would seem to indicate that the Kadets had no special minority interests which would offer a simplistic analysis of its purposes. For the party represented the Russian application of a broad, western, liberal current with its emphasis on individual rights. And since, in this light, it opposed the disabilities, official and unofficial, of the minorities in the Empire, it attracted the sympathies and the support of their parliamentary groupings in most matters.

As representatives of the Party most attractive for the practitioners of the liberal professions it is hardly surprising that almost three-quarters of the Fraction had gained considerable experience in local institutions and the preceding Dumas. Thirteen members (24.5 percent) had served in the first two "popular representations," five in the zemstvos and four in city councils. One had been a mayor, and six had been justices of the peace. In this urban element only five had served in the zemstvo structure and one had been a marshal of the nobility. The disproportionate involvement in the central representative body reflected, perhaps, the broader horizons of the new, "radical" leadership who thought in terms of the possible major accomplishments of national, rather than local, bodies of self government. It also reflected their primarily, non-agrarian orientation. No less predictable was the Fraction's high educational level. Thirty-nine deputies (73.5 percent) had received a higher education and seven (13.2 percent) an intermediate, while seven more had only lower or home schooling.

The relatively youthful nature of this leading oppositional fraction was rather typical of the Russian political scene. Some seventeen deputies (32 percent) were in their thirties, twenty-three (42.4 percent) were in their forties and ten (18.8 percent) in their fifties. There was but one callow youth in his twenties, and two were sexagenarians.

The Kadets hailed from the larger cities in all parts of European Russia with no special areas of concentration. The North Central

provinces with nine deputies (16 percent), the Volga with eight
(15 percent), the Urals with seven (13 percent), and the Don
Oblast with five (9.4 percent, reflecting an interesting attraction
of the Cossacks for the Kadets) afforded the largest clusters of
liberal representatives. Asiatic Russia sent six Kadets, all Russians. And only the Baltic voters, among the minority regions
with a vote, sent four Kadets who were not Russians to St Petersburg. These peoples preferred their own national groups.

The Kadet Fraction, as indicated earlier, was quite stable
throughout all five sessions of the Third Duma. An Octobrist and
a Progressive moved into their ranks, and they lost four deputies
to the Non-party Group and one to the Trudoviki for a total loss
of three deputies in fractional shifts. A. M. Koliubakin was
forced to yield his seat in the Duma but was replaced by the vet-
eran bureacrat-deputy N. N. Kutler. Two Kadet deputies died and
only one was replaced by a Kadet, and one resigned and was replaced. Thus, in toto, by the end of the Third Duma the Kadets
lost only four of their original number, which represents a decline
of less than a quarter of a percentage.

The ethnic and religious minority groups which had been
forming since the First Duma were of such strength as to merit the
especial attention and concern of the larger predominant fractions. No perceptive parliamentary figure could afford to ignore
their attitudes, and political figures of the caliber of V. P. Grabski
and the astute R. V. Dmovski, both of the Polish Kolo, were
widely respected in the Duma. Moreover, in the sessions of the
Second Duma, the minority groups sensed an affinity for the
Kadet program and leadership and generally voted with them except in agricultural matters—if they were dominated by large
landowners, or if their nationalist sensitivities were ruffled (as in
the debates on Polish city government) or insufficiently
supported.

Together, the western border and Moslem groups numbered
twenty-six deputies, a not inconsiderable accretion to the liberal
and constitutionalist opposition. And they were among the most
stable groupings. The name of the northwestern Polish-Lithuanian-Bielorussian Group was misleading. Its seven members were
solidly Polish (at least culturally) except for a lone Lithuanian
peasant. This group was predominantly aristocratic with relatively modest landholdings.[75] Two deputies held under 400
desiatiny but two owned between 1,000 and 2,000, and one listed
a home in Vilna valued at 40,000 rubles. It was entirely Roman
Catholic, with ages ranging from the thirties to the fifties; five
enjoyed a higher education, and the entire membership stemmed

from the predominantly Lithuanian provinces of Vilna, Kovno, and Grodno. Only one of their number, S. A. Tankovich, had seen public service as a justice of the peace and deputy to the Second Duma. The Group was eminently stable; it suffered no losses and had no accretions in the Third Duma.

The essential Polish element in the Duma was, of course, the Polish Kolo. By virtue of the new electoral law, its membership was reduced by over three-fourths as compared with the Second Duma, from forty-six to eleven deputies.[76] It was predominantly noble, but like the Kadets, most of its members practiced the liberal professions. Nine (81.8 percent) were of noble origin. The remaining two designated themselves as peasants but one, actually a physician, belonged to the six in the liberal professions. As a whole, both the rural and urban elements had moderately substantial incomes. The five landowning nobles, with one exception, L. K. Dymsha with 2,200 *desiatiny*, held moderate estates ranging from 300 to 600 *desiatiny*. The lone peasant farmer held seven and a half *desiatiny*. The lawyers, doctors, and publicists enjoyed an average earning of about 4,000 rubles annually. But two were bashful about publicizing their incomes, and the lone businessman, V. V. Zhukovski, with insurance and mining interests, would only indicate that he held 300 *desiatiny* for farming. The Kolo could be none other than Polish and Roman Catholic, and all members hailed from the "Vistula Provinces" and Warsaw. Its vigorous image was confirmed by its youth. Six deputies were in their forties, three in their thirties, one each in the twenties and fifties. All the Polish deputies but the peasant received a higher education, and seven were veterans of the Second Duma. The Kolo suffered no shifts in its membership, and it replaced two deputies who resigned in the course of the Third Duma.

The Moslem Group of eight deputies was drawn from the small band of Russian-accultured intelligentsia of the predominantly Moslem areas of the Empire still included in the franchise: the lower Volga, the Caucasus, and the Urals.[77] All but two were recruited from the liberal professions and public Moslem institutions and hence enjoyed a moderate income, on the average of 2,800 rubles annually. Only one was a noble landowner with over 1,000 *desiatiny*, and one was a farmer-trader. Officially, the Group listed three nobles, three peasants, and two burghers. They represented a melange of Turkic ethnic groups—four Bashkirs, three Tartars, a Daghestani—who were not as well educated as the minority leaders from the western borderlands. Three had a higher education, three an intermediate, and two a lower. Yet,

half of them sat in past Dumas and one was a marshal of the nobility at the *uiezd* level. Half the Group were in their thirties and
forties, three were in their fifties, and one was in his twenties.
Only one new adherent transferred from the Social Democratic
Fraction at the end of the second session. I. I. Gaidarov, a Lezgin
engineer from Daghestan, apparently found the intellectual environment of his Moslem compatriots more attractive. Actually,
the class, economic, and even ethnic backgrounds of the membership were not, at the time, particularly relevant for their basic,
religious, pan-Moslem orientation in the face of Great Russian
nationalism which colored official policy.

Moving into the further and far left, to the Trudovik Group
and the Social Democrats, the familiar phenomena of varied ethnic and geographic origin, along with a relatively lower educational level are apparent. And in occupation and their economic
level they differed not too widely from the other representations
of European Russia and the western borderlands.[78]

The Trudovik Group elected fourteen deputies to the Third
Duma, a devastating reduction from the 104 in the more representative Second Duma. Nine deputies of this traditionally peasant group were designated officially as peasant, but of these one
was a lawyer and one a factory worker. Four members, in all
probability townsmen, were listed only by occupation (three
lawyers and a craftsman) without class designation. Thus, there
were four members from the liberal professions (29 percent of the
Group) and half of the membership were landworking peasants.
The Group also included a *chinovnik*, a tax official, noble by
birth.

The relatively high income of the professional stratum contrasted sharply with the moderate holdings of the allotment peasants. None of the former had an annual income under 3,000
rubles, and one earned up to 6,000 rubles. All of the allotment
holding peasants worked under 100 *desiatiny* and three of these
held less than 20.

Like most groups from the "basic" Russian regions, the Trudoviki were predominantly Russian, only four designating themselves otherwise (three Lithuanian and an Armenian), and all but
one, an Old Believer, were Orthodox. Eight hailed from the
provinces predominantly Great Russian in culture, including
three from the Russian populated areas of Asiatic Russia.[79] One
came from Poland, three from the Caucasus, and two from the
Baltic Region.

The Trudovik deputies were somewhat younger than the average age of most fractions and groups. None had reached his fifties (nine were in their thirties), and one enjoyed twenty-nine summers. In this respect they were not unlike other revolutionary elements in the Duma. And their educational level, reflecting their professions, was higher than might be expected of an element representing the peasantry. Four had a higher education and one an intermediate, while nine of their number had a lower or home education. Three had served in past Dumas, and in the Third Duma four had shifted to the Non-party Group and they welcomed a member from the Kadets, thus representing a relatively stable element.

Finally, to the far left, the Social Democrats with nineteen members in their Fraction were likewise considerably reduced in strength from the sixty-five who sat in the Second Duma.[80] Both Fractions, Menshevik and Bolshevik, had campaigned strenuously despite some reservations on the part of the latter[81] and the Caucasus with its socialist and nationalist leadership, and the North Central industrial area, including the city of St. Petersburg, provided five each of the Marxist deputies. Three hailed from Asiatic Russia, and the Central, Ural, and Baltic Regions sent two each. Yet, only two from the Caucasus identified themselves as Georgians. The two from the Baltic were a Lithuanian and Lett respectively, and one, we saw, was a Lezgin. The remaining fourteen members, three-quarters of the Fraction, were Great Russian. Interestingly enough, these marxists registered their religious preferences, and it followed from their ethnic origins that the great majority, all but four (an Old Believer, a Roman Catholic, a Moslem, and a Lutheran) were Orthodox.

Among the Social Democratic deputies eleven were identified as peasants under a rather rigid, official, corporate class structure. Thus, even in this small but representative segment of the Russian labor movement of the early twentieth century, the transitional nature of the working class was clearly reflected. For eight of the peasants were listed as workers or craftsmen, only two as farmers, and one as a school teacher. One member of the Fraction called himself a Cossack landowner. Two of the three townsmen (one was a worker) and the four nobles pursued the liberal professions —all in good revolutionary tradition. Taken as whole the party could claim an economically comfortable status. The two farmers held under 100 *desiatiny* and five earned under 400 rubles annually, but eight earned between 400 and 3,000 rubles. Yet there were no data listed for four deputies.

The relatively humble social and economic level of the Fraction

is reflected in the eleven deputies who received only a lower education. But as a whole, its educational level was far from mediocre. Five, a quarter of the fraction, graduated from institutions
of higher learning, and three from intermediate schools. After the
arrest or flight of the Fraction in the Second Duma there was none
in the group with political experience.

The Social Democratic Fraction was restless. Every session saw
some movement, and all of the shifts were away from it. Most
losses came between the first and second sessions when three were
lost: one to the Moslems and two to the Non-party Group. Still a
fourth was ousted from the Duma. The third and fourth sessions
suffered one loss apiece—in each case to the Non-party Group.
Thus the Fraction slipped from 4.2 percent of the membership of
the Duma in 1907 to 2.9 percent in 1912, offering an index of sorts
of the sad political estate of the marxists in the "years of reaction."

XI
The Relationship of Forces

The prospects for the Third Duma as a significant factor at the end of the third election campaign were not reassuring. Yet its composition in the perspective of administrative action and policy offered the still hazy potentiality that it might emerge as an independent power base. This might be achieved both in cooperation and in competition with ruling elements which had forcefully demonstrated that they would regard themselves as limited in the use of power only at their pleasure. The crucial problem was the creation of a relatively stable majority on the order of a "victorian compromise." But it would have to be forged in the context of a complex, multiparty system steeped in political dogmatism arising from a prolonged revolutionary effort and opposition to it, and without a parliamentary tradition.

The elections had clarified the power structure within the Duma, and on the surface, at least, they reasserted support for constitutionalism. The moderate Octobrist constitutionalists and Progressives and the more zealous Constitutional Democrats and the national minorities who would perforce seek the protection of the Fundamental Laws numbered almost fifty-eight percent of the Duma's strength. The results could have hardly surprised seasoned observers. The Kadets had, indeed, counted on a broad expression of constitutionalist sentiment to carry forward their program to control the bureaucracy through a parliamentary ministry and to widen the Duma's jurisdiction. The outcome could appear the more impressive as a triumph of sorts over the new electoral law, and the Kadets had demonstrated that they still had the capacity to carry a strong urban vote. But the law probably yielded about what Premier Stolypin had expected, and the artificial nature of the Duma's composition (stemming from the same electoral law) obscured any clear estimate of the strength of its public support.

The Octobrists, resting on a narrow popular base but with considerable influence with the apparently like-minded Stolypin administration, could at best maintain parliament as a holding operation within the limits of the electoral law. They might seek to broaden its jurisdiction and, if they were so inclined, its representational base, until it could establish itself in the public mind as an effective instrument for reform. The Octobrist Party was the loose keystone of a shaky parliamentary structure. For Octobrist political expression and action reflected a wide range of sometimes contradictory conservatism and liberal attitudes. And the Party's constitutionalism might appear—from the right or left—as equivocal as Peter A. Stolypin's.

The Octobrist program was liberal enough. But this was the work of its constitutional-minded leadership whose attitudes might differ vastly from those of the local membership. All Russian parties found a common political strand to their opposition to the bureaucracy but the Octobrist leadership stood closer to the liberal opposition in their reasons therefor. The rightists opposed the new constitutional structure with its legislative, parliamentary foundation, as the devilish work of the bureaucracy. For them the *chinovniki* stood between the voice of the "True Russians," the experienced and "cultured," aristocratic, landowning *zubry*, and the Tsar whose convictions, they were certain, approximated their own. But the Octobrist leadership, committed to constitutionalism, had fairly acute qualms about the Administration's cavalier attitude toward basic provisions of the Fundamental Laws which the regime itself had devised. They were restrained constitutionalists who would promote specific legislation to protect promised civil liberties, the independence of the courts and educational institutions, and they might even foresee a ministry representative of the parliamentary groupings.

Yet, on basic economic and political issues the Octobrists listed noticeably rightward. With the right they supported Stolypin's land reform since it involved no sacrifice on the part of their zemstvo landowner constituents. It was a preferable alternative to liberal land condemnation and socialist expropriation. And it might go far to blunt the edge of peasant opposition to the established economic order. Hence the Law of June 3, 1907, was a "sad necessity" and the field courts martial were needed until they had pacified the active dissident elements. And the Octobrist Party as a whole supported a chavinistic policy, not unlike that of the Administration, for all who were not Great Russians—in the name of an empire "one and indivisible" in the strictist interpretation of that slogan. Still more compromising for the moderate constitutionalists was the identification of their rank and file with the right in the election campaign when party discipline was almost nonexistent. The successful blockage by provincial, predominantly Octobrist, elements of a movement in the Zemstvo

Congress to institute badly needed *volost* zemstvos; their efforts to resurrect the power of the land captains by subordinating the small zemstvos to them; and their vehement opposition to the expansion of middle class influence in them reflected attitudes more nearly reactionary than conservative. The government could discern an apparently dependable ally for the moment. But the obvious question for the popular strata who supported the underrepresented parties of reform and revolution was whether a parliament dominated by the Octobrists would have the will or sufficient political strength, for that matter, to realize vital political and economic reform.

It might be noted that bridgehead groups in parliament more nearly identifiable with the center—mostly grouped in the peaceful Renovationists and the Progressives—were intellectually too rarified to be understood by any but the politically experienced and educated. Their numerical weakness spurred them to seek common ground for all constitutionalists. But they were unable to transmit a sense of urgency or meaningful conviction given their essential, anti-constitutional Slavophilism. They could hope to influence the Duma only with their literacy, the logic of their argument for the obvious need for common action, and their sincerity in promoting it.

The Constitutional Democrats could not reassure themselves that any groups to their right were sincere and dependable constitutionalist, least of all the Octobrists. They were close to the sources of power responsible for the new electoral law and the Kadets were uneasy about the ideological steadfastness of a part of their own electorate, the old zemstvo constitutionalists, should they move perceptibly toward the Octobrists. Basic differences on the all-important agrarian reform were, by themselves, sufficient to inhibit common action. The Octobrists heartily agreed. They could see no cause to move from their preferred political position toward the dogmatic, intellectually snobbish, and "lefting" Kadets with what they adjudged to be their habitual revolutionary spirit—as reflected in their land project. And there was little likelihood that either party leadership could nudge their followings toward each other. The *kto kogo* syndrome in Russian political psychology was too strong for common action even among those elements who by temperament and training should have been the most likely to cooperate. The only real prospect for the success of a constitutional central bloc lay in the potential differentiation within each grouping; particularly if the bureaucracy remained, as it had since the summer of 1906, oversensitive about its prerogatives and insufficiently sensitive to broad, popular pressures.

Cooperation with the administration had been abandoned by the Kadet leadership since the preceding summer. This was largely a matter of temperament, ideology, and practical politics. In an atmosphere in which the repressive element of Stolypin's post-revolutionary program overshadowed every other facet of his broad policy in the public mind there was little foreseeable likelihood of mutual action between the government and political segments to the left of the Octobrists. Stolypin would show that he meant business and the opposition, constitutional or revolutionary, would regard it as overreaction or bloody murder. The field courts martial were only the most blatant element of the official reaction to the revolutionary disturbances. More subtle and meaningful in the long run would be the characteristic reluctance of the regime to legislate guarantees of promised civil liberties and the rigid interpretation of the Duma's rights which meant a progressive circumscription of its activities; in a sense, a repetition of the persistent frustrating experience of the wearied zemstvo leadership. As significant for the politically informed was the regime's unwillingness to differentiate between the parliamentary and revolutionary opposition—as reflected particularly in its refusal to legalize liberal and minority constitutionalists. In these circumstances it was neither morally nor politically feasible to sit in any but a Duma ministry, much less one in which the "public figures" were a minority.

And there were more than traces of a weakened sense of "realpolitik" in the calculations of the Kadet leadership. In reaction to what it regarded as centuries of official lawlessness, it was obsessed by the rule of law—an admirable attitude if it fully assessed the realities of the moment; if, for example, it truly understood the configuration of the Russian "constitutional monarchy" which it insisted did indeed exist in the Fundamental Laws. If the Kadet leaders rested too heavily on legalisms which the regime might easily honor in the breach, they faced a very real danger of the moment—the sort of danger that would overwhelm them in 1917 with their highly legalistic concepts of jurisdiction and obligations.

Then the Kadet leadership overestimated current popular support for the constitutional idea. They were, for example, buoyed up by the sanguine hope that after the first reaction to the events of June 3, 1907, public opinion would be sensible enough to accept the "realistic" Kadet reforms. And their unwillingness to recognize the dimensions of evident apathy toward the unrepresentative Duma was not likely to reinforce their capacity to appreciate current political circumstances, howsoever harsh.

Certainly unrealistic was their reiterated belief that they could attract some of the labor vote since it was more interested in trade union activities of a self-interested nature than in leftist ideologies. By the opening of the Third Duma the Kadets clearly understood that the workers who took the trouble to vote already had determined their ideological-emotional choice. Yet they persistently pressed the argument that significant legislation of a "trade union" order might attract them to support the Duma. But the chances of arousing real interest were remote with the conservative, landlord-entrepreneur Octobrists in key positions because of official fiat of a questionable legal order.

The liberal, long-range view of the Duma as an arena for the presentation and competition of partisan programs was more salutary and hopeful for the future. It was, perhaps, too optimistic after the events surrounding the dissolution of the Second Duma and the administration's rejection of bills and interpellations emanating from the opposition. But in the long run, the normal operation of the parliamentary body was likely to add daily to the experience of the deputies in the new world of parliamentary activity incessantly demanding varying degrees of compromise. For those who were not adamantly doctrinaire, it would offer at least a basis for considering the promise of parliamentary action (even if moderately significant at first) as a channel for reform in Russia of the early twentieth century.

There was little basis, at the moment, for finding common grounds between the government and the national minorities. As one of the major targets of the new electoral law which only sharpened their awareness of their legal disabilities, the official course was calculated to bring these minorities under liberal or independent conservative leadership in opposition to the administration. Their truncated representation added some modest strength to the constitutional center. But the nationalities were riven all too often by long standing animosities which officialdom could easily stimulate. And within each minority there were significant differences on ideological or economic grounds: socialists opposed bourgeois nationalists, and separatists countered automomists seeking to preserve economic ties with the Empire. And the Russian nationalism of the Octobrists inhibited any cordial, binding union of ethnic minority elements with right-wing constitutionalists except on matters of common, primarily economic, interest in country and town. An astute Administration might deftly enlist these interests in economic and political security in a more positive policy.

On the left the Kadets might still attract the Trudoviki. But despite their inclinations there was little likelihood that the liberals could cooperate with the socialist parties and fractions effectively and consistently. And with their severely limited representation and their dogmatic positions, there was little real profit in cooperation as a parliamentary tactic. Kadet interest in parties, fractions and groups on the left lay in their influence on public opinion. More specifically, through them the Kadets would project and protect their image as a sympathetic, zealous, reformist, if non-socialist element in Russian political life. If leftist votes were few in parliament, they represented broad strata of the rural and urban electorate which had to be convinced of the efficacy of the Duma as an instrument for reform. But experience of the past two years indicated that just because of their political strength and capacities the Kadets had become the chief targets of the left as the embodiment of the perfidy and hypocracy of "bourgeois" politics distracting from the pursuit of revolutionary programs. And their strenuous effort to protect parliament against popular bills which would exceed its jurisdiction only widened the breach with marxists and populists alike. Certainly after June 3 the hearts of the leftist deputies lay more with propaganda than parliamentary effect and the "unattainable," liberal projects could serve as an ideal target for propaganda about Kadet "constitutional illusions." There might be electoral agreements to minimize the artificial conservative surge. But neither ideologically, nor tactically, nor, for that matter, temperamentally could the Constitutional Democrats and revolutionaries find consistent common ground for parliamentary action. And the bifurcation within the marxist camp involving the matter of commitment to parliamentary action as such could only complicate the quest for a common effort.

In the past the peasant deputies had generally followed the Kadet lead in the business of the Duma. But the Kadet program for land reform had no special attraction for the peasantry. Obligatory confiscation of surplus lands in large estates at a just remuneration would be billed ultimately to the peasantry, and it could not compare with the promises of the Marxists and populists. It might attract the considerable following of *sredniki* among the Trudoviki, likely to benefit by additions to their relatively profitable holdings. And this served to emphasize what the politically informed understood only too well: that the peasantry were not a monolithic gray mass who would sing in one voice. Furthermore, none of the peasantry were likely to be charmed by the legalistic Kadet stand against parliamentary investigations of the famine relief campaign, which could only feed suspicions emanating from the further left about "deals" with the autocracy for cabinet "armchairs." This drift of the moderate left on the matter of legally questionable proposals could only weaken the positions of both the leftists and liberals. And this could only harden the attitude of the regime toward both representations. For rather indiscriminately it regarded their ultimate purposes as equally revolutionary. And the rightist segment of the administration probably welcomed peasant disenchantment with the Duma.

The focus for the formation of an effective oppositional bloc to the left had to rest on the Trudoviki because they were the only organized parliamentary group representing the peasantry. The Social Revolutionaries had no Duma fraction. They reflected the political essence of those elements on the left who thought so little of the Duma as a legislative and agitational organ, and so feared its potentialities for compromise with the regime, that they would have the population ignore it completely. They could not be disregarded because their attitude was undoubtedly shared by underrepresented or the unrepresented popular elements, and they had the ear of broad peasant and worker-peasant strata as well as the more radical movements among the national minorities. They undoubtedly contributed to the election of deputies who joined the Trudovik Group and Social Democratic Fraction, and some who joined the various, amorphous non-party groups which emerged in the course of the Third Duma. By the fall of 1907 the Social Revolutionary Party commanded the loyalties of a significant sector of the population which had little experience with, understanding of, or concern for the parliamentary campaign. These would be likely to lose interest in the Duma and even renounce it if it proved relatively ineffective for their purpose as a legislative organ, if it acted according to its conservative propensities to restrain the revolutionary process, or behaved indecisively on matters of land reform or peasant juridicial status.

The marxist Social Democrats were officially never more than tolerant of the Duma and largely as a propaganda platform. They were not particularly concerned with its fate or operations, except insofar as it might interfere with or modify the operation of the historical dialectic. But given their program and temperament, the Mensheviki could be interested in labor legislation. They might

utilize the Duma most effectively by articulating their attitudes
toward competitive measures which directly affected labor. And
they would have to offer perforce their own contrasting projects
which could involve them in the parliamentary process. This
could tend to confuse their following who were constantly assured that the Duma was an ineffective *pomiestchik* and bourgeois institution entirely at the mercy of the autocracy. While the
Duma generated some sympathy among the industrial workers, its
prestige among them had suffered severely. The curtailment of
labor representation and the arrest of the Social Democratic Fraction undoubtedly scarred their political consciousness. But the
attitudes of the factory and shop worker toward the Imperial
Duma were likely to be conditioned by the attractiveness of such
legislation as the administration's social insurance, measures
broadening the scope of trade union activities, and guarantees of
civil liberties.

Again, like the Social Revolutionaries, the Social Democrats
were significant to the constitutionalists for the impact they
might have on the parliamentary cause. For one thing, they had
proved adept at disrupting the Duma's activities and arousing
governmental authorities and the excitable extremists on the right
to a degree that threatened the very existence of the parliamentary
idea. As part of a bloc, a factor in counting votes, their impact was
negligible. They were few in number and hopelessly split ideologically. How they might affect the political actions of workers
in factories, shops, and mines was a matter which the liberals
could do little to control. They could only circumspectly promote
tendencies on the left to engage it in legislative activity attractive
to labor.

At the other extreme, on the far right, the danger to the parliamentary idea was even greater at the moment. The rightists
matched the far left in dogmatism and fanaticism. They were more
numerous in the Duma thanks to the electoral law, and they were
influential at court. Like most Russian political parties they were
not of one mind on the proper function of parliament in the political structure. They entered the Duma to discredit it and transform it, at the least, into a *zemskii sobor,* an advisory body of an
order more restricted than that conceived by the Bulygin Project
of 1905. Given the sensitivities of the "ruling circles" after the
intense revolutionary experience, the rightist extremists could
cause serious mischief by demands to honor the fallen police
(offsetting interpellations focusing on police excesses), to arise
and chant the national anthem, or by baiting the left extremists

to attack the army, Great Russian nationalist sensibilities, and autocracy.

For the far right counted heavily on the attraction of court circles to their simplistic *weltanschauung;* an attraction that could be none other than unfortunate in terms of political strategy and the damage done to the impartial "tsar-father" image. Support of official nationalism from the royal family and court and overt demonstration of its political preferences could only alienate broad currents of public opinion from the throne. And if the pinnacle of authority truly regarded the Union of the Russian People as spokesmen for the popular strata, it would penalize severely and circumscribe any effort toward its understanding of even the moderate opposition in the Third Duma. Nor could the administration expect to escape politically unscathed if the public mind suspected it of a liaison with the right, particularly in the dim area of financial subsidization. In the framework of vigorous, counterrevolutionary repression this made even the imaginative, conservative administration of Stolypin appear more reactionary than its actual philosophy and program would warrant and act as a further inhibitor to cooperation with the conservatives and moderate liberal constitutionalists. In fact, Stolypin's restrictive policy toward the URP to minimize its open relations with the crown were hardly suspected by the public. This was a matter of simple political caution on Stolypin's part, but it also indicated more exactly his proper political orientation.

The great body of rightists consisted of a considerable segment of largely landowner deputies standing between the Octobrists and the extremists who found it difficult to realize organizational unity and stability, promoted to a degree in the course of the Third Duma by Stolypin's parliamentary politics. The antics of the extreme right were far too undignified, even too crude, for their tastes, and they were somewhat concerned by extremist efforts to subvert the Duma and interfere with its operation. The Duma, even in its modified form, was for them a necessary evil. But it was the law, the will of the tsar-autocrat which fortified their way of life. And under the circumstances it behooved the moderate right to join in a single bloc to promote a program which protected their agrarian, Great Russian, and Orthodox interests. The extremists would interfere with the formation of a comprehensive and enduring rightist fraction with common, Russian nationalist purposes, and hence were to be differentiated from the moderates.

Actually, chronic, organizational instability and ideological differences militated against any consistent unity among the nationalists. But if the various programs of this intermediate element truly reflected the attitudes of their adherents, they might vote on many issues along with the Octobrists and thus lend some stability to a practical, conservative bloc in the Duma. Like the Octobrists they were concerned with ending revolutionary unrest and like the Octobrists they were Great Russian nationalists—somewhat more avid in promoting their cause. Again, like the conservative center, they could support the Tsar's constitution and claim to be more ardent reformists than the public imagined. But their reformism and constitutionalism were inhibited by the imperative drive to protect their special position and interests in the aftermath of the revolutionary experience. To this end they would still further restrict the suffrage. They maintained that they were concerned with the problems of the national minorities but stressed the traditional statist, Great Russian concept in attributing to the nationalities ethnocentric and parochial tendencies harmful to the interests of the Russian state system. In their union in the Russian National Party, final for most of the moderate rightists in the Third Duma, they articulated a nationalism which was ideologically, if not emotionally, closer to the far right than the Octobrists. And their nationalism was intensified by a considerable infusion of "border Russian" anxiety—characteristic, to a degree, of the entire right of center. In general, their constitutionalism indicated that they were not aware of some basic roots of public discontent, or excluded them from their political consciousness. In a condition of crisis—parliamentary or revolutionary—they were more likely to bend rightward than toward the conservative center with its mildly liberal wing.

The Russian parliamentary scene was a veritable kaleidoscope of attitude, opinion, and dogma bound to promote organizational instability and splintering. Superficially, in this respect it resembled the continental parliamentary systems of other major European states—even the more nearly representative. But the cleavages were deeper, the differences more acute among and within political elements in the wake of the first significant social and political upheaval in the twentieth century and with, at best, a weak tradition of political compromise. The ferment was quickened and extraordinarily complicated by long-standing racial and cultural competitions, animosities and repressions which would have challenged the capacities of less ethnocentric regimes operating under relatively normal circumstances. And with rapid social and economic change accompanying a swift industrial revolution, the magnitude of the task of realizing political stability through compromise assumed awesome dimensions. After six centuries of political life informed by statist, class-corporate concepts in a predominantly agrarian society, the quest for stability through parliamentary procedures was in the first stages of its infancy. Parliament was struggling for survival as an exotic phenomenon. An obvious primary prerequisite for the development and acceptability of the popular representation as an instrument for change was, at the least, a relative tranquility during which the necessity for moderation in the resolution of essential problems could emerge. In circumstances which would prolong or aggravate the basic factors contributing to chronic unrest, those who would promote the parliamentary experiment would of necessity be caught up in a truly vicious circle.

And for the moment, a conservative trend was emergent which certainly transcended the immediate impact of the new electoral law. For in the primary elections, and especially in the elections from the county to the provincial electoral assemblies, a movement of opinion away from the left and toward the center is reflected in the mood of the suffrage at all strata of society. This could be anticipated to some extent with a preponderance of electoral seats assigned to the landlord curia and the creation of the new, first city, category. But the conservative trend was clearly delineated even among the popular elements in country and town. Generated primarily by indifference and political circumspection, it reduced the peasant opposition in the guberniia assemblies from 60 percent of the electors in the second elections to 47 percent in the third, and in the cities the oppositional, and particularly the leftist vote, declined drastically. This is especially evident when the entire city vote in the second election is compared with the mass urban vote in the third. In the second elections 86 percent of all electors from the cities were oppositional while in the third elections the second curia sent but 79 percent from the oppositional elements. While never strong among the landowners, the opposition lost 7 percent of their electoral seats in the *gubernia* assemblies in the third campaign as compared with the second. Only the workers held hard to the left; a significant factor in the course of the decade.[1] Certainly apathy and indifference played havoc with the peasant vote. But it should be noted that in the elections to the Second Duma about 45 percent of the peasant electoral seats were not filled.[2] This was not so much a matter of being dissillusioned with leftist tactics as the Kadets maintained, as a disenchantment with the whole revolutionary effort which really brought the peasantry nothing more ta gible than promises of a better life through enclosure. And the conservative peasant was highly skeptical of so drastic a reorientation of a traditional way of life. Stolypin assumed as much and set in operation a propaganda campaign, largely by deed, involving governors, land captains, and surveyors of the Land Settlement Administration.[3] He must have been aware that this kind of operation had been generally successful in the long history of land enclosure, but he needed a persistent effort without undue interference by domestic and foreign crises. He was convinced that the peasant would decide the course of the revolutionary effort and that under relatively normal circumstances strong measures to repress immediate outbreaks combined with an imaginative policy of reform (e.g., his projected educational and worker insurance measures) could limit and isolate disturbances in the urban arena of the restless workers.

In a word, the government had procured its more or less manageable Duma without a serious reaction and with a strong presumption of a conservative trend in the suffrage. True, it had established a reserve of mistrust by violating the Fundamental Laws, and it could only vaguely estimate the consequences. But that seemed to offer no immediate problem. Its appointed task was basically the same as that of the Kadets, though for different ends. It had to perform effectively through the Duma to enlist the support of broad strata of the population—especially the peasantry and the national minorities whose sensibilities it had sorely wounded. Given the kind of Duma the regime had created, the attraction of the first would be difficult enough and reconciliation with the second most unlikely. Civil liberties, the cry of the oppositional and revolutionary leadership, were less significant in the Russian political tradition than the quest for higher living standards and economic security, and the quest for equal opportunity for all ethnic elements, particularly in the matter of economic welfare and the protection of cultural patterns. And the suffrage of the Russian Empire had to develop a sorely needed sense of confidence in the regime; that it would somehow outgrow its paternalistic habits and patterns of operation; that it would come to trust the popular representation and abide by rules which it had established for itself to meet the "vital needs" of the moment.

The traditional, Russian, statist system, modified to a degree in 1861 and considerably in 1905-1906, had accumulated social and political attitudes for over six centuries. The infant parliament would probably share some of them—a greater faith in the efficacy of a more centralized authority than western Europeans might tolerate, a penchant for social and political suspicion, and a diffidence toward compromise if not an outright aversion for it. And, as the constitutionalists had learned in less than a year, it would have to draw heavily on the traditional patience of the Russian people for a long, undisturbed haul to master the parliamentary process.

Notes

Chapter I

1. For a discussion of the motivation and writing of the Electoral law of June 3, 1907 see Alfred Levin, "June 3, 1907: Action and Reaction," in A.D. Furgeson and A. Levin, editors, *Essays in Russian History; A Collection Dedicated to George Vernadsky,* (Hamden, Connecticut, 1965), pp. 247-251. The statement below on the content of the law is largely excerpted from this study, pp. 251-255. See also a detailed analysis of the contents of the law in Marc Szeftel, "The Reform of the Electoral Law to the State Duma on June 3, 1907: A New Basis for the Formation of the Russian Parliament" in *Liber Memoralis George De Lagarde: Studies Presented to the International Commission for the History of Representative and Parliamentary Institutions,* Vol. XXXVIII (London, 1965).

2. P. N. Miliukov, C. Seignobos and L. Eisenmann, *Histoire de Russie,* 3 vols. (Paris, 1922-1923), vol. III, p. 1156; P. Chasles, *Le Parlement Russe* (Paris, 1910), pp. 71, 73-74; Hereafter cited as Chasles, *Parlement;* Cf. A. Leroy-Beaulieu, "La Russie devant le Troisieme Duma," *Revue des Deux Mondes,* vol. 41 (1907), p. 390. Hereafter cited as Leroy-Beaulieu, *Revue.*

3. Chasles, *Parlement,* pp. 70-71, 73; L. Pasvolsky, *The Russian Review* (London), 1916, No. 2, p. 102. For the text of the Law see *Polnoe sobranie zakonov rossiskoi imperii. Sobranie tretie,* 43 vols. (St. Petersburg, 1885-1916), vol. XXVII, No. 29242. Hereafter cited as *P. S. Z.,* III.

4. See pp. 100-101.

5. This had the obvious affect of increasing the relative strength of the individual landowners. In ninety-three *uiezds* of European Russia they had six times the voting power of the city voters and the large landowners had ten times that of the small. See *Riech,* June 5, 1907, p. 2 c. 4; June 6, 1907, p. 3 c. 1; S. Harper, *The New Electoral Law for the Russian Duma* (Chicago, 1908), pp. 29, 42-44. Hereafter cited as Harper, *New Electoral Law.* Chasles, *Parlement,* p. 92; L. Martov and A. Potresov, editors, *Obshchestvennoe dvizhenie v Rossii v nachalie XX-go vieka,* 4 vols, (St. Petersburg, 1909-1914), IV, pt. 2, p. 145. Hereafter cited as *Ob. dvizh. Viestnik Evropy,* July 1907, pp. 345-346; *P. S. Z.,* III, vol. XXVII, No. 29242, Arts. 28, 29, 61, 62; *Riech,* August 29, 1907, p. 2. c. 2.

6. See Chasles, Parlement, pp. 92, 94-96; *Viestnik Evropy,* July, 1907, p. 345; *Ob. dvizh.,* IV, part 2, p. 145.

7. *Viestnik Evropy,* July, 1907, p. 347; *Riech,* June 5, 1907, p. 2, c. 3; June 8, 1907, p. 1, c. 4.

8. *P. S. Z.,* III vol. XXVII, No. 29242, Arts. 8, 37, 123.

9. In forty-nine provinces the first category elected 688 electors, the second 560. In some cities a first category elector had a constituency of twenty to thirty voters. *P. S. Z.,* III, vol. XXVII, No. 29242. Arts. 8, 27-44, 123; *Viestnik Evropy,* July, 1907, pp. 348-349; A. Petrishchev, "Bez pobiediteli," *Russkoe Bogatstvo,* July, 1907, p. 29; *Riech,* July 29, 1907, p. 2, cc. 2-3; August 28, 1907, p. 1, c. 6.

10. *P. S. Z.*, III, vol. XXVII, No. 29242, Arts 8, 42, 61, 123; Harper, *New Electoral Law*, pp. 29, 44: Chasles, *Parlement*, pp. 89, 90, 92; *Ob. dvizh*, IV, pt. 2, p. 145; Leroy-Beaulieu, *Revue*, pp. 391-392.

11. *P. S. Z.*, III, vol. XXVII, No. 29242, Arts. 30, 35, 38; *Viestnik Evropy*, July, 1907, p. 318; Harper, *New Electoral Law*, pp. 22-27.

12. Polish seats in the Duma were reduced from thirty-three to fourteen and in the cities of Warsaw, Liublin, and Siedlets, and in Vilno and Kovno *gubernii* one deputy was assigned to the Russian population and would, in all probability, be a bureaucrat. The representation of Asiatic Russia was reduced from forty-four to fifteen and half of the deputies from the area east of Lake Baikal had to be Cossack. The Transcaucasus was cut from twenty-nine to ten deputies and the Russian population was provided with a deputy for whom the Orthodox clergy voted with or without electoral qualifications. The "backward" steppe region and Central Asia which lost all representation included several cities with a population of over 100,000. See *P. S. Z.*, III, vol. XXVII, No. 29242, Article 8, Appendix; *Vestnik Evropy*, July, 1907, pp. 353-355; *Riech*, June 7, 1907, p. 1, c. 4; Harper, *New Electoral Law*, pp. 36-38; Leroy-Beaulieu, *Revue*, pp. 383-386; Chasles, *Parlement*, pp. 66-68. Not only were pocket boroughs created for Russians in overwhelmingly non-Russian areas (the 5,789 Polish and Jewish voters in Bielostock named 2 electors as against one for 112 voting Russians), but the conservative Germans in the Baltic and Taganrog regions were favored over other national groups, even over the politically questionable Cossacks. And in Kiev *guberniia* the rigid reduction of the nationality vote hurt the government's own interests as that conservative province lost half its deputies. *Riech*, August 5, 1907, p. 1, c. 6; Aug. 18, 1907, p. 3, c. 6; Aug. 28, 1907, p. 1, c. 6; Oct. 18, 1907, p. 5, c. 1; Oct. 25, 1907, p. 5, cc. 1, 5.

13. *P. S. Z.*, III, vol. XXVII, No. 29242, Arts. 45, 142-147; *Riech*, June 9, 1907, p. 1, c. 6; Harper, *New Electoral Law*, *pp. 35-36*, *Viestnik Evropy*, July, 1907, p. 356.

14. For a discussion of the development of the program and position of the rightist parties see A. Levin, *The Reactionary Tradition in the Election Campaign to the Third Duma, Oklahoma State University Publications. Arts and Sciences Studies. Social Science Series No. 8* (Stillwater, Oklahoma, 1962), pp. 4-8. Cited hereafter as Levin, *The Reactionary Tradition;* Hans Rogger, "The Formation of the Russian Right," *California Slavic Studies*, vol. III, pp. 66-69; Hans Rogger, "Russia," Hans Rogger and Eugen Weber, editors, (University of California Press, 1966), pp. 443-500.

15. Levin, *The Reactionary Tradition*, p. 8.

16. Ibid., pp. 9-10.

17. Ibid., pp. 10-13.

18. Official information on the Union of the Russian People is taken from reports of provincial governors to the Ministry of the Interior which were summarized by the Vice Director of the Police Department May 8, 1908 in "Information on the Numerical Strength of Legal Parties," TsGIAM *(Tsentralnyi Gosudarstvennyi Istoricheskii Arkhiv Moskva), Fona* 102, *Opis* 99, *Ed. Khranenii,* 164 (Fund 102, Section 99, File 164), pp. 280-281 reverse side (R), 292-292R, 298. Hereafter cited according to fund, section, and file or item *(delo)* when pertinent. TsGIAL *(Tsentralnyi Gosudarstvennyi Istoricheskii Arkhiv Leningrad),* 1327, 1, III, pp. 245-246R. This report is for May 20, 1911 but indicates the persistence of the practice of exaggeration.

19. Levin, *The Reactionary Tradition*, pp. 10-13.

20. Ibid., pp. 12, 26-27, 31-33.

21. Ibid., pp. 12-13.

22. Ibid., pp. 13-14.

23. Ibid., pp. 25-28.

24. Ibid., pp. 15-16.

25. Ibid., pp. 31-32.

26. Ibid., pp. 29-31.

27. Other rightist parties formed during the third election campaign or while the Duma was in session will be discussed below in connection with the election campaign and fractional splintering in the Third Duma.

Chapter II

1. M. Ia. Kapustin, *Riechi Kazanskogo Oktiabrista*, p. 76; B. Pares, *History of Russia* (New York, 1926), pp. 443-444: *Ob. dvizh.*, voi. III, p. 17.

2. A number of "Parties of Order" proliferated after October, 1905, the most typical being the Party of Legal Order (L.O.). It stood somewhat to the right of the Octobrists but generally acted with them. And it was recruited from the moderate bureaucracy with a great concern for a strong, central authority. The Party's call for just remuneration to those from whom land would be transferred to the peasantry may have influenced the Kadet program. It regarded the first two Dumas with considerable suspicion and was aroused by the influence of the "aliens" in public life. It stood resolutely against a federative structure of the Empire, fostered imperial as against local interests of any order, and promoted the prestige of government. It claimed no more than 1,390 members, probably in the major centers. See *Ob. dvizh.*, vol. III, p. 206; *Polnoe sobranie podrobnykh programm russkikh i polskikh partii* (Vilno, 1906), pp. 19-24; TsGIAM, 102, 99, 164, pp. 280-281; ibid., 166, pp. 266-267R. During the third campaign it "cursed out" the extremists, noting that the new electoral law only made martyrs of the left, and that the right appeared as paid hirelings. The L. O. Party played a passive role in the elections (to the irritation of some of its membership) and waited for the electorate to determine the complexion of the Duma before deciding on its course of action. See *Slovo*, Sept. 19, 1907, p. 2, c. 7—p. 3, c. 1; Oct. 21, 1907, p. 3, c. 4.

3. The program derives from a combination of the theses issued with the proclamation of its constituent session on November 10, 1905 (when the moderate minority left the Zemstvo Congress) and the resolutions of its First Congress held February 8-12, 1906 and published somewhat later in edited form. The latter were never confirmed by the Party as a whole, hence the theses of the Moscow Proclamation of November 10, 1905, represented the only official platform. See D. N. Shipov, *Vospominaniia i dumy o perezhitom*, (Moscow, 1918), pp. 405-406, 410-442; *Ob. dvizh.*, vol. III, pp. 175-177, 178-189. See also Levin, *The Second Duma* (New Haven, 1940), pp. 30-31.

4. Shipov, op, cit., pp. 423-424.

5. Ibid., pp. 430-431.

6. *Ob. dvizh.*, vol. III, pp. 191-194, 211-213; Levin, *The Second Duma*, passim, especially Chapters VI. XI, XII.

7. See pp. 24-25.

8. He seemed to have a particular fascination for areas in a state of crisis. In the Boer War he fought against Britain and was involved in Red Cross Work in Manchuria during the Japanese War. The Boxer Rebellion found him in North China and he was on the spot during disorders in Armenia and Macedonia. See B. Pares, *The Fall of the Russian Monarchy*, (New York, 1939), p. 105; P. E. Shchegolev et. al., editors, *Padenie tsarskogo rezhima* (Moscow and Leningrad, 1926), vol. VII, pp. 331-332. Cited hereafter as *Padenie*.

9. *Riech*, August 31, 1907, p. 3, c. 1.

10. Two of the Party's major figures stemmed from the world of science. Both M. Ia. Kapustin and L. R. Fon Anrep were professors of medicine, *Riech*, June 30, 1907, p. 2, c. 5; Pares, *The Fall of the Russian Monarchy*, p. 147; *Padenie*, VII, p. 406. Other figures include Iu. N. Miliutin and G. G. Lerkhe, highly placed in the Ministry of Finance, and the eminent Lawyer F. N. Plevako, *Slovo*, Sept. 20, 1907, p. 3. c. 3: *Riech*, July 20, 1907, p. 1, c. 5; Sept. 29, 1907, p. 3, c. 6: *Tretie sozyv gosudarstvennoi dumy Portretv, biografii, avtografii* (St. Petersburg, 1910) This work was organized alphabetically.

11. *Riech*, July 2, 1907, p. 1, c. 6; July 20, 1907, p. 1, c. 6; July 31, 1907, p. 1, c. 3; Aug. 15, 1907, p. 2, c. 1.

12. *Riech*, July 20, 1907, p. 1, cc. 5-6. The independent rightist organ *Grazhdanin* characterized the Octobrist Party as a "repainted false mummy" reflecting the falsity and rot of the old (bureaucratic—A. L.) regime, yet like it, apparently indestructible. Ibid., p. 1, cc. 6-7.

13. *Riech*, Aug. 2, 1907, p. 1, cc. 5-6; Aug. 15, 1907, p. 2, c. 1; Aug. 16, 1907, p. 1, c. 7, p. 2, c. 1; Oct. 10, 1907, p. 3, c. 4; Oct. 14, 1907, p. 2, c. 1.

14. *Riech*, June 24, 1907, p. 4, c. 6; Aug. 2, 1907, p. 3, c. 1; Aug. 5, 1907, p. 2, c. 3. See below pp.

15. *Slovo*, Sept. 9, 1907, p. 3, c. 3; Aug. 30, 1907, p. 3, c. 4; Oct. 14, 1907, p. 3, cc. 3, 4; Oct. 20, 1907, p. 3, c. 3. Other branches such as that in Kishenev were paralyzed by the ideological split. *Riech*, June 22, 1907, p. 4, c. 1.

16. *Slovo*, Sept. 14, 1907, p. 3, c. 2; *Riech*, July 17, 1907, p. 3, c. 7. In Dvinsk, Vice chairman Ia. K. Molchanov declared that he intended to leave the Octobrist Party. Ibid., Aug. 31, 1907, p. 5, c. 2-3.

17. *Riech*, June 24, 1907, p. 4, c. 6; Aug. 2, 1907, p. 3, c. 1; Aug. 5, 1907, p. 2, c. 3. See below pp. 18-19.

18. Cf. Leroy-Beaulieu, *Revue*, p. 399. *Grazhdanin* remarked that the Octobrists are indestructible because they were on all sides at once. Today they "rage for the freedom of the crowd" and establish field courts martial tomorrow. They present their left cheek to the Kadets and their right to the URP, wink with one eye at the government and with the other at the constitution. *Riech*, July 20, 1907, p. 1, c. 7.

19. *Riech*, Oct. 9, 1907, p. 2, c. 4; *Slovo*, Oct. 14, 1907, p. 3, c. 3.

20. The Octobrists recognized that they were not likely to attract the "impressionable" youth and extremists with such a philosophy. Kapustin, op. cit., pp. 79-80; *Riech*, Oct. 9, 1907, p. 2, c. 4.

21. *Riech*, July 7, 1907, p. 2, c. 6; Oct. 18, 1907, p. 2, cc. 2-3.

22. *Slovo*, Sept. 29, 1907, p. 3, c. 2; *Riech*, July 20, 1907, p. 1, c. 6; Oct. 4, 1907, p. 1, cc. 5-6; Oct. 13, 1907, p. 2, c. 3; *Novoe Vremia*, Oct. 15, 1907, p. 1, cc. 5-6; Kapustin, op. cit., p. 83; P. Chasles, *Parlement*, p. 71.

23. *Riech*, June 5, 1907, p. 3, cc. 2-3; *Golos Moskvy*, June 5, 1907, Supplement, p. 2, c. 7. It should be noted that the version in *Golos Moskvy* quoting an official Octobrist statement from *Novoe Vremia* did not include the words "and the necessity for it regrettable." Levin, *The Reactionary Tradition*, pp. 256-258.

24. *Riech*, June 13, 1907, p. 1, c. 5; Aug. 17, 1907, p. 1, c. 7; Ia. Miketov, *Chto sdielala narodnoe predstavitelstvo tretiago sozyva* (St. Petersburg, 1912), pp. 61-62.

25. *Viestnik Evropy*, Oct. 1907, p. 783. Support for the regime was not unanimous within the Party. Some felt that it was playing a hazardous game in coddling the Kadets; others, that repression could lead to a dangerous explosion. *Slovo*, July 11, 1907, p. 3, c. 2: *Riech*, Aug. 18, 1907, p. 1, cc. 4-5.

26. *Riech*, July 31, 1907, p. 3, c. 1; Sept. 3, 1907, p. 1, c. 4; Oct. 13, 1907, p. 2, c. 3. See also A. Leroy-Beaulieu, *Revue*, p. 399.

27. *Riech*, June 4, 1907, p. 1, c. 5; June 13, 1907, p. 2, c. 5; A. Savitskii, "P. A. Stolypin," *Monde Slave*, (Paris, 1917-1918, 1924-1938), vol. IV, 1934, pp. 393-394; *Ob. dvizh.*, III, pp. 207-208.

28. *Ob. dvizh.*, III, pp. 207-208; Savitskii, loc. cit., pp. 393-394; Shipov, *Vospominaniia*, p. 417: *Riech*, Aug. 17, 1907, p. 1, c. 7: Aug. 31, 1907, p. 1, c. 1.

29. *Riech*, June 13, 1907, p. 2, cc. 4-5: June 14, 1907, p. 1, c. 5, p. 2, c. 6.

30. *Riech*, June 12, 1907, p. 2, cc. 2-3; June 13, 1907, p. 1, c. 4, p. 2, c. 7; *Golos Moskvy*, June 12, 1907, p. 2, c. 1; June 14, 1907, p. 3, c. 1.

31. In this connection, N. E. Markov (II) lamented that the "cultured" nobility had disappeared—even as the aurochsen (bison—A. L.) of the Bieloviezh Forest, and identified those beasts, the *zubry*, henceforth with the conservative and reactionary landlordry. *Golos Moskvy*, June 12, 1907, p. 2, c. 1.

32. *Riech*, June 20, 1907, p. 1, c. 7; *Golos Moskvy*, Aug. 26, 1907, p. 5, cc. 6-7; Aug. 29, 1907, p. 4, c. 1.

33. *Riech*, June 20, 1907, p. 1, c. 7; Aug. 29, 1907, p. 2, cc. 1-4; Aug. 30, 1907, p. 2, c. 4; *Golos Moskvy*, Aug. 26, 1907, p. 5, c. 7; Aug. 29, 1907, p. 2, c. 4, p. 4, cc. 2-3.

34. *Golos Moskvy*, Aug. 23, 1907, p. 3, cc. 4-6; *Riech*, Aug. 30, 1907, p. 2, c. 4.

35. *Riech*, June 13, 1907, p. 2, cc. 5-6; June 14, 1907, p. 1, cc. 1, 5-6, p. 2, cc. 4-5; June 15, 1907, p. 2, cc. 5-7.

36. *Riech*, July 1, 1907, p. 4, c. 5; Aug. 24, 1907, p. 3, c. 3; Aug. 31, 1907, p. 1, c. 7. Premier Stolypin's project was not available to the author. A project of a governmental commission of December, 1905, and January, 1906, in all probability known to Stolypin, defined the nature of local "public organizations with the character of zemstvo institutions . . . about the size of the district of the present land captain." Taxable real estate and businesses were to be the bases for representation in an assembly. Its elected board and chairman were not to be subject to official confirmation. The local zemstvo was to have the same general powers as the *uiezd* zemstvo and the latter was to have powers of "general guidance" over the former. Unlike the *uiezd* zemstvos, the district zemstvos could meet to discuss common purposes. But they were to be subordinated to the administration and supervision of an *"uiezd* captain" appointed by the government as its highest representative in the *uiezd*. TsGIAL, 1921, 50, 33, p. 135R.

37. *Slovo*, July 6, 1907, p. 3, c. 2; July 13, 1907, p. 3, c. 3; July 25, 1907, p. 3, cc. 1-2; *Riech*, July 2, 1907, p. 3, c. 1; July 26, 1907, p. 1, c. 5; Aug. 5, 1907, p. 2, c. 3.

38. *Slovo*, July 6, 1907, p. 3, c. 2; Aug. 11, 1907, p. 3, c. 4; Aug. 14, 1907, p. 3, cc. 3-4; Aug. 21, 1907, p. 3, c. 5; *Riech*, June 23, 1907, p. 2, c. 5; June 29, 1907, p. 2, c. 7.

39. *Slovo*, Aug. 12, 1907, p. 3, c. 1; Aug. 23, 1907, p. 3, cc. 5-6; Aug. 28, 1907, p. 4, c. 5; Aug. 29, 1907, p. 3, c. 4; Aug. 30, 1907, p. 3, c. 4; Sept. 2, 1907, p. 2, c. 7.

40. A rift developed over the question of supporting the government in the spirit of the statement on the events of June 3. The St. Petersburg proclamation was critical of the regime's arbitrary procedures but called on parliament to support its measures for reform. *Riech*, Sept. 16, 1907, p. 4, c. 2. The proclamation appeared in *Golos Moskvy*, Sept. 16, 1907, p. 3, cc. 1-2; Sept. 20, 1907, p. 2, cc. 1-3; *Slovo*, Sept. 16, 1907, p. 2, cc. 5-6; Sept. 19, 1907, p. 3, cc. 1-2.

41. *Slovo*, July 5, 1907, p. 3, cc. 2-3; July 11, 1907, p. 3, c. 2; July 21, 1907, p. 3, c. 4; July 24, 1907, p. 3, cc. 4-5; July 29, 1907, p. 3, cc. 4-5; Aug. 8, 1907, p. 3, c. 4; Aug. 11, 1907, p. 3, c. 4; Aug. 19, 1907, p. 3, cc. 4-5; Aug. 21, 1907, p. 3, c. 5; Aug. 29, 1907, p. 3, c. 4; Sept. 12, 1907, p. 3, c. 1; *Riech*, Aug. 2, 1907, p. 3, c. 1; Aug. 18, 1907, p. 3, c. 2. Despite numerous plaintive calls for contributions from wealthy adherents, the campaign fund was always deplorably inadequate. *Riech*, July 28, 1907, p. 2, c. 5; *Slovo*, Aug. 3, 1907, p. 3, c. 4; Aug. 21, 1907, p. 3, cc. 4-5; Aug. 24, 1907, p. 3, c. 4.

42. All data are taken from the Report of the Vice Director of the Ministry of the Interior "Information on the Numerical Strength of Legal Parties," May 8, 1908, TsGIAM 102, 99, 164, pp. 266-267R, 280-281R; 166, pp. 266-267R.

43. *Riech*, July 1, 1907, p. 4, cc. 5-6; *Slovo*, July 15, 1907, p. 3, c. 1; Aug. 24, 1907, p. 3, c. 4.

44. *Riech*, June 10, 1907, p. 2, c. 6; July 1, 1907, p. 4, cc. 5-6; *Slovo*, July 27, 1907, p. 3, c. 3; Aug. 11, 1907, p. 3, 4; Sept. 15, 1907, p. 3, c. 4.

45. *Riech*, June 10, 1907, p. 2, c. 2; *Slovo*, Aug. 24, 1907, p. 3, c. 4.

46. *Riech*, Aug. 9, 1907, p. 3, c. 2; Sept. 29, 1907, p. 3, c. 4; *Slovo*, Sept. 20, 1907, p. 3, c. 3.

47. *Slovo*, July 4, 1907, p. 3, c. 3; July 17, 1907, p. 3, c. 3; July 21, 1907, p. 3, c. 4; Aug. 29, 1907, p. 3, c. 4; Oct. 20, 1907, p. 3, c. 6; *Riech*, July 14, 1907, p. 3, cc. 4-5; Aug. 23, 1907, p. 2, c. 2. Here again, those with transferable qualifications were urged to validate them. *Riech*, Aug. 9, 1907, p. 3, c. 2.

48. *Slovo*, July 14, 1907, p. 3, c. 4; July 22, 1907, p. 3, c. 4; Sept. 8, 1907, p. 3, cc. 2-3; *Riech*, Aug. 9, 1907, p. 3, c. 4; S. M. Sidelnikov, *Obrazovanie i deiatel'nost pervoi gosudarstvennoi dumy* (Moscow, 1967), p. 146. The Party gave some thought to organization along occupational lines—including peasant and worker sections—united under *guberniia* and *oblast* councils. *Slovo*, Sept. 8, 1907, p. 3, cc. 2-3.

49. *Viestnik Evropy*, August, 1907, p. 755; *Slovo*, July 4, 1907, p. 3, c. 3; July 14, 1907, p. 3, c. 4; Sept. 16, 1907, p. 2, c. 6; *Riech*, Aug. 31, 1907, p. 5, cc. 2-3; Sept. 19, 1907, p. 2, c. 7.

50. *Riech*, June 29, 1907, p. 4, c. 1; Aug. 31, 1907, p. 5, cc. 2-3; Sept. 22, 1907, p. 5, c. 5.

51. *Riech*, Aug. 9, 1907, p. 3, c. 2; Aug. 17, 1907, p. 3, c. 6; Sept. 27, 1907, p. 3, c. 4; *Slovo*, Aug. 22, 1907, p. 3, c. 4; Sept. 9, 1907, p. 3, c. 3; Sept. 13, 1907, p. 4, c. 5; Sept. 28, 1907, p. 3, c. 4; Oct. 23, 1907, p. 4, c. 1. Differences among the German Octobrists resembled those of the Party as a whole. The St. Petersburg organiza-

tion was more liberal than the Muscovite, and the St. Petersburg Party was cleft by a moderate-liberal schism. *Slovo,* Aug. 22, 1907, p. 3, c. 4; Aug. 30, 1907, p. 3, c. 4; Sept. 5, 1907, p. 3, c. 5. It should be noted that the German branches on the Volga (and in Novorossiisk) were composed largely of commune peasants. Chasles, *Parlement,* pp. 106, ff. In the Baltic Region the German Octobrist group was involved in the sharp ethnic-class animosities characteristic of the area. *Slovo,* July 4, 1907, p. 3, c. 3; *Riech,* Sept. 2, 1907, p. 5, c. 5.

52. A special bureau was set up to arrange for pre-election meetings and tactics. *Slovo,* Sept. 4, 1907, p. 3, c. 2. See also *Slovo,* Aug. 11, 1907, p. 3, c. 4; Aug. 19, 1907, p. 3, c. 5; Aug. 21, 1907, p. 3, c. 5; Aug. 24, 1907, p. 3, c. 4; *Riech,* July 1, 1907, p. 4, cc. 5-6; Oct. 7, 1907, p. 4, c. 4.

53. *Riech,* July 14, 1907, p. 3, c. 5; *Slovo,* Aug. 24, 1907, p. 3, c. 4; Sept. 20, 1907, p. 3, c. 3.

54. *Slovo,* Aug. 1, 1907, p. 3, c. 2; Sept. 13, 1907, p. 4, c. 4; Sept. 15, 1907, p. 3, c. 4; Sept. 20, 1907, p. 3, c. 3.

55. *Riech,* Sept. 23, 1907, p. 3, c. 2; Sept. 25, 1907, p. 4, c. 6; Sept. 29, 1907, p. 3, c. 6; *Slovo,* Sept. 30, 1907, p. 2, c. 4; Oct. 4, 1907, p. 4, c. 5. The Muscovites were somewhat more lively, concentrating at least four meetings into the first half of October as the campaign reached a climax. *Golos Moskvy,* Oct. 6, 1907, p. 2, cc. 1-3; Oct. 7, 1907, p. 2, c. 2; Oct. 10, 1907, p. 2, cc. 5-7; Oct. 11, 1907, p. 2, c. 6.

56. *Slovo,* July 19, 1907, p. 3, c. 3; July 24, 1907, p. 3, cc. 4-5; Aug. 30, 1907, p. 3, c. 4; Sept. 12, 1907, p. 3, c. 1; *Riech,* July 27, 1907, p. 2, c. 5; Sept. 20, 1907, p. 3, c. 4; Oct. 4, 1907, p. 2, c. 7.

57. E.g., Iu. N. Miliutin and F. N. Adoratskii with a wide following among the clergy. See *Slovo,* July 19, 1907, p. 3, c. 3; July 27, 1907, p. 3, cc. 3-4; Aug. 10, 1907, p. 3, c. 3; Aug. 15, 1907, p. 3, cc. 4-5; Aug. 29, 1907, p. 3, c. 4; Aug. 30, 1907, p. 3, c. 4; Sept. 4, 1907, p. 3, c. 2; Sept. 12, 1907, p. 3, c. 1; Sept. 22, 1907, p. 3, c. 3; Sept. 23, 1907, p. 3, c. 1; Sept. 27, 1907, p. 3, c. 3; Oct. 4, 1907, p. 4, c. 5; Oct. 11, 1907, p. 5, c. 1; Oct. 21, 1907, p. 3, c. 4; *Riech,* Sept. 22, 1907, p. 4, c. 4.

58. Faced with opposition from the URP in Warsaw, they named a constitutionalist. *Slovo,* Aug. 11. 1907, p. 3. c. 4; *Riech.* Aug. 10, 1907, p. 3, c. 7; Aug. 29 1907, p. 3, c. 7; Aug. 31, p. 5, cc. 2-3; Sept. 9, 1907, p. 5, c. 4; Sept. 23, 1907, p. 3, c. 2.

Chapter III

1. *Ob. divzh.,* vol. III, p. 195; Shipov, *Vospominaniia* p. 478.

2. Shipov was basically a Slavophile in his conviction that only advisory representation was needed. Shipov, *Vospominaniia,* pp. 448-491, 497; *Ob. dvizh.,* vol. III, pp. 195, 200-202.

3. *Riech,* June 21, 1907, p. 1, c. 7; Shipov, *Vospominaniia,* pp. 513-514.

4. Shipov, *Vospominaniia,* pp. 510, 513-515; V. V. Vodovozov, *Sbornik programm politicheskikh partii v Rossii* (n.p., 1906), p. 47; *Polnoe sobranie podrobnykh programm,* pp. 25-26; *Riech,* Aug. 11, 1907, p. 1, c. 7. p. 2, c. 1; V. I. Gurko, *Features and Figures of the Past. Government and opinion in the Reign of Nicholas II,* J. E. Wallace Sterling. Xenia J. Eudin, H. H. Fisher, editors, and L. Matveev, Translator (Stanford University California and London, 1939), p. 49.

5. Shipov, *Vospominaniia,* pp. 510-515; *Sbornik programm politcheskikh partii,* p. 47.

6. *Slovo*, Aug. 29, 1907, p. 3, c. 5. See below pp. 61-64, 130.

7. Shipov, *Vospominaniia*, pp. 516-518; *Sbornik programm politicheskikh partii*, p. 47; *Riech*, June 8, 1907, p. 2, c. 6; July 10, 1907, p. 1, c. 3; June 24, 1907, p. 2, c. 3; July 20, 1907, p. 2, c. 5; Aug. 1, 1907, p. 2, c. 3; Aug. 3, 1907. p. 3, cc. 4-5; Aug. 31. 1907, p. 4, c. 3; *Golos Moskvy*, Aug. 30, 1907, p. 2, c. 3; TsGIAM, 102. 99, 164, pp. 280-281R.

8. For a discussion of the Kadet reaction to the new electoral law see Levin, "June 3, 1907; Action and Reaction," loc. cit., pp. 259-261.

9. V. Obninskii, *Novy Stroi* (Moscow, 1909), p. 207.

10. *Viestnik Evropy*, November, 1907, pp. 354-356.

11. Ibid., August, 1907, pp. 843-844; November, 1907, pp. 442-444; *Riech*, Oct. 17, 1907, p. 1, c. 7.

12. *Riech*, July 1, 1907, p. 1, c. 3; Aug. 9, 1907, p. 1, c. 3, Sept. 13, 1907, p. 1, c. 7, p. 2, c. 1; Oct. 17, 1907, p. 1, cc. 6-7, p. 2, c. 1.

13. *Viestnik Evropy*, October 7, 1907, p. 778; December, 1907, p. 891; *Riech*, June 30, 1907, p. 1, cc. 3-4; July 8, 1907, p. 1, c. 7; A. Levin, "Peter Arkad'evich Stolypin: a Political Appraisal", *The Journal of Modern History*, December, 1965, p. 457.

14. *Riech*, Aug. 11, 1907, p. 2, c. 4.

15. *Viestnik Evropy*, November 1907, pp. 364-365. Bernard Pares, *The Fall of the Russian Monarchy*, pp. 104-105.

16. *Viestnik Evropy*, August, 1907, p. 846.

17. Ibid., January, 1908, pp. 350-352; *Riech*, Sept. 18, 1907, p. 2, c. 4; Sept. 28, 1907, p. 5, c. 1-2.

18. *Riech*, June 8, 1907, p. 1, c. 3; Sept. 18, 1907, p. 2, c. 2; *Slovo*, Oct. 2, 1907, p. 3, cc. 3-4; Oct. 12, 1907, p. 3, c. 5.

19. *Riech*, Oct. 13, 1907, p. 2, cc. 1-5; Oct. 16, 1907, p. 4, c. 3.

20. In "attainable" legislation the Kadets evidently included bills on local government, church affairs, and a land bill on which their committees were at work by mid-September. *Riech*, Aug. 31, 1907, p. 1, c. 7; Sept. 11, 1907, p. 3, c. 7, p. 4, c. 1; Sept. 26, 1907, p. 2, c. 6. See also ibid., June 21, 1907, p. 1, cc. 5-6; Aug. 14, 1907, p. 1, cc. 5-6; Sept. 9, 1907, p. 2, c. 5; Oct. 12, 1907, p. 3, c. 5; Oct. 13, 1907, p. 3, cc. 3-4; Oct. 16, 1907, p. 4, c. 4; Oct. 17, 1907, p. 3, c. 6.

21. This will be discussed in connection with the assessment of election results. The Kadets held that their following was growing and that their sincere constitutionalism had generated broad sympathy in the electorate. *Riech*, July 1, 1907, p. 1, c. 3; Sept. 14, 1907, p. 1, c. 3.

22. *Riech*, June 10, 1907, p. 1, cc. 4-5; June 12, 1907, p. 1, c. 3; Levin, *The Second Duma*, pp. 338-339.

23. *Riech*, June 12, 1907, p. 1, c. 3; Sept. 18, 1907, p. 2, c. 4; Levin, *The Second Duma*, Chaps. VI, VII.

24. The definitive arguments of the Maklakov, Miliukov schools are entirely of post-revolutionary vintage. The biographical article on V. A. Maklakov in the Granat Encyclopedia notes his conservative-oppositional trend. *Entsiklopedicheskii slovar*, (T-va Br. A. I. Granat i Ko. St. Petersburg, 1890-1917), vol XVII,

see article "Chleny Gosudarstv. Dumy pervogo, vtorogo i tret'iago sozyva," pp. 39-40. Cited hereafter as Granat, *Entsik. slovar.* See also A. Ia. Avrekh, *Stolypin i tret'ia duma,* (Moscow, 1968), pp. 292-294, 438 on Maklakov's conservatism.

25. For a detailed elaboration of these views see V. A. Maklakov, *Vlast i obshchestvennost na zaktie staroi rossii* (Paris, 1928), 3 vols, and *Iz vospominanii, Pervaia Gosudarstvennaia Duma. Vospominaniia sovremennika* (Paris, 1938). This has been translated as *The First State Duma. Contemporary Reminiscences, by Mary Belkin. Indiana University Publications, Russian and East European Series, vol. 30 (Bloomington Indiana, 1964); Vtoraia Gosudarstvennaia Duma* (New York, 1954); P. N. Miliukov, *God borby* (St. Petersburg 1907); P. N. Miliukov, *Vospominaniia* (New York, 1955) 2 vols. See also D. W. Treadgold, *Lenin and His Rivals,* (New York, 1955), Chaps. VI, X, XIII.

26. Cf. A. Levin, "Foreword" in V. A. Maklakov, *The First State Duma.*

27. P. N. Miliukov, *Vospominaniia,* vol. I, pp. 240-241. For a discussion of efforts to woo liberals into the Witte and Stolypin cabinets see P. N. Miliukov, *Tri popytki* (Paris, 1921), V. I. Gurko, *Features and Figures of the Past,* pp. 711-712, 718, 724; N. A. Savitskii, "P. A. Stolypin," *Monde Slave,* 1933, No. 4, pp. 362-367; V. N. Kokovtsov, *Out of My Past, Memoires of Count Kokovtsov,* translated by L. Matveev (Palo Alto, California, 1935), pp. 150-151.

28. *Riech,* Sept. 21, 1907, p. 2, cc. 2-3; Sept. 25, 1907, p. 2, cc. 1-2.

29. *Riech,* June 12, 1907, p. 3, c. 5; Aug. 16, 1907, p. 3, c. 5; Aug. 24, 1907, p. 3, c. 2. For the Kadet platform see "Novaia duma, platforma partii narodnoi svobody," in V. Ivanovich, *Rossiiskaia partii, soiuzy i ligi* (St. Petersburg, 1906), pp. 15-18.

30. *Riech,* July 3, 1907, p. 1, cc. 4-5.

31. These had been offered as a conservative and rightist gambit with varying degrees of sincerity and the Kadets had opposed it on the legal grounds that the law and morality already controlled it; on the political grounds that the government was in some measure responsible for it; and on the practical grounds that such action would indicate a rightist turn which could cost the party considerable popular support. See Levin, *The Second Duma,* Chap. XII; *Riech,* Aug. 12, 1907, p. 1, c. 7.

32. *Riech,* June 12, 1907, p. 3, c. 5.

33. *Riech,* Aug. 21, 1907, p. 1, c. 7, p. 2, c. 1.

34. *Riech,* Sept. 28, 1907, p. 4, c. 3; Sept. 30, 1907, p. 3, c. 4.

35. The Odessa chairman, Shchepkin, objected to the candidacy of Nikolaev for deputy to the Duma. *Riech,* Aug. 28, 1907, p. 4, c. 3; Aug. 29, 1907, p. 3, cc. 1-2; Oct. 25, 1907, p. 4, c. 3.

36. *Riech,* June 6, 1907, p. 1, cc. 6-7; Aug. 1, 1907, p. 3, c. 7; Aug. 16, 1907, p. 3, c. 5; Aug. 25, 1907, p. 2, c. 5; Aug. 25, 1907, p. 2, cc. 3-4; Aug. 30, 1907, p. 3, c. 1; Sept. 8, 1907, p. 4, c. 3; Sept. 9, 1907, p. 4, c. 2; Sept. 11, 1907, p. 4, c. 1; Sept. 12, 1907, p. 7, c. 1; Sept. 21, 1907, p. 4, c. 1; Oct. 2, 1907, p. 2, cc. 1-2; Oct. 3, 1907, p. 5, c. 1; Oct. 4, 1907, p. 4, c. 3; Oct. 5, 1907, p. 4, c. 1; Oct. 7, 1907, p. 1, c. 7.

37. *Riech,* Aug. 25, 1907, p. 2, c. 3; Aug. 28, 1907, p. 4, c. 3; Sept. 4, 1907, p. 4, c. 3; Sept. 6, 1907, p. 3, c. 7; Sept. 9, 1907, p. 4, c. 2.

38. *Riech,* Sept. 11, 1907, p. 4, c. 1; Oct. 3, 1907, p. 3, c. 3; Oct. 6, 1907, p. 2, c. 3.

39. *Riech,* Aug. 11, 1907, p. 3, c. 2; Aug. 28, 1907, p. 3, c. 3; Aug. 29, 1907, p. 3, cc. 1-2; Aug. 30, 1907, p. 3, c. 1; Sept. 2, 1907, p. 3, c. 6; Sept. 6, 1907, p. 3, c. 3.

40. *Riech,* Aug. 28, 1907, p. 4, c. 3; Aug. 31, 1907, p. 3, c. 4; Sept. 1, 1907, p. 3, c. 4; Sept. 4, 1907, p. 4, cc. 2-3; Oct. 6, 1907, p. 2, c. 3; Oct. 21, 1907, p. 2, cc. 2-5; Oct. 23, 1907, p. 4, c. 7; Oct. 30, 1907, p. 3, c. 4.

41. *Riech,* Sept. 13, 1907, p. 3, c. 3.

42. *Reich,* June 6, 1907, p. 3, c. 5; June 14, 1907, p. 2, c. 7; June 21, 1907, p. 1, c. 7, p. 2, c. 5; Aug. 16, 1907, p. 3, c. 5.

43. *Riech,* July 8, 1907, p. 3, c. 6; July 11, 1907, p. 3, c. 1; July 24, 1907, p. 3, c. 2; Aug. 4, 1907, p. 3, c. 3; Aug. 11, 1907, p. 3, cc. 1-2; Sept. 26, 1907, p. 4, cc. 1-2.

44. In St. Petersburg some 2,000 of a possible 20,000 workers were registered. *Riech,* July 17, 1907, p. 3, c. 6.

45. *Riech,* July 17, 1907, p. 3, c. 6; July 25, 1907, p. 1, cc. 6-7; July 31, 1907, p. 1, c. 6; Aug. 9, 1907, p. 1, c. 5; Sept. 12, 1907, p. 3, c. 7; Oct. 11, 1907, p. 1, cc. 5-7.

46. *Riech,* Aug. 4, 1907, p. 3, c. 3; Sept. 12, 1907, p. 3, c. 1; Sept. 22, 1907, p. 3, c. 6. In the Polish-Lithuanian area they won the deep gratitude of the Polish nationalists (the National-Democrats) for eschewing an independent campaign in Warsaw because of their compassion for the Polish position in the revised electoral structure. And in Grodno they were disturbed by the political fervor of charitable-religious Russian organizations. *Riech,* July 31, 1907, p. 3, cc. 6-7; Sept. 12, 1907, p. 3, c. 6; Sept. 26, 1907, p. 5, cc. 1-2; Oct. 17, 1907, p. 3, c. 4.

47. *Riech,* Aug. 21, 1907, p. 2, c. 1; Aug. 26, 1907, p. 3, c. 7.

48. *Riech,* Aug. 23, 1907, p. 1, c. 7.

49. *Riech,* Aug. 29, 1907, p. 3, c. 2; Sept. 4, 1907, p. 1, c. 2.

50. Chasles, *Parlement,* pp. 71-72; V. I. Gurko, *Features and Figures of the Past,* p. 491; A. Levin, *The Second Duma,* p. 34n; B. Pares, *Russia and Reform,* pp. 542, 551; *Polnoe sobranie podrobnykh programm,* pp. 60-68; *Viestnik Evropy,* October, 1907, p. 779 and 779n; D. W. Treadgold, *Lenin and his Rivals,* p. 242.

51. Samuel Harper, as a relatively new observer of the Russian political scene from the American academic world, regarded the formation of the "non-party peasant party" in the Duma as an indication of the political inexperience of the Russian electorate. S. N. Harper, *The Russia I Believe In* (Chicago, 1945), p. 38.

52. *Riech,* July 25, 1907, p. 1, cc. 5-6.

53. They chided the Kadets for not naming Father G. S. Petrov as a candidate, and were, in turn, assailed by the Social Democrats for placing Sokolov on the list. *Slovo,* Aug. 24, 1907, p. 3, c. 5; Oct. 12, 1907, p. 3, c. 3; Oct. 13, 1907, p. 3, c. 4.

54. *Slovo,* Aug. 29, 1907, p. 3, c. 5; Oct. 27, 1907, p. 3, c. 4, p. 4, c. 2.

55. *Riech,* Apr. 4, 1907, p. 3, c. 1; Sept. 9, 1907, p. 4, c. 3; Sept. 23, 1907, p. 4, cc. 4-5; Sept. 29, 1907, p. 5, cc. 4-5.

Chapter IV

1. *Ob. dvizh.* vol. III, pp. 151-158; Levin, *The Second Duma,* pp. 34-36, 57-59; Treadgold, *Lenin and his Rivals,* p. 211; *Riech,* Sept. 6, 1907, p. 2, cc. 1-3.

2. *Riech*, July 6, 1907, p. 3, c. 3; Mar. 24, 1907, p. 3, c. 2.

3. *Riech*, July 1, 1907, p. 3, cc. 3-4; July 24, 1907, p. 1, c. 3.

4. *Riech*, July 31, 1907, p. 3, c. 1; *Slovo*, July 27, 1907, p. 3, cc. 4-5.

5. *Slovo*, July 31, 1907, p. 3, c. 3; Aug. 5, 1907, p. 3, c. 4; *Riech*, July 31, 1907, p. 3, c. 2.

6. Those named were V. A. Miakotin, E. V. Sviatlovskii, A. V. Pieshekhonov, A. A. Demianov, A. A. Leontiev, A. E. Kalistratov, I. L. Lutiugin, N. F Anenskii, A. F. Nikolai. *Slovo*. Sept. 13, 1907, p. 4, c. 5. See also ibid., Aug. 26 1907, p. 3, c. 4; Sept. 9, 1907, p. 3, c. 3; *Riech*, Sept. 13, 1907, p. 3, c. 5.

7. *Riech*, Sept. 25, 1907, p. 4, c. 6.

8. *Ob. dvizh.*, vol. III, pp. 138-151; Pares, *Russia and Reform*, pp. 543, 558; Levin, *The Second Duma*, pp. 36-37, 106-107, 132, 139, 141, 167-168.

9. *Riech*, July 19, 1907, p. 3, c. 3; July 28, 1907, p. 3, c. 3.

10. The Kadets countered with the argument that their parliamentary action was not inherently illusory but was so rendered by the leftists, including the Trudoviki, with unattainable proposals presented for agitational affect. Such measures raised the prospect of sharp peasant disappointment with Duma activity, even that of the Trudoviki, if they failed to realize demands they raised. The Kadets were not at all certain that the peasants tied their fate to the coming revolution. *Riech*, July 9, 1907, p. 1, cc. 4-5; July 14, 1907, p. 2, cc. 2-5; July 19, 1907, p. 3, c. 3; Aug. 2, 1907, p. 1, cc. 1-3; Aug. 7, 1907, p. 1, cc. 5-6; Oct. 2, 1907, p. 4, c. 7.

11. *Slovo*, July 19, 1907, p. 3, c. 4; Aug. 3, 1907, p. 3, c. 4; Aug. 8, 1907, p. 3, cc. 4-5; *Riech*, July 14, 1907, p. 3, c. 4; July 27, 1907, p. 3, c. 5. As efforts to form a "left bloc" of all socialists dragged on, the Turdoviki took matters into their own hands and named candidates for the town categories. After a canvass of local organizations, I. L. Lutiugin, V. I. de Planson, A. S. Zarudnovo, and V. V. Vodovozov were named for St. Petersburg. *Riech*, Aug. 26, 1907, p. 4, c. 4; Sept. 1, 1907, p. 3, c. 7; Sept. 15, 1907, p. 3, c. 2.

12. *Slovo*, Aug. 5, 1907, p. 3, c. 4; Aug. 17, p. 3, cc. 4-5.

13. *Partiia sotsialistov revoliutsionerov. Rezoliutsii ekstrennogo siezda P. S. R. po voprosu o dumskoi i vnie dumskoi taktiki.* N. d., n. p.

14. *Riech*, July 24, 1907, p. 1, cc. 3-4.

15. *Slovo*, July 4, 1907, p. 3, cc. 3-4; Aug. 1, 1907, p. 1, c. 2; Sept. 5, 1907, p. 3, c. 5; *Riech*, July 6, 1907, p. 2, c. 5; Aug. 11, 1907, p. 3, c. 4; Aug. 25, 1907, p. 2, c. 4; Aug. 28, 1907, p. 4, cc. 4-5; Sept. 1, 1907, p. 3, c. 7; Sept. 13, 1907, p. 3, c. 7; Oct. 16, 1907, p. 3, c. 4.

16. *Riech*, July 20, 1907, p. 3, c. 4; Aug. 10, 1907, p. 3, c. 3; *Slovo*, Aug. 14, 1907, p. 3, c. 4.

17. O. H. Radkey, *The Agrarian Foes of Bolshevism: Promise and Default of the Russian Socialist Revolutionaries, March to October 1917* (New York, 1958), pp. 70-74; *Riech*, Aug. 12, 1907, p. 1, c. 6.

18. J. A. Reshetar, *A Concise History of the Communist Party of the Soviet Union* (New York, 1964), p. 81; G. Vernadsky, *Lenin Red Dictator*, pp. 73, 77; L. Fischer. *The Life of Lenin* (New York, 1964), p. 51; *Riech*, July 22, 1907, p. 5, c. 1.

19. Reshetar, op, cit., p. 78; L. Schapiro, *The Communist Party of the Soviet Union* (New York, 1959), pp. 97-98; E. Iaroslavskii, editor, *Protokoly s'ezdov i konferentsii VKP (b)*. *Piataia s'ezd RSDRP* (Moscow, 1935), pp. 624, 629, 853-860.

20. V. I. Lenin, *Sobranie sochinenii* (Moscow, 1921-1925), vol. VIII, note 193, p. 650.

21. *Riech*, Sept. 4, 1907, p. 5, c. 1.

22. *Riech*, June 28, 1907, p. 2, c. 6; July 11, 1907, p. 3, c. 7; Aug. 16, 1907, p. 2, c. 5; Aug. 21, 1907, p. 2, c. 4, p. 6, c. 4. Some concern was aroused by the apprehension of an editor of *Proletarii* as he returned from an international congress at Stuttgart with compromising and detailed records of Party activities. Ibid., Aug. 11, 1907, p. 3, c. 7.

23. See Levin, *The Second Duma*, pp. 40-50. Reshetar, op. cit., pp. 72-79.

24. E. Iaroslavskii, *Istoriia VKP (b)* 4 vols., (Moscow, 1926-1930), vol. I, p. 201; Lenin, *Sobranie sochinenii*, vol. VIII, p. 411.

25. Ibid.

26. See "Partizanskaia voina" in *Proletarii*, Sept. 30, 1906; Lenin, *Sobranie sochinenii*, vol. VII, pp. 77-86.

27. Reshetar, op. cit., 64,77.

28. The P. P. S. called for concentration on legal, political, and trade union activities as well as fundamental reform to obviate disorder. *Riech*, June 23, 1907, p. 5, c. 7; Aug. 8, 1907, p. 1, cc. 2-4, p. 3, c. 4; Aug. 31, 1907, p. 3, c. 1; Sept. 18, 1907, p. 4, cc. 4-5; Oct. 4, 1907, p. 4, c. 5; *Slovo*, Aug. 8, 1907, p. 3, c. 5; Aug. 11, 1907, p. 3, c. 4. Terroristic elements withdrew from the Polish Socialist Party but the majority at its Tenth Congress condemned "militia" activities, sometimes operating for personal ends. Earlier in the summer the Party indicated the seriousness of its purpose by "executing" six members who had been tried by a Party court for banditry and disregard of orders to leave the Kingdom of Poland within twenty-four hours. *Riech*, July 22, 1907, p. 5, c. 7; Oct 28, 1907, p. 5, cc. 3-4; Oct. 30, 1907, p. 3, c. 6.

29. *Riech*, Aug. 9, 1907, p. 2, c. 6.

30. Kadet analysts were certain that Lenin's Blanquism was driving labor to a spontaneous "economism" and into the arms of the Social Revolutionaries and the anarcho-syndicalists (Makhaevists). *Riech*, Aug. 1, 1907, p. 1, cc. 3-4.

31. *Riech*, Sept. 13, 1907, p. 3, c. 6.

32. *Slovo*, Sept. 12, 1909, p. 3, c. 2 has the text of the Menshevik resolution on trade unions offered at the Party Central conference held in St. Petersburg in mid-September. *Riech*, June 12, 1907, p. 4, c. 3; July 1, 1907, p. 4, c. 4; Sept. 28, 1907, p. 4, cc. 3-4. The Mensheviks recommended that Social Democrats join mutual aid societies and create them where they did not exist. Ibid., Sept. 29, 1907, p. 4, c. 3. The majority of the Stuttgart Conference of the Second International held in August, had assumed approximately the same position as the Mensheviks on trade union—Party relations. Ibid., Oct. 28, 1907, p. 5, c. 4. The important Baltic and Polish Social Democratic Parties also stood on the Menshevik position. The Baltic conference in August suggested the creation of Social Democratic sections in the trade unions and that their representatives seek administrative positions with advisory votes. Ibid., Aug. 24, 1907, p. 3, c. 4. The Poles emphasized that the union were to make no distinctions of a national, religious, or political order.

They would exclude only "Christian" unions which introduced elements of religious and racial intolerance. Ibid., Oct. 28, 1907, p. 3, c. 4.

33. *Riech*, July 1, 1907, p. 4, c. 4; July 21, 1907, p. 2, cc. 4-5.

34. It is perhaps notable that some trade union elements were all too ready to co-operate with management and that the feeling was widespread that the unions were too weakly organized to participate in an international trade union congress. *Riech*, July 6, 1907, p. 3, c. 3; July 7, 1907, p. 3, c. 4.

35. *Slovo*, Sept. 18, 1907, p. 3, c. 4; Lenin, *Sobranie sochinenii*, vol. VIII, p. 418.

36. *Riech*, Oct. 21, 1907, p. 3, cc. 1, 3.

37. S. M. Sidelnikov, *Obrazovanie i deiatel'nosti pervoi gosudarstvennoi* dumy, p. 21.

38. See Lenin, *Sobranie sochinenii*, vol. VII, pp. 77-86. The article "Partisan Warfare" is translated in *Orbis, a Quarterly Journal of World Affairs*, July 1958, p. 205.

39. J. A. Reshetar, *A Concise History of the Communist Party of the Soviet Union*, pp. 60, 68-69; L. Schapiro, *The Communist Party of the Soviet Union*, pp. 83-85.

40. A. Levin, *The Second Duma*, pp. 51-52.

41. Lenin, *Sobranie sochinenii*, vol. XVII, pp. 109, 152, 452n. Levin. *The Second Duma*, p. 51.

42. *Riech*, June 28, 1907, p. 3, c. 1, p. 4, c. 1; July 3, 1907, p. 3, cc. 1-2; July 7, 1907, p. 4, c. 1; July 8, 1907, p. 3, cc. 6-7.

43. Lenin, *Sobranie sochinenii*, vol. VIII, pp. 434-461; *Riech*, July 22, 1907, p. 4, cc. 4-5. He elaborated these ideas in a "Project of an Electoral Platform for the RSDLP," Lenin, *Sobranie sochinenii*, vol. VIII, see especially p. 633.

44. Note Lenin's consistency in his characterization of the immediate post 1905 period in connection with expropriations.

45. Lenin, *Sobranie sochinenii*, vol. VIII, p. 449.

46. The Menshevik leader, L. Martov, arguing against the boycott, condemned expectations for revolutionary action when there was "no revolution of the mood." He apparently feared the same indifferentism that haunted Lenin, though Martov blamed it on the bourgeois campaign for concessions. *Riech*, July 25, 1907, p. 1, cc. 6-7, p. 2, c. 1.

47. At the same meeting (in mid-July) the Bolshevik argument against the boycott was repeated in detail by the "most talented leader of the Bolsheviks, a leader of the boycott in the first election campaign," apparently referring to Lenin. *Riech*, July 12, 1907, p. 2, c. 4; *Slovo*, July 15, 1907, p. 3, cc. 1-2.

48. Kamenev renounced his stand in the course of the campaign. E. Iaroslavskii. *Istoria VKP (b)*, p. 201; Iurii Kamenev, "Za boikota." This was published together with Lenin's "Protiv boikotie" in *O boikotie tretei dumy* (Moscow, 1907). See pp. 24-27; *Riech*, Aug. 11, 1907, p. 1, c. 6.

49. "Za boikot", loc. cit., p. 25.

50. *Slovo*, July 17, 1907, p. 3, c. 4; *Riech*, July 25, 1907, p. 3, c. 4. The majority of 59 was all Bolshevik. While ten Bolsheviks voted with six Mensheviks against the boycott, the whole district, including Ivanovo, went along with the capital city. *Slovo*, July 20, 1907, p. 2, c. 3.

51. *Slovo,* July 19, 1907, p. 3, c. 4; *Riech,* July 20, 1907, p. 3, cc. 4-5; Aug. 14, 1907, p. 3, c. 5.

52. The Conference was composed of representatives of the Central Committee and all local organizations: the center, south Russia, the Crimea, the Caucasus, Siberia, Turkestan, and other *oblasts.* It also included representatives of the Bund, Lettish, Polish, and Armenian Party organizations. There were 27 participants in all including two with an advisory vote. Other items on the agenda were the tasks of the campaign, election agreements, the election platform. See immediately below. Relations with the Trade Union Council were also discussed here. See pp. 44-45. *Slovo,* July 22, 1907, p. 3, c. 5; *Riech,* July 27, 1907, p. 3, c. 2. The Polish Socialists were divided between a predominant moderate "left" and a boycottist "right". The former joined with other "progressive elements" to offer serious opposition to the nationalists. *Riech,* July 11, 1907, p. 3, c. 7.

53. *Riech,* July 28, 1907, p. 3, c. 4.

54. *Riech,* July 29, 1907, p. 4, c. 2; Aug. 4, 1907, p. 3, c. 2; *Slovo,* July 27, 1907, p. 3, c. 5; Aug. 23, 1907, p. 3, c. 6. Lenin, *Sobranie sochinenii,* vol. VIII, pp. 632-638. The preamble gave no attention to the individual rightist parties or the smaller conservative or moderate elements to the right of the Kadets. It may have regarded them as too insignificant politically or subsumed them under the generic title "Black Hundreds." It reflects an obvious element of dogmatism and intellectual impatience in analyzing the forces which would dominate the legislative process, and thus the welfare of their constituents.

55. *Riech,* July 28, 1907, p. 2, c. 6; Aug. 5, 1907, p. 3, c. 3.

56. *Riech,* Aug. 9, 1907, p. 3, c. 2.

57. The Party journal *Vpered* reminded it brusquely of the obligation to mobilize for elections. *Vpered,* Aug. 29, 1907, pp. 2-3.

58. *Riech,* Sept. 4, 1907, p. 4, c. 4; Sept. 8, 1907, p. 4, c. 4. The city organization actually tried to press its slight advantage in the second curia. Ibid., Sept. 9, 1907, p. 3, cc. 5-6.

59. *Slovo,* Aug. 16, 1907, p. 5, c. 6; *Riech,* Aug. 22, 1907, p. 3, c. 1. Intra-party discussion of the boycott allowed the Ministry of the Interior to identify Social Democratic organizations as they were reported in the press for and against the boycott. *Riech,* Aug. 17, 1907, p. 3, c. 4.

60. *Riech,* Sept. 4, 1907, pp. 5-6.

Chapter V

1. *Riech,* July 21, 1907, p. 3, c. 6.

2. *Riech,* July 29, 1907, p. 4, c. 1.

3. *Riech,* July 10, 1907, p. 3, c. 7, p. 4, c. 1; July 25, 1907, p. 4, c. 1; July 29, 1907, p. 5, c. 7.

4. *Riech,* July 25, 1907, p. 4, c. 1; Aug. 29, 1907, p. 3, c. 7.

5. *Riech,* July 1, 1907, p. 1, c. 7, p. 2, c. 1.

6. *Riech,* June 13, 1907, p. 3, c. 7; June 19, 1907, p. 3, c. 7; July 7, 1907, p. 4, c. 1.

7. *Riech,* June 28, 1907, p. 4, c. 1.

8. *Riech,* June 30, 1907, p. 3, c. 7.

9. *Riech,* July 8, 1907, p. 5, cc. 5-6.

10. *Riech,* Aug. 5, 1907, p. 3, c. 3; Aug. 7, 1907, p. 3, c. 7, p. 4, c. 1; Sept. 1, 1907, p. 4, c. 1; Sept. 8, 1907, p. 5, c. 2.

11. *Riech,* Sept. 9, 1907, p. 5, c. 4. For a discussion of the Polish Kolo see pp. 53-54 and A. Levin, *The Second Duma,* pp. 34n, 77-78.

12. *Riech,* July 10, 1907, p. 4, c. 1.

13. *Riech,* Sept. 1, 1907, p. 4, c. 1.

14. *Riech,* Sept. 18, 1907, p. 5, c. 2; Sept. 20, 1907, p. 5, c. 2; Sept. 25, 1907, p. 5, c. 3.

15. *Gosudarstvennaia duma, ukazatel k stenograficheskim otchetam, vtoroi sozyv,* 1907, g., p. 30; *Chast I-IV, tretii sozyv, sessiia III, 1909-1910 gg.,* p. 16.

16. *Riech,* Oct. 17, 1907, p. 3, c. 2.

17. *Riech,* Oct. 12, 1907, p. 5, c. 3; Oct. 17, 1907, p. 3, cc. 1, 4.

18. *Riech,* Oct. 4, 1907, p. 3, c. 3; Oct. 24, 1907, p. 2, c. 3. In fact, neither the Polish Progressives nor the Kolo included specific agrarian platforms in their 1906 program. *Polnoe sobranie podrobnykh programm,* pp. 113-114.

19. *Riech,* June 12, 1907, p. 4, cc. 1-2; June 27, 1907, p. 3, c. 7; June 28, 1907, p. 4, c. 1; Sept. 8, 1907, p. 5, c. 4; Oct. 7, 1907, p. 5, c. 2. It is not surprising that in the first groundswell of reaction against the measures of June 3, both the Bund and Judophobic Polish papers called for common Polish-Jewish action. *Riech,* June 28, 1907, p. 4, c. 1; June 29, 1907, p. 4, c. 1.

20. The Society for Equal Rights held its constituent convention March 25-27, 1905 in Vilna and established a permanent bureau in St. Petersburg. It dominated Jewish activity in the "liberation movement" until the second election campaign when (in December, 1906), it fragmented on the question of a separate Jewish fraction in the Duma. Elements of the core group of the Society favoring a special fraction formed the Jewish Popular Group and organized for an independent campaign. The Zionists also withdrew and did likewise. *Evreiskaia Entsiklopediia,* (Izdatel'stvo Brokgauz i Efron, St. Petersburg, 1906-1913), vol. VII, pp. 438-439, vol. XIV, pp. 515-517.

21. As "bourgeoisie," most Jews could not vote with the left and the Octobrists would not grant them equal rights.

22. *Slovo,* Sept. 21, 1907, p. 3, c. 2; *Riech,* Oct. 2, 1907, p. 2, c. 7; Oct. 6, 1907, p. 3, c. 2.

23. *Riech,* Oct. 6, 1907, p. 3, c. 2; Oct. 11, 1907, p. 3, c. 3; Oct. 12, 1907, p. 3, c. 5; Oct. 24, 1907, p. 2, c. 3.

24. *Riech,* Oct. 14, 1907, p. 4, cc. 2-3.

25. *Riech,* Sept. 4, 1907, p. 5. c. 2; G. B. Sliozberg, *Diela minuvshikh dnei: zapiski russkago evreia,* (Paris, 1933-1934), vol. III, pp. 255-256.

26. Sliozberg, op. cit., pp. 252-253, 257-258.

27. Ibid., pp. 210-213; *Riech,* June 23, 1907, p. 3, c. 7; July 26, 1907, p. 3, c. 1.

28. *Evreiskaia entsiklopediia,* vol. V, p. 100; *Riech,* June 29, 1907, p. 4, c. 1.

29. *Riech,* June 27, 1907, p. 3, c. 7; Aug. 23, 1907, p. 2, c. 4; Sept. 5, 1907, p. 5, cc. 2-3; Oct. 16, 1907, p. 5, c. 4.

30. *Riech*, Aug. 8, 1907, p. 5, c. 6.

31. *Riech*, Sept. 22, 1907, p. 5, c. 4; Sept. 26, 1907, p. 5, c. 4; Oct. 3, 1907, p. 4, c. 7.

32. The leftist Moslem press begged abject pardon from the government for having sent Kadets to the Second Duma. *Riech*, Aug. 2, 1907, p. 1, c. 7; Oct. 3, 1907, p. 4, c. 7; Oct. 4, 1907, p. 4, c. 4.

33. For a discussion of the legalization effort see *Riech*, Sept. 19, 1907, p. 2, cc. 5-6.

34. Article 6, Section 1, of the Provisional Rules of March 4, 1906 on Societies and Unions prohibited those which pursued goals opposed to social morality, which were forbidden by criminal law, or which threatened public order and security. *Spravochnaia kniga ob obshchestvakh i soiuzov*, V. N. Charnolutskii, editor (St. Petersburg, 1912), pp. 28-29.

35. Ibid., *Riech*, October 27, 1907, p. 2, c. 3.

36. In a footnote, as it were, to the seemingly unreal world of Russian politics, the Moslem Party announced late in October that it would call a nationwide congress in Kazan "in the near future" to work out the directives for their Duma fraction. *Riech*, Oct. 21, 1907, p. 3, c. 3.

Chapter VI

1. Much of the material on the Rightist effort to form blocs is taken from A. Levin, *The Reactionary Tradition*, pp. 38-40.

2. *Riech*, Aug. 2, 1907, p. 2, c. 7, p. 3, c. 1; Aug. 18, 1907, p. 2, c. 4; Aug. 28, 1907, p. 4, c. 5; *Slovo*, July 7, 1907, p. 3, c. 4; Aug. 26, 1907, p. 3, c. 4.

3. *Riech*, July 1, 1907, p. 2, c. 1, p. 4, c. 1; July 8, 1907, p. 3, c. 1; July 15, 1907, p. 3, c. 5; July 27, 1907, p. 4, c. 1; July 31, 1907, p. 1, c. 3; Aug. 7, 1907, p. 1, c. 3; *Slovo*, July 7, 1907, p. 3, c. 4; July 18, 1907, p. 3, c. 2; Aug. 21, 1907. p. 3, c. 6. The Peaceful Renovationist leader M. A. Stakhovich charged that the Octobrists were quite aware that the "zubry" were of one mind with the URP and did not join them out of political timidity. And in this perspective he questioned the firmness of *Golos Moskvy's* constitutionalism. *Riech*, Oct. 12, 1907, p. 2, cc. 3-4. The Democratic Reformist spokesman, V. O. Kuzmin-Karavaev, likewise doubted that the rank and file of the Octobrist Party were real constitutionalists. *Viestnik Evropy*, August, 1907, p. 744.

4. *Riech*, July 22, 1907, p. 5, c. 3; Aug. 1, 1907, p. 2, c. 3; Aug. 7, 1907, p. 1, c. 7; *Slovo*, July 18, 1907, p. 3, c. 2; July 29, 1907, p. 3, c. 3; July 31, p. 3, c. 3; Aug. 21, 1907, p. 3, c. 5.

5. *Riech*, July 15, 1907, p. 3, c. 6; Aug. 12, 1907, p. 5, c. 4; Sept. 4, 1907, p. 5, c. 1; Sept. 9, 1907, p. 4, c. 3; Sept. 13, 1907, p. 5, c. 3; Sept. 21, 1907, p. 4, c. 2; Sept. 22, 1907, p. 3, c. 7; *Slovo*, July 31, 1907, p. 3, c. 3; Sept. 5, 1907, p. 3, c. 5.

6. *Riech*, July 1, 1907, p. 2, c. 1, p. 3, c. 7, p. 4, c. 1; July 12, 1907, p. 2, c. 7; Aug. 22, 1907, p. 2, c. 5; Sept. 25, 1907, p. 3, c. 5; Sept. 27, 1907, p. 2, c. 7, p. 4, c. 4.

7. *Riech*, July 27, 1907, p. 4, c. 1; July 31, 1907, p. 3, c. 7; Aug. 3, 1907, p. 4, c. 1; Aug. 16, 1907, p. 3, c. 6; Aug. 28, 1907, p. 5, cc. 2-3; Sept. 4, 1907, p. 5, c. 2; Sept. 19. 1907, p. 3, c. 7; Oct. 30, 1907, p. 3, c. 6. See pp. 7-8.

8. *Riech*, Aug. 2, 1907, p. 1, c. 6; Aug. 5, 1907, p. 3, c. 5; Aug. 29, 1907, p. 3, c. 6; Aug. 30, 1907, p. 2, c. 4; Sept. 20, 1907, p. 1, c. 5; Sept. 26, 1907, p. 3, c. 3, p. 5, c. 4; Oct. 17, 1907, p. 3, c. 6; *Slovo* Aug. 31, 1907, p. 3, c. 6; Sept. 4, 1907, p. 3, c. 1.

9. *Riech*, Oct. 16, 1907, p. 2, c. 1; Oct. 18, 1907, p. 3, c. 3; Oct. 20, 1907, p. 4, c. 1; Oct. 25, 1907, p. 2, c. 4; Oct. 27, p. 4, cc. 1-2.

10. As noted above, the Peaceful Renovationists were constitutionalist in principle and were philosophically near the Kadets. See pp. 24-25.

11. *Golos Moskvy*, June 19, 1907, p. 2, c. 2; *Riech*, June 21, 1907, p. 1, c. 7, p. 2, cc. 1-2; June 28, 1907, p. 1, c. 6.

12. *Riech*, Sept. 30, 1907, p. 2, cc. 1-7.

13. *Riech*, June 22, 1907, p. 2, cc. 1-5; June 29, 1907, p. 2, cc. 1-7.

14. Professor Miliukov resented a current of anti-intellectualism which he regarded as a characteristic Octobrist attitude. *Vestnik Evropy*, August, 1907, pp. 786-787.

15. *Riech*, June 29, 1907, p. 2, c. 2; Oct. 16, 1907, p. 2, c. 6.

16. *Viestnik Evropy*, October, 1907, p. 782; *Riech*, June 20, 1907, p. 2, c. 4; June 21, 1907, p. 1, c. 6; July 14, 1907, p. 1, c. 7.

17. *Riech*, July 1, 1907, p. 3, cc. 1-2; Oct. 6, 1907, p. 2, cc. 3-5.

18. *Riech*, Oct. 5, 1907, p. 3, c. 5.

19. See above, note no. 9.

20. *Riech*, Oct. 6, 1907, p. 1, c. 6.

21. See Miliukov's statement in *Riech*, June 11, 1907, p. 2, cc. 3-4. He observed bitterly that the government had only recently made its position clear by refusing to grant the Kadets permission to hold a Party convention. Ibid., p. 2, c. 3.

22. *Riech*, July 22, 1907, p. 3, c. 6.

23. *Riech*, July 11, 1907, p. 2, cc. 3-4.

24. *Riech*, June 12, 1907, p. 4, c. 3; July 22, 1907, p. 3, c. 4.

25. *Riech*, June 28, 1907, p. 1, cc. 4-5; July 11, 1907, p. 2, cc. 2-4; July 22, 1907, p. 3, c. 4; Oct. 2, 1907, p. 4, c. 6; Oct. 12, 1907, p. 2, c. 3.

26. *Riech*, July 4, 1907, p. 1, cc. 5-6.

27. *Riech*, July 22, 1907, p. 3, cc. 4-6.

28. *Riech*, Oct. 14, 1907, p. 1, c. 7, p. 2, c. 3.

29. See above pp. 44-45; *Riech*, Oct. 7. 1907, p. 2, c. 5.

30. *Slovo*, July 3, 1907, p. 3, c. 3.

31. *Riech*, July 3, 1907, p. 3, c. 2.

32. Lenin, "Attitudes toward bourgeois parties," *Sobranie Sochinenii* vol. VIII pp. 410-427. This article was essentially a critique of the Menshevik attitude toward the Kadets at the Fifth (London) S. D. Party Congress just concluded, and repeated arguments pressed since 1905 on relations with constitutionalists.

33. Lenin, *Sobranie sochinenii*, vol. VIII, pp. 462-472.

34. *Slovo*, July 21, 1907, p. 3, c. 4; Sept. 13, 1907, p. 4, c. 5; *Riech*, July 25, 1907, p. 3, cc. 3-4; July 27, 1907, p. 3, c. 2; Sept. 12, 1907, p. 3, c. 4.

35. *Riech*, Aug. 30, 1907, p. 3, c. 2; Sept. 12, 1907, p. 3, c. 5; *Slovo*, Sept. 13, 1907, p. 4, c. 5.

36. *Riech*, Sept. 22, 1907, p. 5, c. 6.

37. *Slovo*, Oct. 4, 1907, p. 4, c. 5.

38. *Slovo*, July 3, 1907, p. 3, c. 3; July 20, 1907, p. 3, c. 4. In August, representatives of the Jewish Bund and the Lettish Social Democrats were coopted into the Central Election Committee. Ibid., Aug. 23, 1907, p. 3, c. 5.

39. *Slovo*, Aug. 25, 1907, p. 3, c. 5.

40. *Slovo*, July 5, 1907, p. 3, c. 3; July 20, 1907, p. 3, c. 4; Aug. 2, 1907, p. 2, c. 7; Aug. 12, 1907, p. 3, c. 2.

41. *Riech*, Aug. 7, 1907, p. 3, c. 3.

42. Lenin, *Sobranie sochinenii*, vol. VIII, 649-650; *Riech*, Aug. 7, 1907, p. 3, c. 3; Aug. 8, 1907, p. 3, c. 5.

43. *Slovo*, Sept. 26, 1907, p. 3, c. 6. The Bolshevik-dominated St. Petersburg organization named six Bolshevik electors for the worker category. See pp. 48-49, 103-104 for Social Democratic activity in the left bloc.

44. *Slovo*, Aug. 21, 1907, p. 3, c. 6.

45. *Riech*, Aug. 30, 1907, p. 1, cc. 1-2; p. 3, c. 2; Sept. 26, 1907, p. 4, c. 2. The "national" Marxist parties operated in approximately the same fashion as the Russian Social Democrats, establishing executive bureaus which carried on intensive propaganda in conferences and meetings for workers and peasants and coordinated activities between all Marxist groups. *Riech*, Aug. 16, 1907, p. 3, c. 2; Aug. 20, 1907, p. 3, c. 7; Aug. 21, 1907, p. 2, c. 5; Aug. 31, 1907, p. 3, c. 1.

46. *Riech*, Aug. 14, 1907, p. 2, c. 7; Oct. 7, 1907, p. 5, c. 2; Oct. 14, 1907, p. 3, c. 6, p. 4, c. 1; Oct. 16, 1907, p. 5, c. 2.

47. *Riech*, July 19, 1907, p. 3, c. 3; *Slovo*, July 31, 1907, p. 3, c. 3; Aug. 2, 1907, p. 2, c. 7; Aug. 30, 1907, p. 3, c. 4; Sept. 11, 1907, p. 3, cc. 1-2; Sept. 23, 1907, p. 3, cc. 1-2.

48. *Vpered*, November, 1907, No. 18, p. 1.

49. *Riech*, Sept. 26, 1907, p. 4, c. 2; Sept. 28, 1907, p. 4, cc. 3-4; Oct. 2, 1907, p. 4, c. 4; *Slovo*, Sept. 27, 1907, p. 3, cc. 4-5; Sept. 29, 1907, p. 3, cc. 3-4; Sept. 30, 1907, p. 2, c. 4.

50. *Riech*, Oct. 12, 1907, p. 3, c. 7; *Slovo*, Oct. 12, 1907, p. 3, c. 3; Oct. 20, 1907, p. 3, c. 6; Oct. 21, 1907, p. 3, c. 6; Oct. 23, 1907, p. 4, c. 1.

51. *Riech*, Oct. 7, 1907, p. 4, c. 4.

52. *Riech*, Oct. 12, 1907, p. 3, c. 5; *Slovo*, Oct. 7, 1907, p. 4, c. 5.

53. *Riech*, Oct. 6, 1907, p. 3, c. 3; Oct. 12, 1907, p. 3, c. 5. The liberal *Riech* and moderate leftist *Tovarishch* reacted negatively toward the bloc on grounds that it would accomplish little but would weaken the respective candidates by scattering votes and was no more than a propaganda gambit. *Riech*, Oct. 21, 1907, p. 2, c. 7.

Chapter VII

1. *Riech*, June 13, 1907, p. 3, c. 3; June 14, 1907, p. 3, c. 1; July 15, 1907, p. 5, c. 1.

2. *Riech,* June 5, 1907, p. 2, c. 5; June 6, 1907, p. 3, c. 1; June 7, 1907, p. 2, c. 1; June 26, 1907, p. 3, c. 6, p. 4, c. 1.

3. *Riech,* June 7, 1907, p. 3, c. 2; July 14, 1907, p. 2, c. 7; July 15, 1907, p. 4, c. 3; Aug. 5, 1907, p. 3, c. 1; Aug. 8, 1907, p. 2, c. 4; Aug. 26, 1907, p. 3, c. 7, p. 4, c. 1; Oct. 26, 1907, p. 3, c. 4. *Vybory po gorodu Moskvie v gosudarstvennuiu dumu tret'iago pryzyva* (Moscow, 1908), p. 30. Hereafter cited as *Vybory po gorodu Moskvie.*

4. *Riech,* Aug. 23, 1907, p. 2, cc. 2-3.

5. *Riech,* June 5, 1907, p. 2, c. 5; June 6, 1907, p. 3, c. 1; June 13, 1907, p. 3, c. 3; June 28, 1907, p. 2, c. 5.

6. *Riech,* June 10, 1907, p. 3, c. 2; June 13, 1907, p. 3, c. 3; June 15, 1907, p. 4, c. 3; June 19, 1907, p. 2, c. 5; June 21, 1907, p. 2, c. 7; June 22, 1907, p. 2, c. 6; July 8, 1907, p. 3, c. 6; July 15, 1907, p. 4, c. 3; July 19, 1907, p. 3, c. 5; Aug. 22, 1907, p. 3, c. 4.

7. *P. S. Z.,* vol. XXVII, No. 29242, Arts. 9, 10, 11.

8. *Riech,* June 7, 1907, p. 3, c. 1; June 15, 1907, p. 3, c. 3.

9. *Riech,* June 8, 1907, p. 3, c. 1.

10. *Riech,* June 14, 1907, p. 3, c. 1; June 23, 1907, p. 3, c. 3.

11. Excluded were military surgeons, usually liberal in politics, who were permitted to register in the second elections. *Riech,* June 20, 1907, p. 3, c. 5; June 24, 1907, p. 4, c. 4; July 7, 1907, p. 2, c. 3. The tendency of the bureaucracy to interpret the law narrowly is evident, for example, in the action of the governor general of Elets in allowing suffrage only to those whose names appeared on the registration lists; that is, the basic employees of an institution. This eliminated school teachers serving chancelleries of railways, and city and zemstvo boards. *Ibid.,* June 20, 1907, p. 3, c. 3.

12. *Riech,* June 27, 1907, p. 2, c. 2; Aug. 3, 1907, p. 2, c. 5; Aug. 8, 1907, p. 1, c. 6.

13. *Riech,* July 10, 1907, p. 1, c. 7; July 25, 1907, p. 2, cc. 1-2. There were 307,930 voters in the cities canvassed in the second elections and 195,000 in the third. See note no. 6, Chap. IX, for specific designation of general areas (Central, Volga, etc.).

14. *Riech,* July 2, 1907, p. 2, c. 5; July 12, 1907, p. 2, c. 7; July 15, 1907, p. 5, c. 1; July 19, 1907, p. 2, c. 3; July 22, 1907, p. 4, c. 4; July 25, 1907, p. 3, c. 7; July 27, 1907, p. 2, c. 6; July 28, 1907, p. 2, c. 6; Aug. 2, 1907, p. 2, c. 4; Aug. 8, 1907, p. 2, c. 6; Aug. 17, 1907, p. 3, c. 7.

15. *Riech,* July 8, 1907, p. 3, c. 7; July 10, 1907, p. 1, c. 7.

16. In Moscow the decrease was evident in all categories. Registration among apartment holders who paid no taxes (small) fell 73.3 percent; payers of a professional tax 83.7 percent; owners of commercial enterprises 83.7 percent; apartment renters paying a tax, 83.4 percent; pensioners and employees of government and public institutions, 7.5 percent, the overall decline being 78.8 percent. *Vybory po gorodu Moskvie,* pp. 12-13. *Riech,* July 17, 1907, p. 3, c. 6; Aug. 5, 1907, p. 4, c. 1; Aug. 9, 1907, p. 2, c. 3; Aug. 14, 1907, p. 2, c. 6; Aug. 26, 1907, p. 3, c. 7, p. 4, c. 1.

17. *Riech,* June 29, 1907, p. 2, c. 7; July 3, 1907, p. 2, c. 1; July 10, 1907, p. 2, cc. 1-2; July 15, 1907, p. 5, c. 1; July 25, 1907, p. 2, c. 6, p. 3, c. 7; Aug. 17, 1907, p. 3, c. 7.

18. In Vladimir, the first category elector represented 90 votes, the second some 800. In Minsk 330 votes were represented by an elector in the first category and 6,300 in the second. *Riech,* July 10, 1907, p. 2, cc. 1-2.

19. *Riech,* June 30, 1907, p. 3, c. 1; July 1, 1907, p. 4, cc. 1, 5; July 8, 1907, p. 5, c. 5; July 10, 1907, p. 2, cc. 1, 4; July 11, 1907, p. 2, c. 4, p. 3, c. 1; July 26, 1907, p. 1, c. 5.

20. *Riech,* June 15, 1907, p. 4, cc. 3-4; June 22, 1907, p. 3, c. 1.

21. *Riech,* June 29, 1907, p. 3, c. 7; July 10, 1907, p. 1, c. 7, p. 2, cc. 1-2; July 20, 1907, p. 1, cc. 4-5.

22. *Riech,* June 27, 1907, p. 2, c. 3; June 29, 1907, p. 3, cc. 6-7; July 7, 1907, p. 2, cc. 3-5; July 8, 1907, p. 3, c. 4.

23. Elizavetgrad reported on July 10 that 600 small apartment renters had enrolled "in the past few days" and Simferopol noted 200 registrants in the two-day period preceding July 12. *Riech,* July 10, 1907, p. 2, c. 4; July 12, 1907, p. 2, c. 6; July 19, 1907, p. 2, c. 2.

24. *Riech,* July 15, 1907, p. 5, c. 1; Aug. 5, 1907, p. 3, c. 1; Aug. 14, 1907, p. 2, c. 6.

25. *Riech,* June 28, 1907, p. 3, c. 5; July 2, 1907, p. 2, c. 4; July 7, 1907, p. 2, c. 4; July 14, 1907, p. 2, c. 7; July 15, 1907, p. 5, c. 1; July 19, 1907, p. 2, c. 2.

26. *Riech,* June 27, 1907, p. 2, c. 2; June 28, 1907, p. 3, c. 3; June 29, 1907, p. 2, c. 2; July 1, 1907, p. 4, c. 5; July 8, 1907, p. 3, c. 7; July 12, 1907, p. 2, cc. 3-4; July 23, 1907, p. 3, c. 6.

27. *Riech,* June 22, 1907, p. 2, c. 6; July 12, 1907, p. 2, c. 7.

28. *Riech,* June 21, 1907, p. 2, c. 7; June 29, 1907, p. 2, cc. 5-6; June 30, 1907, p. 3, cc. 1-2; July 4, 1907, p. 1, cc. 5-7; July 14, 1907, p. 3, c. 7; Sept. 9, 1907, p. 4, c. 7.

29. *P. S. Z.,* vol. XXVII, No. 29242, Arts. 42, 43, 61, 71, 72; Chasles, *Parlement,* p. 90; S. N. Harper, *The New Electoral Law,* p. 11; *Riech,* June 8, 1907, p. 3, c. 1. In Moscow it was estimated that of some 40,000 workers "only several hundred at most" could qualify as apartment renters who paid no tax. Ibid., July 27, 1907, p. 2, c. 5.

30. *Vybory po gorodu Moskvie,* p. 104.

31. *Riech,* June 8, 1907, p. 3, c. 1; June 23, 1907, p. 3, c. 2; June 28, 1907, p. 2, c. 7; July 27, 1907, p. 2, c. 5; July 29, 1907, p. 3, c. 7; Aug. 15, 1907, p. 2, cc. 6-7.

32. The pretext of work interruption, presumably due to strikes or layoffs, was interpreted as noncompliance with the requirement of employment for six months in one locality, and plant officials in an enterprise operated by the state might fail to register workers on grounds that they were civil servants. *Riech,* July 31, 1907, p. 2, c. 6.

33. *P. S. Z.,* vol. XXVII, No. 29242, Art. 32.

34. *Riech,* July 15, 1907, p. 4, c. 3; Aug. 17, 1907, p. 3, c. 3.

35. In Moscow, the first category list numbered 6,674; St. Petersburg, 3,833; Kiev, 2,423; Odessa 1,534; Minsk, 1,372; Kazan, 1,200, and 502 in Stavropol. *Riech,* July 14, 1907, p. 2, c. 7; July 15, 1907, p. 5, c. 1; Aug. 14, 1907, p. 3, c. 3; Oct. 19, 1907, p. 3, c. 7, p. 4, c. 2; *Vybory po gorodu Moskvie,* p. 35.

36. *Riech,* July 7, 1907, p. 3, c. 7; July 15, 1907, p. 5, c. 3; July 17, 1907, p. 2, c. 7; July 20, 1907, p. 2, c. 5; July 25, 1907, p. 2, c. 2.

37. *Riech,* June 15, 1907, p. 3, c. 2; June 24, 1907, p. 4, cc. 3, 4; June 29, 1907, p. 2, cc. 6-7; July 1, 1907, p. 4, c. 5; July 11, 1907, p. 2, c. 7; July 17, 1907, p. 2, c. 7; Aug. 14, 1907, p. 3, c. 3.

38. Fifteen percent in the first election, 12 percent in the second. *Riech*, July 10, 1907, p. 2, c. 1.

39. *Riech*, July 7, 1907, p. 3, c. 7; July 8, 1907, p. 3, c. 4; July 15, 1907, p. 5, c. 3; July 20, 1907, p. 2, c. 5; July 25, 1907, p. 2, c. 2; July 26, 1907, p. 4, c. 1; Aug. 9, 1907, p. 2, c. 3: Aug. 17, 1907, p. 3. c. 7: Aug. 28, 1907. p. 4, c. 5. On the strength of the clergy in the landholding category see p. 88.

40. *Riech*, July 10, 1907, p. 1, c. 7.

41. The law of June 3, 1907, provided that peasant homeowners (i.e., family heads, a restriction not included in the 1905 law) of each *volost* meet to elect two delegates to an *uiezd* electoral meeting. *P. S. Z.*, vol. XXVII, No. 29242, Art. 37.

42. In Nizhni Novgorod, one third of the voters in this category in the first elections (over 1,000) lost their suffrage in the third. *Riech*, June 14, 1907, p. 3, c. 7; June 19, 1907, p. 2, c. 2.

43. *P. S. Z.*, vol. XXVII, No. 29242, Arts. 35, 38.

44. *Riech*, July 3, 1907, p. 3, c. 2; July 4, 1907, p. 3, c. 2; July 8, p. 3, c. 6; July 10, 1907, p. 3, c. 2; July 12, 1907, p. 2, c. 5; July 15, 1907, p. 4, c. 3; July 20, 1907, p. 3, c. 1; July 26, 1907, p. 3, c. 1; Aug. 8, 1907, p. 2, c. 6; Aug. 10, 1907, p. 3, c. 2.

45. *Riech*, July 6, 1907, p. 2, c. 4; July 19, 1907, p. 3, c. 4; July 31, 1907, p. 3, c. 2; Aug. 2, 1907, p. 2, cc. 2-3. The Kharkov Provincial Judicial Administration vigorously warned the governor that his appointment of the Chief of the Provincial Gendarme Administration to the provincial electoral committee would bring public opposition, and a replacement was found outside the police administration. Ibid., Aug. 16, 1907, p. 3, c. 6.

46. *Riech*, Aug. 8, 1907, p. 1, c. 6; Aug. 30, 1907, p. 3, c. 2.

47. *Riech*, Sept. 4, 1907, p. 3, cc. 3-4; Sept. 18, 1907, p. 3, c. 3.

48. E. g. Kadet candidate Obolianinov from Gdovsk *uiezd*, St. Petersburg *guberniia*, was protested by the governor on grounds that he visited the town of Gdovsk only infrequently from his estate. *Riech*, Oct. 16, 1907, p. 4, c. 2.

49. *Riech*, Sept. 30, 1907, p. 3, c. 2; Oct. 14, p. 4, cc. 2, 7; Oct. 23, p. 5, c. 4.

50. *Riech*, Sept. 21, 1907, p. 3, cc. 6-7; Sept. 23, p. 3, c. 5; Oct. 4, p. 4, c. 5; Oct. 14, p. 4, c. 2.

51. *Riech*, Sept. 29, 1907, p. 3, c. 4; Oct. 5, 1907, p. 2, c. 3; Oct. 6, 1907, p. 3, c. 3; Oct. 7, 1907, p. 4, c. 3; Oct. 14, 1907, p. 4, c. 7. Bobin's case was considered by a provincial committee which included his Octobrist rival A. I. Iakovlev.

52. *Riech*, Sept. 2, 1907, p. 3, c. 3; Sept. 25, 1907, p. 3, cc. 5-6; Sept. 29, 1907, p. 3, c. 6; Oct. 2, 1907, p. 5, c. 4.

53. *Riech*, Oct. 2, 1907, p. 1, c. 7; Oct. 14, 1907, p. 4, c. 3.

54. *Riech*, July 20, 1907, p. 2, c. 5; Oct. 5, 1907, p. 4, c. 2.

55. *Riech*, Oct. 2, 1907, p. 1, cc. 6-7; Oct. 5, 1907, p. 2, c. 3.

56. For information concerning the affair see *Riech*, Sept. 29, 1907, p. 1, c. 3; Sept. 30, 1907, p. 4, c. 3; Oct. 2, 1907, p. 5, c. 1; Oct. 6, 1907, p. 2, c. 7. *Viestnik Evropy*, November, 1907, pp. 446-449.

57. *Riech*, Oct. 2, 1907, p. 1, c. 6. The first session of the Third Duma investigated Shmidt's qualifications and refused to seat him. *Gosudarstvennaia duma; Tretii Sozyv. Stenograficheskie otchety 1907-1908 gg. Sessia pervaia, Chast'* I (St. Petersburg, 1908), pp. 1753-1761. Cited hereafter as *G. D. III. Stenog. Ot.*

Chapter VIII

1. *Riech*, Sept. 6, 1907, p. 2, c. 7; Sept. 13, 1907, p. 3, c. 1; Sept. 18, 1907, p. 3, c. 6; Sept. 20, 1907, p. 4, c. 7, p. 5, cc. 1, 3; Oct. 14, 1907, p. 1, c. 4; Oct. 18, 1907, p. 3, c. 7, p. 4, c. 1; Oct. 19, 1907, p. 2, c. 5.

2. *Riech*, Sept. 28, 1907, p. 2, c. 7, p. 3, c. 1.

3. The villagers in Vladimir *guberniia* felt that nothing would come of the Duma and were more concerned with the potato harvest. *Riech*, Sept. 13, 1907, p. 5, c. 2; Oct. 10, 1907, p. 5, c. 2; Oct. 16, p. 4, c. 2.

4. *Riech*, Sept. 4, 1907, p. 2, c. 3; Sept. 12, 1907, p. 1, c. 6.

5. A. I. Shingarev went to Saratov, Klets to Tambov and Voronezh, N. N. Shchepkin to Tula, Dukovskii to Nizhni Novgorod, Iordanskii to Smolensk, and R. I. Astrov to Tomsk. *Riech*, Sept. 14, 1907, p. 2, cc. 2-3; Sept. 16, p. 4, c. 2.

6. *Riech*, Sept. 28, 1907, p. 1, c. 6.

7. *Riech*, Oct. 20, 1907, p. 2, c. 4; Oct. 23, 1907, p. 4, c. 7.

8. See Circular of July 6, 1907, from the Minister of the Interior to the "Marshals of the Nobility, the Mayor of St. Petersburg, City boards, Prefects and Burgomasters on the electoral qualifications of the clergy," and of Aug. 25, 1907, to "*Guberniia* election chairmen on the limitations and rights of the Marshals of the Nobility as chairmen of the provincial election committees" in *Riech*, July 7, 1907, p. 3, c. 2; Aug. 25, 1907, p. 3. c. 7.

9. *Riech*, Aug. 28, 1907, p. 3, c. 4.

10. See the "Circular of the Ministry of the Interior on the order of voting in meetings of city voters and divisions of these meetings with over 500 voters and also in the wards of Warsaw and Lvov," *Riech*, Aug. 28, 1907, p. 2, c. 7, p. 3, cc. 1-2; Aug. 29, 1907, p. 2, cc. 4-5. See also Minister P. A. Stolypin's "Instructions on the order of holding elections to the Imperial Duma in cities named in the second supreme regulation on elections confirmed June 3, 1907," *Riech*, Sept. 12, 1907, p. 3, cc. 2-3; Sept. 13, 1907, p. 4, cc. 5-6; Sept. 16, 1907, p. 4, cc. 5-6.

11. See also *Riech*, Aug. 29, 1907, p. 1, c. 2.

12. See report on an article from the *Manchester Guardian* in *Riech*, Sept. 26, 1907, p. 2, c. 5.

13. *Viestnik Evropy*, September, 1907, pp. 437-440.

14. *Riech*, Aug. 4, 1907, p. 3, c. 2.

15. The data on the voting qualifications and elections offered below are derived, unless otherwise stated, from materials in TsGIAL. They include governors' reports on local elections to the Minister of the Interior from provinces of European Russia exclusive of Poland and the Caucasus and include Tomsk and the Don Army Oblast. They indicate the distribution of the electors named by the *uiezd* assemblies to the *guberniia* assemblies in some 518 *uiezdy* by categories. The reports list 1,095 electors of the *volost* delegates at the *uiezd* assemblies, 2,458 electors for the landowners, 798 for the city voters, 535 for the second city electorate, some 50 for both the first and second categories, undifferentiated, and 94 for the workers. These reports designate the subdivisions of the categories by geographic area within an *uiezd*, ethnic groups and their property qualifications, and property and tax qualifications for *volost*, landowner, and city categories. See TsGIAL, 1327, 1, 111-116, chasti I-VI, MVD, *Delo osobago proizvodstvo v gosudarstvennuiu dumu I, II, i III sozyvov i vyborshchikov chlenov gosudarstvennoi dumy.*

16. Special preliminary elections for clerical delegates to the *uiezd* electoral assemblies took place in Bessarabia, Voronezh, Vitebsk, Vladimir, Viatka, the Oblast of the Don Army, Ekaterinoslav, Kazan, Kaluga, Kostroma, Moscow, Mogilev, Nizhegorod, Orenburg, Orel, St. Petersburg, Poltava, Penza, Podolsk, Perm, Pskov, Riazan, Samara, Saratov, Smolensk, Tambov, Tver, Tula, Kherson, Chernigov, and Iaroslavl *gubernii*. There were no data available for the division of curiae in Moscow *guberniia*, but this undoubtedly took place because of the large clerical population. The clergy were not assigned qualifications different from other landholders except for those with less than a full qualification in St. Petersburg *guberniia*. The election law established a complex of qualifications which most frequently designated one-tenth of a qualification or less, one-fifth or less, one-third or less, and two-thirds or less. The smaller landowners held up to 20 or 30 *desiatiny*, the middle element held 30 to 150 and the more affluent over 150 *desiatiny*. The latter also included landed estates with a minimum evaluation set by the zemstvo agencies at 5,000 rubles and homeowners whose real estate was valued by zemstvo and town governments at 3,000 to 15,000 rubles.

17. In Minsk *guberniia* some 1,068 large landowners with 2,740,283 *des.* (These included their renters and administrators and their lands) together with 4,213 small Orthodox landowners with 90,793 *des.* had seventy-one delegates in the *uiezd* assembly while 531 priests with 47,785 *des.* sent twenty-three delegates to landowners' meetings of the *uiezd* assemblies. See TsGIAL, 1327, 1, 113, chast' III, pp. 39-53. A Smirnov, an election "expert" for *Riech*, maintained that in six *uiezdy* of Vladimir *guberniia* the middle landowners held three times the voting power of the clergy and eight times that of the small landowners. The latter held only half the voting strength of the large landowners. *Riech*, Aug. 14, 1907, p. 1, cc. 2-3.

18. The clergy made their best showing in the provinces north of the Volga, in the western borderlands and in the Urals. They were a particularly negligible factor in the Baltic Region and the north west borderlands. See below p. 102.

19. The governor suggested an intricate gerrymandering system by limiting their representation at each preliminary meeting to two full qualifications thus reducing their number by two to five delegates in each such meeting. This would beget representations closer to the "real expression" of the state structure. TsGIAL, 1327, 1, 114, chast' IV, pp. 196-196R, 197, 197R, 199-199R.

20. Ibid., pp. 1, 171, 178-179, 197-197R, 232-233, 234-235, 240-241.

21. In Tambov the second category included small property owners, traders, and craftsmen in one divifion and bureaucrats, pensioners and payers of apartment taxes in another. In the second category in Vladimir real estate owners and merchants were segregated from office workers and those paying apartment taxes. *Riech*, Sept. 9, 1907, p. 5, c. 3; Sept. 11, 1907, p. 5, c. 1; Sept. 12, 1907, p. 3, c. 6; Sept. 18, 1907, p. 5, c. 1.

22. TsGIAL, 1327, 1, 111-116, Chast'i I-VI, passim.

23. For difficulties encountered in defining "Russian" and Orthodox" voters see A. Levin, "The Russian Voter in the Elections to the Third Duma", *Slavic Review*, December, 1962, pp. 672-673.

24. Christian and Jewish categories were established in Kishenev, Kovno, Elizavetgrad, Poltava Kremenchug. *Riech*, Aug. 29, 1907, p. 2, c. 7; Sept. 1, 1907, p. 3, c. 1; Sept. 12, 1907, p. 2, c. 5; Sept. 15, 1907, p. 2, cc. 6; Sept. 18, 1907, p. 3, c. 5; Sept. 22, 1907, p. 5, c. 4.

25. *Riech*, Sept. 15, 1907, p. 2, c. 6; Sept. 18, 1907, p. 3, c. 5; Sept. 22, 1907, p. 5, c. 4.

26. *Riech*, Sept. 25, 1907, p. 4, c. 3; Oct. 13, 1907, p. 3, c. 6; Oct. 22, 1907, p. 5, c. 4.

27. *Riech*, Oct. 11, 1907, p. 4, c. 6; Oct. 19, 1907, p. 5, c. 4.

28. *Viestnik Evropy*, September, 1907, pp. 437-440.

29. *Riech*, Oct. 18, 1907, p. 3, c. 4; Oct. 20, 1907, p. 5, cc. 2-3.

30. *Riech*, Oct. 18, 1907, p. 3, cc. 1, 2, 4.

31. *Riech*, Sept. 29, 1907, p. 3, cc. 4-5; Sept. 30, 1907, p. 3, c. 1; Oct. 19, 1907, p. 3, cc. 1-5.

32. *Riech*, Sept. 26, 1907, p. 3, c. 2; Sept. 27, 1907, p. 4, c. 2; Oct. 4, 1907, p. 5, c. 1; Oct. 7, 1907, p. 5, c. 3; Oct. 9, 1907, p. 5, c. 3.

33. *Riech*, Oct. 5, 1907, p. 5, c. 1.

34. *Riech*, Oct. 20, 1907, p. 3, c. 6; Oct. 25, 1907, p. 2, c. 3.

35. *Riech*, June 30, 1907, p. 2, cc. 6-7; Aug. 30, 1907, p. 3, c. 7. In at least one instance a land captain sought to destroy the lists of rural delegates. Ibid., Sept. 15, 1907, p. 3, cc. 6-7.

36. *Riech*, June 5, 1907, p. 2, c. 3; June 8, 1907, p. 1, c. 4; Sept. 6, 1907, p. 3, c. 7; Sept. 8, 1907, p. 3, c. 5; Sept. 16, 1907, p. 3, cc. 5, 6; Sept. 18, 1907, p. 5, c. 1; Sept. 20, 1907, p. 1, c. 7; *Viestnik Evropy*, July, 1907, p. 347.

37. *Riech*, Sept. 11, 1907, p. 5, c. 1; Oct. 20, 1907, p. 3, c. 6.

38. *Riech*, Oct. 23, 1907, p. 5, c. 5; Oct. 25, 1907, p. 5, c. 1. See *P. S. Z.;* III, vol. XXVII, No. 29242, Art. 1 for cities with direct vote.

39. *Riech*, Sept. 18, 1907, p. 5, c. 4; Sept. 30, 1907, p. 2, c. 2; Oct. 3, 1907, p. 5, c. 2; Oct. 14, 1907, p. 4, c. 3; Oct. 31, 1907, p. 4, c. 1.

40. *Riech*, July 6, 1907, p. 3, c. 1; Aug. 26, 1907, p. 4, c. 5.

41. *Riech*, Sept. 20, 1907, p. 5, c. 1; Sept. 26, 1907, p. 5, c. 3; TsGIAL, 1327, 1, 116, pp. 202-203.

42. *Riech*, Oct. 18, 1907, p. 3, c. 6; Oct. 21, 1907, p. 3, c. 7. The campaign to arrest opposition leaders assumed almost mass proportions in some localities, as in Voronezh. And in Narva so many Kadet leaders were arrested that the Party charged the government with carrying out a *"chistka"*. *Riech*, Sept. 9, 1907, p. 5, c. 3; Aug. 12, 1907, p. 3, c. 7; Aug. 14, 1907, p. 2, c. 7; Aug. 19, 1907, p. 2, c. 6.

43. *Riech*, Oct. 3, 1907, p. 5, c. 1; Oct. 20, 1907, p. 5, c. 2; Oct. 28, 1907, p. 5, cc. 1-2.

44. *Riech*, Oct. 16, 1907, p. 2, c. 4; Oct. 25, 1907, p. 3, c. 7.

45. The St. Petersburg Telegraphic Agency was in the Ministry of Finance under Count Kokovtsov. V. N. Kokovtsov, *Out of My Past*, p. 169. *Riech*, Sept. 15, 1907, p. 2, c. 5; Sept. 23, 1907, p. 3, c. 5; *Viestnik Evropy*, October, 1907, p. 867.

46. *Riech*, Sept. 9, 1907, p. 2, cc. 1-2; Sept. 20, 1907, p. 3, c. 5. Wide differences were noted between reportage of results by the Agency and such widely read liberal and progressive, independent papers as *Riech, Russkoe Slovo* and *Russkoe Viedomosti*. Ibid., Sept. 29, 1907, p. 2, c. 5.

47. *Viestnik Evropy*, October, 1907, p. 867; *Riech*, Sept. 13, 1907, p. 3, c. 3.

48. *Riech*, Oct. 16, 1907, p. 1, c. 3.

49. *Riech*, Aug. 25, 1907, p. 3, c. 6.

50. *Riech*, Oct. 24, 1907, p. 4, c. 7; *Viestnik Evropy*, October, 1907, pp. 784-785.

51. *Riech*, Oct. 13, 1907, p. 3, c. 5; Oct. 16, 1907, p. 2, cc. 1-2, p. 5, cc. 2; Oct. 18, 1907, p. 4, c. 5; Oct. 19, 1907, p. 5, cc. 2-3; Oct. 20, 1907, p. 5, c. 4; Oct. 23, 1907, p. 5, c. 3. In Kiev the liberal press reported that political combinations had been formed in the Pecherskii and Mikhailovskii Monasteries among the rightists who controlled the electoral assemblies. Ibid., Oct. 20, 1907, p. 5, c. 4. Prayer meetings similar to those described above were reported in Zhitomir, central Volyn Province, and in Tiflis. *Riech*, Oct. 20, 1907, p. 5, c. 2; Oct. 24, 1907, p. 4, c. 6.

52. Compare *Riech*, Oct. 20, 1907, p. 5, c. 4.

53. *Riech*, Oct. 26, 1907, p. 1, c. 6.

Chapter IX

1. In widely separated *gubernii* the preliminary elections of delegates to the *uiezd* assemblies and of workers in the cities (from industrial and commercial units) were held between Sept. 2, and 11, 1907. And the election of *uiezd* electors of all categories to the guberniia assemblies were held from September 21 to 28. The *gubernii* concerned are Nizhegorod, Novosibirsk, Penza, Pskov, Tula, Tver, Vilno, Voronezh, Zhitomir. *Riech*, Aug. 23, 1907, p. 2, c. 4; Aug. 25, 1907, p. 2, c. 5.

2. *Riech*, June 6, 1907, p. 3, c. 6.

3. *Riech*, June 9, 1907, p. 1, cc. 3-4. Early in the campaign *Rus* offered almost a stereotype for this kind of analysis. It guessed that 131 deputies would adhere to the opposition. *Riech*, June 9, 1907, p. 1, cc. 6-7.

4. *Riech*, Sept. 11, 1907, p. 1, cc. 6-7; Smirnov indicated that of the 48 percent of the vote with the opposition in the European provinces, some 12 percent would come from the peasantry, 2.5 percent from the workers and 30 percent from' the landowner and city categories.

5. *Riech*, June 27, 1907, p. 1, cc. 6-7; *Viestnik Evropy*, October, 1907, p. 782.

6. Compare *Riech*, June 9, 1907, p. 1, c. 7. See also ibid., June 8, 1907, p. 1, c. 6; Sept. 11, 1907, p. 1, c. 7.

7. *Riech*, Oct. 14, 1907, p. 1, cc. 3-4.

8. *Riech*, June 8, 1907, p. 1, c. 6; Sept. 11, 1907, p. 1, c. 7.

9. *Slovo*, Sept. 26, 1907, p. 3, c. 5; Sept. 28, 1907, p. 3, c. 3.

10. *Vpered*, Sept. 10, 1907, p. 1; *Riech*, Oct. 25, 1907, p. 2, c. 3.

11. *Riech*, Oct. 3, 1907, p. 2, c. 2.

12. *Riech*, Oct. 9, 1907, p. 1, c. 7; *Golos Moskvy*, Aug. 6, 1907, p. 2, c. 2.

13. *Riech*, Oct. 9, 1907, p. 1, c. 7., p. 3, c. 6.

14. See A. Levin, *The Second Duma*, pp. 69-70.

15. *P. S. Z.*, vol. XXVII, No. 29242, Art. 37; *Riech*, Aug. 23, 1907, p. 3, c. 5; Sept. 18, 1907, p. 3, c. 3. The St. Petersburg Telegraphic Agency (PTA) report indicated that 8,639 of 14,000 peasant delegates listed themselves as right, left, or progressive non partisans. *Golos Moskvy*, Sept. 29, 1907, p. 2, cc. 4-5.

16. In the elections to the Second Duma the peasants named 1246 of 2258 electors alloted them—some 55 percent. A. Levin, *The Second Duma*, p. 65.

17. *Viestnik Evropy*, October, 1907, p. 863; *Riech*, Sept. 30, 1907, p. 2, c. 3.

18. *Riech*, Sept. 7, 1907, p. 1, c. 7.

19. A number of reports noted that less than one quarter of the voters from the peasants appeared. *Riech*, Sept. 11, 1907, p. 3, c. 1; Sept. 19, 1907, p. 2, c. 3.

20. The information was probably gathered in 1908, during the first session of the Third Duma, and submitted February 11, 1909. See TsGIAM, 102, 8, 580-1907, pp. 136-137.

21. All data on local elections for the Third Duma are taken from *Golos Moskvy*, Sept. 25, 1907, p. 3, c. 1. For the most complete data from oppositional elements see *Riech*, Sept. 21, 1907, p. 3, c. 1. The conservative delegates were sent from the Moderate Non-partisans, the Moderates, and the Union of October 17. The progressives and liberals include the Progressive Non-partisans, the Peaceful Renovationists, the parties of most national minorities and the Kadets. Since the data are not always comparable, it is difficult to compare the peasant vote in the elections to the Third Duma with its vote in the second elections. Certain it is that the center and right gained a considerable peasant vote in the third elections to the local electoral assemblies; according to the estimates of early Soviet scholars by 52.7 percent to the right of the Kadets, while the Kadets lost 23.9 percent, and the left 20 percent. As nearly as homologous elements can be identified, the right and center held 83.6 percent of the peasant seats in the *uiezd* assemblies in the third campaign, while the same element won 30.9 percent in the second elections. The Progressives and Kadets held 13.2 percent of the *uiezd* seats in the third elections and 37.1 percent in the second. The leftists fell to 3 percent of the peasantry in the third elections as against 23 percent in the second. It should be noted that *Riech* estimates for elections to the Second Duma allowed the rightist peasants 26 percent of the *uiezd* assembly seats, the conservatives 20.8 percent, the Progressives and Kadets 30.8 percent, and the left 23.3 percent. According to official estimates the elements to the right of the Kadets gained 36.8 percent among the *uiezd* peasantry in the third elections as compared with the second, the Progressives and Kadets lost 17.6 percent, and the left lost 19.2 percent. The Moderates, Moderate Non-partisans, and the Octobrists in the *Riech* data are reckoned to the right of the Kadets and the Progressives and Center Non-party Progressives are calculated with the Kadets. See A. Levin, *The Second Duma*, p. 65, 42n.

22. The delegates allowable were calculated on the basis of the aggregate landholdings of the small landowners present and voting. *Riech* held that they were one fourth of their former strength. *Riech*, Sept. 9, 1907, p. 3, c. 6.

23. *Viestnik Evropy*, October, 1907, p. 863; *Riech*, Sept. 11, 1907, p. 5, c. 1; Sept. 12. 1907, p. 3, c. 5; Sept. 16, 1907, p. 3, c. 4; Sept. 23, p. 4, c. 4.

24. *Riech*, Sept. 18, 1907, p. 3, c. 4; Sept. 22, 1907, p. 2, c. 6.

25. Reports from correspondents of *Riech* indicated that the rightist clergy polled a considerably larger percentage of the votes than the official PTA would admit for the small landowner element as a whole. Of some 745 clerical delegates, the rightists, according to *Riech*, numbered 410, the moderates 67, the Octobrists 17, the progressives 20, and the left 96, and 118 non-party clerical delegates were listed with the right. *Riech* asserted that 21 percent of the clergy were "progressives," presumably liberals and moderate leftists. The liberal correspondents of *Riech* allowed the Kadets 40 percent more votes in the small landowner category than PTA. *Riech*, Sept. 22, 1907, p. 3, c. 5; *Golos Moskvy*, Sept. 25, 1907, p. 2, c. 4. The tendency to exaggerate rightist strength was characteristic of Kadet propaganda and probably conviction.

26. *Golos Moskvy*, Sept. 25, 1907, p. 2, cc. 4-5.

27. *Riech*, Sept. 8, 1907, p. 3, c. 3; Sept. 18, 1907, p. 3, cc. 3-4; Sept. 21, 1907, p. 5, c. 3; Sept. 24, 1907, p. 1, cc. 1, 3; Oct. 17, p. 4, c. 1.

28. *Golos Moskvy*, Sept. 25, 1907, p. 2, cc. 4-5; *Riech*, Sept. 21, 1907, p. 3, c. 1, E. D. Cheremenskii, *Burzhuaziia i tsarizm v Pervoi russkoi revoliutsii* (Moscow, 1970), pp. 166-167.

29. *P. S. Z.*, vol. XXV, No. 27029; vol. XXVII, No. 29242. See S. N. Harper, *New Electoral Law*, pp. 16-17, 42-49. The prescribed procedure called for the election of a deputy from each of the categories. In the Empire this meant fifty-three peasant deputies, fifty from the landowners, thirty-five from the first city curia, thirty-five from the second, and six workers' deputies. The undesignated seats would, in all likelihood, be landowners and merchants or manufacturers chosen by the majority of the assembly. The procedure was honored largely in the breach by the conservative majorities in the *guberniia* assemblies. P. Chasles, *Parlement*, p. 99.

30. *Riech*, Oct. 12, 1907, p. 3, c. 2; Oct. 14, 1907, p. 1, c. 6.

31. The following results were reported in *Golos Moskvy*, Oct. 10, 1907, p. 2, cc. 4-5 and in *Riech*, Oct. 12, 1907, p. 3, c. 2. PTA figures appeared in the Octobrist organ *Golos Moskvy*. The data in *Riech* consist largely of reports from its own correspondents and additional information from PTA, all analyzed by its election specialist, A. Smirnov. A rich lode of material on the regional, economic, and social composition of the electors appears in the reports of the provincial governors, TsGIAL, 1327, 1, 111-115. The names of 5,120 electors from all categories are provided. The official PTA reports are the most complete on 5,858 electors as against 4,897 in *Riech*.

32. *Riech*, Aug. 31, 1907, p. 1, c. 5; Oct. 14, 1907, p. 1, c. 6; TsGIAL, 1327, 1, 114, pp. 21-34.

33. *P. S. Z.*, XXVI, No. 27805, Art. 62.

34. TsGIAL, 1327, 1, 111-115, *chast'* I-V.

35. Ibid., 113, *Chast'* II, p. 143; 115, *Chast'* V, pp. 230-236; 116, *Chast'* IV, pp. 5-29. The borderlands are not included.

36. *Viestnik Evropy*, October 1907, pp. 867-868.

37. *Riech*, Oct. 12, 1907, p. 3, c. 2; *Golos Moskvy*, Oct. 5, p. 2, cc. 4-5.

38. *P. S. Z.*, vol. XXV, No. 27029, vol. XXVII, No. 29242.

39. Opposition elements could take some consolation from the circumstance that the peasant merchants who generally voted with the URP were eliminated from the first city category. *Riech*, Sept. 1, 1907, p. 3, c. 7; Sept. 2, 1907, p. 2, cc. 1-2; *P. S. Z.*, vol. XXVI, No. 27805, Art. 62.

40. *Riech*, Oct. 14, 1907, p. 1, c. 6; P. N. Miliukov calculated that 230 landowners sent a single elector and one elector represented a thousand industrial-commercial votes, the middle bourgeois named one for 15,000 voters, the peasants named one for 60,000 and the workers one for 125,000. P. N. Miliukov, *Vospominanii*, vol. II, p. 8.

41. See *Golos Moskvy*, Oct. 5, 1907, p. 2, cc. 4-5; *Riech*, Oct. 12, 1907, p. 3, c. 2.

42. *Riech*, Sept. 30, 1907, p. 2, cc. 1-2.

43. Compare S. N. Harper, *Electoral Law*, pp. 50-51. Professor Harper's figures were taken from *Riech*, Oct. 12, 1907, p. 3, c. 2.

44. *Riech*, Oct. 11, 1907, p. 1, c. 7; Oct. 12, 1907, p. 3, c. 2.

45. *Riech*, Sept. 18, 1907, p. 3, cc. 3-4, p. 5, c. 1; Oct. 12, 1907, p. 3, c. 2; *Vpered*, Oct. 24, 1907, p. 1, c. 3; *Golos Moskvy*, Oct. 5, 1907, p. 2, cc. 4-5.

46. *Riech*, Sept. 8, 1907, p. 3, c. 3; Sept. 14, 1907, p. 2, c. 3; Sept. 17, 1907, p. 4, c. 1; Sept. 19, 1907, p. 2, c. 3; Sept. 22, 1907, p. 4, c. 7; Sept. 25, 1907, p. 3, c. 5; *Vpered*, Sept. 24, 1907, p. 1, cc. 1, 3.

47. Considerable data on the voting of the minorities, not readily available elsewhere, are to be found in the governors' reports to the Ministry of the Interior, TsGIAL, 1, 111-115. The exact number of minority electors is difficult to determine. Family names, with all of the uncertainties they presented, are still the best index available, particularly in the border regions. Hence, both maximum and minimum estimates are cited. The overall differential between the determinable minority members and the doubtful is 2.9 percent of those reported by the governors to the MVD (604 to 622). The largest differentials among the minority electors were 5.7 percent in the first city curia and 4.7 percent in the *volost* elections. The landowner and the city curiae differed by 4.4 percent and 5.4 percent respectively. The largest significant differentials among the ethnic groups were 4.4 percent for the Jews and 6.7 percent for the Germans. The various small minorities, predominantly Moslem, are grouped by religion because they voted as Moslems rather than Tartars, Daghestani, Bashkirs, etc.

48. The ethno-religious minority delegates from the *volost* sent 82 to 86 electors from the *uiezd* to the *guberniia* assemblies, the landowner minority elements sent 291 to 297, the first city category 101 to 107, the second city category 94 to 96, and 28 were listed simply as city electors while the workers sent 8 electors.

49. The minimum and maximum strengths are given for all nationalities for reasons indicated in note no. 47.

50. *Riech*, Oct. 14, 1907, p. 1, cc. 3-5.

51. *Riech*, Oct. 18, 1907, p. 4, c. 5; Oct. 20, 1907, p. 3, c. 6, p. 5, c. 5; Oct. 23, 1907, p. 5, c. 3; Oct. 23, 1907, p. 5, cc. 5-6.

52. *Viestnik Evropy*, November 1907, pp. 367-368; *Riech*, Oct. 18, 1907, p. 4, c. 5; Oct. 20, 1907, p. 3, c. 6; Oct. 21, 1907, p. 5, cc. 1, 3.

53. *Riech*, Oct. 20, 1907, p. 3, cc. 5-6; Oct. 21, 1907, p. 5, cc. 1-2, p. 6, c. 7; Oct. 23, 1907, p. 5, cc. 5-6; Oct. 27, 1907, p. 2, c. 1; Oct. 28, 1907, p. 5, c. 2.

54. See p. 109 for actual voting in Moscow. *Riech*, Oct. 18, 1907, p. 2, c. 6; Oct. 21, 1907, p. 5, cc. 3-4; *Vybory po gorodu Moskvie*, pp. 51-52, 106, 109, 113.

55. These election statistics were compiled and analyzed in 1908 in *Vybory po gorodu Moskvie*.

56. Ibid., pp. 78-79.

57. Two thirds of the owners of commercial establishments were in the second category as were nearly all employees of industrial establishments, transport workers and inn workers as well as employees and workers of commercial establishments. Ibid., pp. 80, 88-89, 91-92, 99.

58. Ibid., 94-95. These included teachers (3.6 percent), physicians (3.5 percent), technicians (1.6 percent), lawyers and notaries (1.2 percent), artists (0.8 percent) and literaeurs (0.29 percent).

59. The professional structure of the first category of Moscow consisted of:

	(percent)
Industrial-commercial entrepreneurs	53.9
Income from rent or investment capital	21.5
Employees of industrial-commercial enterprises	8.5
Employees of state and public enterprises	6.1
Liberal professions	7.4
Undefined elements including homeowners	24.6

The dominant elements in the second category included:

	(percent)
Industrial-commercial employees	37.2
State and public employees	20.2
Owners of commercial-industrial enterprises	21.7
Liberal professions	13.3
Renters, homeowners, capitalists	1.0

See *Vybory po gorodu Moskvie,* pp. 95-96.

60. Of a total of 281,106 persons with a right to vote in Moscow, some 74,199 registrants (26.3 percent) were not allowed to vote. Of these, 26,000 had not voted in the second elections and lost their suffrage right, and 47,584 failed to present the proper documents. The groups which suffered most from these regulations were apartment taxpayers (32.4 percent, chiefly in the second category), and those who paid a professional tax (27.9 percent, largely in the second category). Ibid., pp. 101-102, 105-106.

61. Ibid., p. 108-109.

62. Age Group   Percentage of age group voting in three elections

Age Group	First	Second	Third
30 to 39	76.8	75.8	69.8
40 to 49	75.8	74.1	70.0

Ibid., pp. 112-113.

63. Ibid., pp. 115-117.

64. Ibid., p. 119. In the first category the average participation of the liberal professions was 65 to 69 percent, varying with the different professions, and in the second they averaged 69 percent.

65. Ibid.

66. Ibid., p. 135.

67. Ibid., p. 125.

68. A higher percentage of the first category participated (73.9) than the second (69.1). But the second category shows more interest in the basic elections (69.1) than the voters in the first category (65.1). Ibid., p. 130.

69. *Riech,* Oct. 18, 1907, p. 3, c. 1, p. 4, c. 7; Oct. 24, 1907, p. 2, c. 5, p. 3, cc. 1, 5, p. 5, c. 7.

70. *Obzor dieiatel'nosti gosudarstvennoi dumy tret'iago sozyva. 1907-1912 gg. Chast'pervaia. Obshchiia sviedieniia sostavlen kantseliariei gosudarstvennoi dumy* (St. Petersburg, 1912), pp. 13-18. Cited hereafter as *Obzor dieiat, Chast'* I.

71. *Riech,* Oct. 16, 1907, p. 2, c. 3.

Chapter X

1. Statistics on each fraction and group given below include those deputies listed in *Ukazatel' k stenograficheskim otchetam (chast'i I-III). Tretei sozyv. Sessiia I. 1907-1908 gg. Zasiedaniia 1-98 (1 Noiabria 1907 g. — 28 Iiunia 1908 g.)* (St. Petersburg, 1908). Cited hereafter as *Ukazatel' k sten. ot.* Those who transferred from one group to another are listed in the fractions and groups to which they were elected. The Law of June 3, 1907, assigned 446 members to the Third Imperial Duma but in the course of its five-year duration it numbered in all some 497 deputies due to deaths, resignations, absenteeism, exclusions, and replacements. The election of four deputies from Finland was never held to assure that the centennial autonomy of the Grand Duchy would remain unclouded. Thirty deputies died in the course of the sessions of the Third Duma, nineteen resigned, the election of G. K. Shmidt from Minsk was declared invalid because of an earlier conviction for espionage, and two Kadets were expelled for misconduct. These fifty-two personages (the four Finns were always included in official figures) were replaced by only forty-four deputies since eight seats were never filled in by-elections. *Obzor dieat., Prilozhenie 4(a). Grupp za piat sesan.*

2. G. N. Navrotskii, a large landowner of noble origin, died shortly after the opening session of the Third Duma, and with the ouster of Captain Shmidt, the Rightist Fraction numbered forty-nine during most of the first session. *Ukazatel' k sten. ot. Chast' II. Spisok Chlenov gosudarstvennoi dumy po partiinym gruppirovkam* (St. Petersburg, 1908), p. 11.

3. *Golos Moskvy,* Oct. 23, 1907, p. 2, cc. 5-6.

4. *Riech,* Oct. 14, 1907, p. 2, c. 2; Oct. 21, 1907, p. 5, c. 1; Oct. 27, 1907, p. 5, c. 6; Oct. 28, 1907, p. 5, c. 2. *Viestnik Evropy,* November 1907, pp. 367-368; *Ukazatel' k sten. ot. Chast' II,* pp. 13-14, 51-311. *Obzor dieist. Chast' pervaia. Prilozhenie* 2, 3, 4(a), 4(b).

5. *Ukazatel' k sten. ot. Chast' II,* pp. 13-14, 51-311; *Obzor dieiat. Chast' I.* Prilozhenie 2, pp. 68-70.

6. *Ukzatel k sten. ot. Chast' II.* pp. 13-14, 51-311; *Obzor dieiat. Chast' I. Prilozhenie 2.* For the purposes of this study the provinces are grouped in the following geographic areas: The North includes Arkhangel, Olonets and Vologda *gubernii.* The North Central region encompasses St. Petersburg, Pskov, Novgorod, Tver, Iaroslavl, Kostroma, Viatka, and Vladimir *gubernii.* Smolensk, Moscow, Kaluga, Riazan, Penza, Tambov, Tula, Orel, Voronezh, Kursk and Kharkov are in the Central region. The Northwest Border region includes Vitebsk and Minsk provinces and the Southwest Border region embraces Volyn, Podolia, Bessarabia, Kherson. Estliand, Lifliand, Kurliand, Kovno, Vilno, and Grodno compose the Baltic region. Poland or the Vistula region includes the provinces of Suvalki, Siedlets, Lomzh, Warsaw, Liublin, Plotsk, Kalish, Petrokovsk, Radom, and Kielsk. The Dnieper region is made up of Mogilev, Kiev, Poltava, Chernigov, and Ekaterinoslav *gubernii.* The Crimean region is officially entitled the Taurida province, and the Don Region is officially the Oblast of the Don Army. The Volga region includes Nizhegorod, Kazan, Simbrisk, Samara, Saratov, and Astrakahan *gubernii.* Perm, Ufa, and Orenburg are in the Ural region and the Caucasus includes Stavropol, Kutais, Tiflis, Kars, Kuban, Erivan, Elizavetpol, Dagestan, Baku, Terek, and Chernomorsk provinces. The provinces of Asiatic Russia which retained their franchise were Tobolsk, Tomsk, Irkutsk, and Eniseisk.

7. *Ukazatel'k sten. ot. Chast' II,* pp. 13-14, 51-311; *Obzor dieiat. Chast' I.*

Prilozhenie 2e; Tretiia gosudarstvennaia duma v kartogrammakh (St. Petersburg). 1910, Charts VIII, IX, X.

8. A desiatin is 2.7 acres.

9. *Obzor dieiat. Chast' I. Prilozhenie* 1-e, pp. 2-6, *Prilozhenie* 3-e, pp. 72-93, *Prilozhenie* 4 (b), pp. 102-129.

10. Ibid., *Prilozhenie* 4 (a), pp. 98-99.

11. *Riech*, Oct. 2, 1907, p. 2, c. 5; Oct. 31, 1907, p. 3, c. 6.

12. *Riech*, Nov. 3, 1907, p. 3, cc. 3-4; Nov. 8, 1907, p. 3, c. 6.

13. *Riech*, Nov. 10, 1907, p. 3, cc. 5-7.

14. *Riech*, Nov. 10, 1907, p. 3, cc. 5-7; Nov. 13, 1907, p. 3, c. 6; Nov. 14, 1907, p. 1, c. 5; Nov. 25, 1907, p. 3, cc. 3-4.

15. *Riech*, Nov. 14, 1907, p. 1, c. 5; Dec. 1, 1907, p. 4, c. 1.

16. *Riech*, Nov. 10, 1907, p. 3, cc. 5-7; Nov. 14, p. 2, cc. 6-7.

17. *Riech*, Dec. 1, 1907, p. 4, c. 4; Dec. 4, 1907, p. 3, c. 7; Jan. 25, 1908, p. 4, c. 3.

18. *Obzor dieiat. Chast' I. Prolozhenie* I-e, pp. 10-11; *Prilozhenie* 4 (a), pp. 98-99; *Prilozhenie* 4 (b), pp. 107-108. *Ukazatel' k Sten. ot. Chast' II*, p. 14. Biographical material, unless otherwise cited is taken from Granat, *Entsik. Slovar*, vol. XVII. The statistical information concerns the sixty-nine members of the Moderate Rightist Fraction cited in the *Ukazatel'*. Later adherents do not materially change the "profile."

19. *Riech*, Nov. 24, 1907, p. 4, c. 2; Dec. 6, 1907, p. 3, c. 4; Jan. 17, 1908, p. 3, c. 7; Jan. 25, 1908, p. 4, c. 3.

20. *Riech*, January 25, 1908, p. 4, c. 3.

21. *Riech*, Dec. 8, 1907, p. 2, c. 5.

22. *Riech*, Feb. 1, 1908, p. 3, c. 4; Feb. 3, 1908, p. 3, c. 6; P. N. Miliukov, *Vospominaniia*, vol. II, pp. 23-27.

23. *Ukazatel' k sten. ot. Chast' II*, pp. 13-14; *Obzor dieiat. Chast' I. Prilozhenie* 1-e, 2-e, 4 (a), 4 (b), p. 106; *Granat, Entsik. slovar*, vol. XVII.

24. Balashov claimed a bloc of 230 deputies in the new traction and the Octobrist Fraction. He expected the Octobrists and Nationalists to vote together on basic questions even though they had differed on bills concerning the propagation of the faith and the condemnation of political crime. *Riech*. Oct. 27, 1909, p. 4, cc. 2, 4. *Gosudarstvennaia duma. Fraktsiia narodnoi svobody v period 10 Oktiabria 1909 goda—5 Iiunia 1910 goda* p. 14. Cited hereafter as *Otchet fraktsiia narodnoi svobody.*

25. V. N. Kokovtsov, *Out of My Past*, p. 274; *Obzor dieiat. Chast' I. Prilozhenie* 4 (b), pp. 108-110.

26. *Riech*, Oct. 20, 1909, p. 4, c. 2; Oct. 24, 1909, p. 4, cc. 2-3.

27. *Riech*, Oct. 28, 1909, p. 1, c. 7; *Golos Moskvy*, Oct. 27, 1909, p. 4, c. 1. The text of the program also appears in *Sbornik Kluba Russkikh Natsionalistov*, 6 IV 1909-6 IV 1910, pp. 7-8.

28. *Golos Moskvy*, Oct. 27, 1909, p. 4, c. 1. The new combined bureau consisted of V. G. Vetchinin. A. A. Motovilov, N. K. fon Giubernet from the National Group

and Professor S. M. Bogdanov, P. N. Krupenskii, A. A. Pototskii, Bishop Evlogii, and I. E. Anan'ev from the Moderate Rightists. L. V. Plovtsov had come over from the Octobrists. *Golos Moskvy*, ibid.; *Riech*, Oct. 30, 1909, p. 4, c. 2; *Obzor dieiat. Chast' I. Prilozhenie* 4 (b), pp. 106, 107-108, 112-118. Stolypin, with the help of P. N. Krupenskii, was to create a rightist bloc around the Russian Nationalists which was to include the Rightists and the Right Octobrists. This bloc was to assure Stolypin a rightist majority in the face of the central bloc he had built around the Octobrists after the latter opposed him, along with the Kadets, on the budget, the reestablishment of the justices of the peace, and the western zemstvos. P. N. Miliukov, C. S. Seignobos, L. Eisenmann, *Histoire de la Russie* (Paris, 1922-1923), vol. III, pp. 1164-1168.

29. See interview of Balashov with correspondents of the Octobrist press in *Golos Moskvy*, Oct. 27, 1909, p. 4, c. 1 and his letter of March 20, 1911, to Stolypin in connection with the crisis accompanying legislation on the institution of the zemstvos in non-Russian western provinces, *Krasnyi Arkhiv*, No. 9 (1925), pp. 291-294.

30. *Krasnyi Arkhiv*, No. 9 (1925), pp. 291-294.

31. *Golos Moskvy*, Oct. 27, 1909, p. 4, c. 1.

32. *Golos Moskvy*, Oct. 31, 1909, p. 2, c. 6. See also *Natsionalisty v tretei gosudarstvennoi dumie* pp. 3-4 and *Riech*, Nov. 3, 1909, p. 3, c. 2 on the general attitude toward cooperation of centrist elements along with differences in the Duma and cooperation with liberals.

33. *Obzor dieiat. Chast' I. Prilozhenie* 1-e, 2-e, pp. 68-70, 4 (b), pp. 108-110; *Ukazatel' k sten. ot. Sessia* III, pp. 53-250, Sessia IV, pp. 55-240, *Sessia* V, pp. 67-276. These statistics concern the original 91 members.

34. *Riech*, April 30, 1911, p. 6, c. 3; *Golos Moskvy*, April 30, 1911, p. 3, c. 3.

35. *Golos Moskvy*, April 30, 1911, p. 3, c. 3.

36. *Obzor dieiat. Chast' I*, p. 11; *Otchet fraktsii narodnoi svobody*, Section IV, pp. 7-8.

37. Statistical materials are derived from *Obzor dieiat. Chast' I. Prilozhenie* 1-e, pp. 2-65; 2-e, pp. 68-70; 4 (b), p. 111; *Ukazatel' k Sten. ot. Sessiia* IV, pp. 55-246; *Sessiia* V, pp. 67-276.

38. *Otchet fraktsii narodnoi svobody*, Section IV, p. 7.

39. See pp. 35-36, Chap. III. *Obzor dieiat. Chast' I. Prilozhenie* 4 (b), pp. 128-129.

40. *Riech*, Oct. 18, 1909, p. 2, c. 6; See *Obzor dieiat. Chast' I. Prilozhenie* 4 (b), pp. 128-129 for development. The names of the leadership as reported here and in the press do not always coincide but the evolution toward a predominance of peasant elements is evident.

41. *Riech*, Oct. 15, 1909, p. 4, c. 1; Oct. 16, 1909, p. 4, c. 3; Oct. 21, 1909, p. 3, c. 5.

42. *Riech*, Oct. 20, 1909, p. 4, c. 2; *Golos Moskvy*, Oct. 22, 1909, p. 3, c. 6.

43. Statistical information based on all 29 adherents, is derived primiarily from *Obzor dieiat. Chast I. Prilozhenie* 1-e, 2-e, 3-e, 4 (a), and 4 (b), pp. 128-129; *Ukazatel' k sten. ot. Sessiia* I, pp. 59-311; *Sessiia* II, pp. 49-230; *Sessiia* III, pp. 53-250; *Sessiia* IV, pp. 55-240; *Sessiia* V, pp. 67-276.

44. Data are based on the 148 members of the Party at the end of the first session of the Third Duma. *Obzor dieiat, Chast' I*, p. 9; *Prilozhenie* 1-e, 4 (a), 4 (b), pp. 112-118; *Ukzkatel' k sten. ot.* for all five sessions.

45. C. J. Smith, "The Third State Duma," *The Russian Review*, July, 1958, p. 204.

46. See above pp. 59-60. Cf. *Golos Moskvy*, Oct. 7, 1909, p. 1, cc. 4-5.

47. *Riech*, Nov. 14, 1909, p. 6, c. 4.

48. *G. D. III, Sten. ot. Sessiia II, Chast' I*, pp. 2466-2469.

49. *Novaia Vremia*, March 13, 1909, p. 3, c. 2, p. 4, c. 5.

50. Ibid., March 17, 1909, p. 2, c. 8.

51. *Riech*, May 11, 1909, p. 4, c. 3.

52. Ibid.

53. See *Otchet fraktsii narodnoi svobody, 15 Oktiabria 1908—2 Iiuniia 1909*, p. 49.

54. *Riech*, May 20, 1909, p. 1, c. 5, p. 4, c. 2.

55. *Riech*, May 23, 1909, p. 2, c. 5.

56. *Riech*, May 27, 1909, p. 2, c. 7.

57. *Riech*, Sept. 10, 1909, p. 2, c. 7; Sept. 14, 1909, p. 2, c. 3.

58. *Golos Moskvy*, Oct. 4, 1909, p. 3, cc. 3-4, 6; Oct. 9, 1909, p. 5, cc. 4-5; Oct. 10, 1909, p. 4, c. 2; *Riech*, Oct. 8, 1909, p. 2, c. 7.

59. *Golos Moskvy*, Oct. 13, 1909, p. 2, c. 3.

60. *Riech*, Oct. 15, 1909, p. 4, c. 1; Oct. 17, 1909, p. 4, c. 3. The Right Octobrists were concerned about clerical attitudes toward religion and public education, *Riech*, Nov. 18, 1909, p. 4, cc. 2-3.

61. *Riech*, Oct. 29, 1909, p. 4, cc. 2-3.

62. *Riech*, Oct. 30, 1909, p. 1, c. 2; Oct. 23, 1909, p. 1, c. 7.

63. *Riech*, Dec. 5, 1909, p. 6, c. 2.

64. All statistics for the Right Octobrist Fraction are derived from *Obzor dieiat. Chast' I. Prilozhenie* 1-e, 2-e, 4 (a), 4 (b), p. 111; *Ukazatel' k sten. ot. Sessiia* III, IV, V.

65. See p. 61ff.

66. *Slovo*, Nov. 7, 1907, p. 4, c. 7; Nov. 8, 1907, p. 3, c. 4; Jan. 8, 1908, p. 4, c. 4.

67. *Slovo*, Nov. 2, 1907, p. 3, c. 4; Nov. 7, 1907, p. 4, c. 7; Nov. 8, 1907, p. 3, c. 4; Nov. 11, 1907, p. 4, c. 5; *Obzor dieiat. Chast' I. Prilozhenie* 4-e. Some of those named, including S. Z. Shidlovskii and N. I. Rotermel, were Octobrists who remained with their Party. *Slovo*, Nov. 8, 1907, p. 3, c. 4.

68. *Slovo*, Nov. 8, 1907, p. 3, c. 4; Jan. 8, 1908, p. 4, cc. 4-5.

69. Slovo, Nov. 8, 1907, p. 3, c. 4.

70. *Slovo*, Jan. 8, 1908, p. 4, cc. 4-5.

71. *Slovo*, Nov. 8, 1907, p. 3, c. 4.

72. On a number of occasions Efremov took pains to deny rumors of this order in open letters to *Slovo*. See Nov. 14, 1907, p. 6, c. 6; Nov. 27, 1907, p. 3, c. 3.

73. Sources for statistics on the Progressive and Peaceful Renovationists Group (as it appeared at the end of the first session) are derived from *Obzor dieiat. Chast' I. Prilozhenie* 1-e, 2-e, 3-e, 4-e, 4 (a), and 4 (b), pp. 120-123; *Ukazatel' k sten. ot.* for all five sessions.

74. Statistical data on the Kadets are derived from the sources indicated for other parties and groups, especially *Obzor dieiat. Chast' I. Prilozhenie 2-e, 4 (a), and 4 (b), pp. 124-126. Granat, Entsik. slovar,* vol. XVII.

75. The statistical data are derived from the same sources as those for other fractions and groups. Special information on the Polish-Lithuanian-Bielorussian Group is listed in *Obzor dieiat. Chast' I. Prilozhenie* 4 (b), pp. 118-119.

76. All data are derived from the same sources as indicated for other groups and fractions. Special information on the Kolo is listed in *Obzor dieiat. Chast' I. Prilozhenie* 4 (b), pp. 120-121.

77. Special data on the Moslem Group are listed in *Obzor dieiat. Chast' I. Prilozhenie* 4 (b), pp. 122-123.

78. For special information on the Trudoviki see *Obzor dieiat. Chast' I. Prilozhenie* 4 (b), pp. 126-127.

79. The Maritime Provinces were 67 percent Russian in 1893. See Department of Trade and Manufactures, Ministry of Finance, *The Industries of Russia. Siberia and the Great Siberian Railway,* (St. Petersburg, 1893), vol. V, p. 69.

80. Data for the Social Democrats are derived from the same sources noted for other groups and fractions. Special information for the Social Democrats is listed in *Obzor dieiat. Chast' I. Prilozhenienie* 4 (b), pp. 128-129.

81. See pp. 70-71.

Chapter XI

1. *Riech,* Oct. 11, 1907, p. 2, c. 2; Oct. 12, 1907, p. 3, c. 2.

2. See A. Levin, *The Second Duma,* p. 65.

3. See TsGIAL, 1284, 194, *delo* no. 101, February 2, 1912, pp. 7, 7R; *delo* no. 70, Nov. 13, 1909, pp. 6R-7; *delo* no. 81, Dec. 8, 1911, pp. 8-9R; *delo* no. 75, Dec. 14, 1912, pp. 9R-13; *delo* no. 75, Sept. 12, 1913, pp. 13R-15.

Bibliographical Note

GENERAL

The following is a selective bibliography of materials and studies most pertinent for an examination of the elections and political profile of the Third Duma. A number of textbooks offer material unusual for works of this broad nature and purpose because of the significant relation of their authors to the period an developments concerned. Sir Bernard Pares, as an informed correspondent for the *Westminister Gazette* in 1905-1906, offers the results of his direct observations in Chapter XXIII on the Liberation Movement in his *History of Russia*, New York, 1926, as well as in his *Fall of the Russian Monarchy*, New York, 1939, in his discussion of the Revolution of 1905 and the period of the First and Second Dumas. Observations in the chapters on the revolutionary movement and Duma period written by P. N. Miliukov in vol. III, of P. N. Miliukov, C. Seignobos and L. Eisenmann, *Histoire de la Russie*, 3 vols., Paris, 1922-1923, assume the nature of a commentary and analysis by a major participant within a relatively brief period after the events concerned.

In more specialized studies of the Duma period, A. Levin, *The Second Duma: A Study of the Social Democratic Party and the Russian Constitutional Experiment*, Yale Historical Publications, Vol. XXXVI, New Haven, 1940; second printing, Hamden, Connecticut, 1966, offers a detailed background for the Third Duma in an analysis of the legislation establishing the Dumas and the parties and proceedings of the Second Duma. Soviet historiography of the Duma period has been sparse and sporadic. E. D. Chermenskii's *Burzhuaziia i tsarizm v pervoi russkoi revoliutsii* was originally published in 1939 and has recently appeared in a considerably enlarged second edition, Moscow, 1970. It is replete with detailed material, primarily from the State Historical Archives, concerning the policies, considerations, and attitudes of the government, business circles, conservative and liberal parties in the period from 1904 to 1907. The author's interpretations are entirely informed by Bolshevik theory and policy. S. M. Sidelnikov, *Obrazovanie i deiatelnost' pervoi gosudarstvennoi dumy* presents the same sort of material for the organization, parties, and proceedings of the First Duma. Again, all the complex ideological, parliamentary, and social problems are solved quite simply—according to Lenin. The chief analysis by a Soviet author of the activities of the Third duma is that of A. Ia. Avrekh, *Stolypin i tret'ia duma*, Moscow, 1968. While this study, like that of Chermenskii, provides considerable information garnered from the State Central Historical Archives, it hews close to the Leninist line in depicting the "crash" of Stolypin's policy and the policies of all elements of the Duma other than the Bolshevik.

THE THIRD DUMA

The basic source for any study of the Russian Imperial Duma is *Gosudarstvennaia duma. Stenograficheskie otchety*. St. Petersburg, 1906-1916, 126 volumes. Of particular interest for this study are the indexes to the respective sessions of the Third Duma, *Ukazatel' k stenografisheskim otchetam tretii sozyv. Sessiia I 1907-1908 gg.; Sessiia II 1908-1909 gg.; Sessiia III, 1909-1910 gg.; Sessiia IV 1910-1911 gg.; Sessiia V 1911-1912 gg.* The most useful section in each of the sessions is the personal alphabetical index, *Lichnyi alfavitnyi ukazatel'*, Session I, pp. 49-311; Session II, pp. 49-230; Session III, pp. 53-250; Session IV, pp. 55;240; Session V, pp. 67-276. Each includes information concerning the electoral constituency, fraction or group affiliation, and references to the activities and positions of each member in the Third Duma. A rich lode of materials on the membership of the Third Duma for all five sessions is available in *Obzor dieiatel'-nosti gosudarstvennoi dumy tret'iago sozyva 1907-1912 gg.* Its first part, *Chast' pervaia. Obshchiia svideieniia. Sostavlen kantseli-ariiu gosudarstvennoi dumy*, St. Petersburg, 1912, a review of the general activities of the Third Duma, is concerned with detailed information on its membership. The appendices to part I are especially useful. The most important for this study is Appendix 1 which lists all members of the Duma for all five sessions, the age, faith, nationality, education, class, electoral district, political experience, and property holdings or income of each. Appendix 2 lists those members of the Third Duma who died, resigned, or were expelled, or whose elections were considered invalid. The fraction or group and pertinent dates are noted for each member. Appendix 3 notes the category from which each member was elected. Appendix 4 (a) indicates the strength of each fraction or group in each session by percentage and the net gain or loss in membership as compared with the preceeding session. And Appendix 4 (b) lists alphabetically the membership in each fraction or group by sessions.

The Central State Historical Archives, *Tsentral'nyi Gosudarstvennyi Istoricheskii Arkhiv* in Moscow (TsGIAM) and Leningrad (TsGIAL) offer additional voluminous materials on the Duma membership. In general, they hold reports of provincial governors to the Ministry of the Interior on all matters pertaining to their jurisdictions (financial, agricultural, administrative, police, judicial, and on public opinion, among others). The most useful materials for this study are in TsGIAL, *Fond* (Fund) 1327, *Opis* (Section) 1, *Edinitsi khranenii* (File) 111-116. *Chast'i* (Part) I-IV, MVD, *Dielo osobavo proizvodstvo v gosudarstvennuiu dumu I II i III sozyvov i vyborshchikov chlenov gosudarstvennoi dumy.* This fund includes reports of provincial governors to their superiors in the Ministry of the Interior from the provinces of European Russia exclusive of Poland and the Caucasus, and includes Tomsk Province in Western Siberia and the Oblast of the Don Army. The reports list the distribution of delegates from *volosts* and electors from *uiezdi* for some 518 *uiezdi* by name and category. They designate the subdivisions of categories by geographic areas and ethnic groups, the property qualifications for *volost*, landowner, and city categories. TsGIAM, *Fond* 102, *Opis* 99, *Ed. khr.* 164, includes a long report and statistical summary on the numerical strength of legal parties.

Vybory po gorodu Moskvie v gosudarstvennuiu dumoiu tret'iago sozyva, Moscow, 1908, is another official account, from the Moscow City Council, of the elections in Moscow, covering all aspects of the elections, administratively and statistically, in the greatest detail. This is a remarkably comprehensive analysis of the socioeconomic strata of the city as they participated in, or absented themselves from, the elections.

Contemporary examinations of the third election campaign include *Tret'iia gosudarstvennaia duma v kartogrammakh, izdanii A. V. Bashkirev*, St. Petersburg, 1910, an analysis of the membership of the Third Duma in a series of charts, and *Tret'iia gousdarstvennaia duma. Fraktsiia narodnoi svobody*, St. Petersburg, 1908-1912, 5 vols, renders an account of the activities of the Kadets in each session, explaining their positions and analyzing those of other fractions and groups and of the government. A populist view is presented in A. Patrischev's article "Bez pobiediteli" in *Russkoe Bogatstvo*, July, 1907, pp. 113-115. The author has analyzed public opinion during the elections to the Third Duma

in A. Levin, "The Russian Voter in the Elections to the Third
Duma," *Slavic Review,* December, 1962, pp. 660-677, and in "The
Reactionary Tradition in the Election Campaign to the Third
Duma," A. Levin, Editor, *Oklahoma State University Publications, Arts and Science Studies,* Social Sciences Series No. 8,
Stillwater, Oklahoma, 1962. This monographic article examines
the purposes and tactics of the extreme rightist elements in the
third elections. C. J. Smith, "The Third State Duma; an Ana-
lytical Profile," *The Russian Review,* July, 1958, pp. 201-210,
presents an analysis of the personnel of the Third Duma similar
to that in Chap. IX of the present work which has treated the
statistical material offered in *Obzor dieiatel'nosti* somewhat dif-
ferently with additional material on specific geographic distribution, party strengths by sessions, and statistics on new and
splinter parties formed in the course of the Third Duma. And
Warren B. Walsh presents a study of the membership of the Third
Duma in "Political Parties of the Russian Duma," *Journal of
Modern History,* June 1950, pp. 144-150.

LAWS

The basic source for laws pertaining to this investigation is
Polnoe sobranie zakonov rossiiskoi imperii. Sobranie tret'ie, St.
Petersburg, 1885-1916, 34 vols. This collection lists all imperial
laws and decrees by date. The election law of June 3, 1907, is in
vol. XXVII, No. 29242. Contemporary studies of this crucial
legislation were executed by A. Leroy-Beaulieu, "La Russie
devant la Troisieme Duma", *Revue des Deux Mondes,* vol. 41
(1907), and S. N. Harper, *The New Electoral Law for the Russian
Duma,* Chicago, 1908. Recent studies of the law and its impact are
in A. Levin, "June 3, 1907: Action and Reaction," A. D. Ferguson
and A. Levin, editors, *Essays in Russian History: A Collection
Dedicated to George Vernadsky,* Hamden, Connecticut, 1965,
pp. 233-273; Marc Szeftel, "The Reform of the Electoral Law to
the State Duma on June 3, 1907: a new basis for the Formation of
the Russian Parliament," *Liber Memoralis George de Lagarde:
Studies Presented to the International Commission for the History
of Representative and Parliamentary Institutions,* XXXVIII,
London, 1965. V. Charnolutskii offers a guide to Russian laws
on societies and unions in *Spravochnaia kniga ob obshchestvakh
i soiuzov,* St. Petersburg, 1912.

POLITICAL PARTIES

Numerous, more or less comprehensive collections of Party programs appeared in 1906. These include *Polnoe sobranie podrobnykh programm russkikh i pol'skikh partii*, Vilno, 1906; V. Ivanovich, *Rossiiskaia partii, soiuzi i ligi*, St. Petersburg, 1906; and V. V. Vodovozov, *Sbornik programm politicheskikh partii v rossii*, n.p., 1906. These are collections of programs with little or no analysis of their content. The major contemporary study of the organization and activities of the various parties, particularly in the period 1906-1908, is L. Martov and A. Potresov, editors, *Obshchestvennoe dvizhenie v Rossii v nachale xx-go vieka*, St. Petersburg, 1909-1914, 4 vols. This work has a marked Menshevik coloration but offers considerable information gleaned from the press and party records.

The programs and attitudes of the rightist parties are treated in A. Levin, "The Reactionary Tradition in the Election Campaign to the Third Duma" noted above. And two significant investigations by H. Rogger are "The Formation of the Russian Right," *California Slavic Studies*, vol. III, pp. 66-94, and "Russia" in H. Rogger and E. Weber, *The European Right*, Berkeley, California, 1966, pp. 443-500. The activities of the more moderate, nationalist right are detailed and evolved in *Sbornik kluba russkikh natsionalistov*. Five issues appeared in St. Petersburg from 1907 to 1913. The second issue covering the period from April 6, 1909 to April 6, 1910 has the program of the Russian National Fraction. A careful treatment of the relations between the government and the Stolypin administration appears in A. Hosking, "P. A. Stolypin and the Octobrist Party," *The Slavonic and East European Review*, January, 1969, pp. 137-160.

The attitudes of the Social Revolutionary Party are set forth in *Partiia sotsialistov revoliutsionerov. Rezoliutsii ekstrennogo siezda P. S. R. po voprosu o dumskoi i vnie dumskoi taktiki*, n.p., n.d. S. R. activities are examined by O. H. Radkey, *The Agrarian Foes of Bolshevism: Promise and Default of the Russian Social Revolutionaries, March 6 to October 1917*, New York, 1958. The period indicated is placed in the perspective of the development of the Party's ideology.

There is, of course, a considerable body of material on the Social Democrats, particularly the Bolsheviki, for the Duma period. This study utilized V. I. Lenin, *Sobranie sochinenii*, Moscow, 1921-1925. This is the second edition of Lenin's works, less complete than later editions but with a dependable text and valuable footnotes. An official translation of Lenin's writings, now in the process of publication, is V. I. Lenin, *Collected Works*, Moscow, 1962—. Volume 8 of the Second Edition and volumes 9 to 13 of the *Collected Works* include the articles, brochures, and speeches reflecting the development of Lenin's ideas on the significance of the Duma for the Russian Marxists and his tactics for the Duma. *O boikota tretei dumy*, Moscow, 1907, includes I. Kamenev's "za boikota" and Lenin's "Protiv boikotie" defending his arguments for participation in the third elections. In the *Collected Works* this appears in vol. 13, pp. 14-79. The stenographic reports of the Fifth Social Democratic Party Congress appear in E. Iaroslavskii, editor, *Protokoly s'ezdov i konferentsii VKP (b). Piataia s'ezd RSDRP*, Moscow, 1935. Iaroslavskii's *Istoriia V. K. P. (b)*, Moscow, 1926-1930, 4 vols, is a detailed official history of the Party. Volumes II and III are useful for this study. A convenient and dependable general study of the Social Democrats is J. Reshetar, *A Concise History of the Communist Party of the Soviet Union*, New York, 1964. D. W. Treadgold in *Lenin and His Rivals*, New York, 1955, has placed Lenin in the perspective of the entire opposition from the Kadets leftward. G. Vernadsky's *Lenin, Red Dictator*, New Haven, 1931, is still among the few scholarly portrayals of Lenin and his Party. For a survey of Lenin's attitude toward the Duma and parliamentary activity see A. Levin, "Lenin and Parliament" in Bernard W. Eissenstat, Editor, *Lenin and Leninism: State, Law, and Society*, Lexington, Massachusetts, 1971, pp. 111-135.

There is still considerable investigation to be done of the attitudes of the ethnic minorities as expressed in the Duma debates. The complex Polish problem as seen by deputies from the "Vistula Provinces" is capably analyzed by E. Chmielewski in *The Polish Question in the Russian State Duma*, Knoxville, Tennessee, 1970. The complexity of views expressed by the Jewish leadership on contemporary problems is developed in *Evreiskaia entsiklopediia. Izdatel'stvo Brokgauz i Efron*, St. Petersburg, 1906-1912, vol. VIII, pp. 438-439, vol. XIV, pp. 515-517.

BIOGRAPHIES, SPEECHES, MEMOIRES

A considerable fund of information concerning the deputies to the Third Duma is included in "Chlenyi gosudarstvennoi dumy pervago, vtorogo i tret'iago sozyva" at the end of vol. XVII of T-va br. A. I. Granat i ko., *Entsiklopedicheskii slovar*, St. Petersburg, 1890-1920, 40 vols. Brief biographical sketches of the membership of the First, Second, and Third Dumas include their political and professional careers and considerable statistical data. Cross-references are noted for members who have served in more than one session. Similar, but briefer, thumbnail descriptions of many of the leading political figures are included at the end of vol. VII of P. E. Shchegolev, editor, *Padenie tsarskogo rezhima*, Leningrad and Moscow, 1924-1927, 7 vols. This is the official verbatim report of the proceedings of the Extraordinary Investigating Committee of the Provisional Government to examine former government officials and "public figures" on their connections with, or knowledge of, salient developments which transpired largely in the Duma period. Portraits, biographies, and autobiographies of the deputies to the Third Duma are compiled in *Tret'ie sozyv gosudarstvennoi dumy. Portrety, biografii, avtografii*, St. Petersburg, 1910.

There are significant materials available for the ideas and activities of P. A. Stolypin. His speeches and the events with which they are connected are collected in two compilations: *Predsiedatel' sovieta ministrov Petr Arkad'evich Stolypin, sostavleno E. V. po soobshcheniiam pressa za tri goda [8 Iiulia 1906-8 Iiulia 1909 gg.]*, St. Petersburg, 1909, and *Gosudarstvennaia dieiatel'nost' predsiedatel sovieta ministrov Petra Arkad'evicha Stolypina*, St. Petersburg, 1911. Stolypin's daughter, M. Bok, has rendered an intimate presentation, if not a profound analysis, of her renowned parent in *Vospominaniia o moem otse, P. A. Stolypine*, New York, 1953. More comprehensive analyses of Stolypin by his contemporaries are offered by S. Syromatnikov, his secretary, in "Reminiscences of Stolypin," *The Russian Review* [London], Vol. I, 1912, No. 2, pp. 2-87; by the Premier's brother and publicist, A. A. Stolypin, in *P. A. Stolypin: 1862-1911 gg.*, Paris, 1927; by A. Izgoev, *P. A. Stolypin: Ocherk zhizni i dieiatel'nosti*, Moscow, 1912. And N. Savitskii has done the most extensive of these reviews in "P. A. Stolypin," *Monde Slave*, No. IV, 1933, pp. 229-233; No. IV, 1934, pp. 363-399; No. II, 1935, pp. 42-54; No. II, 1936, pp. 347-386. More recent estimates include L. Strakhovsky, "The Statesmanship of P. A. Stolypin: a Political Reappraisal," *Slavonic and East European Review*, Vol. XXXVII, No. 89, June 1959, pp. 348-371; and A. Levin, "P. A. Stolypin: A Political Appraisal," *The Journal of Modern History*, December, 1965. pp. 445-463.

Officialdom of the Duma period have left several significant memoires. V. I. Gurko, *Features and Figures of the Past: Government and Opinion in the Reign of Nicholas II*, J. E. Wallace

Sterling, Xenia J. Eudin, H. H. Fischer, editors, and L. Matveev, translator, Stanford University, California and London, 1934, is important for the 1905 Revolution and the period of the first two Dumas. V. N. Kokovtsov, *Out of My Past: Memoires of Count Kokovtsov*, L. Matveev, Translator, Palo Alto California, 1935, presents a vivid account of his stewardship as Minister of Finance and Chairman of the Council of Ministers from 1905 to 1914. S. E. Kryzhanovskii, *Vospominaniia iz bumag S. E. Kryzhanovskago*, Berlin, 1938, is a detailed, impassioned account by the Vice Minister of the Interior who wrote the Law of June 3, 1907. These writings depict consistently the official mind and the atmosphere in which it operated—generally hostile to the "popular representation."

Some leaders of the various parties, fractions and groups have collected their speeches or authored reminiscences which allow us a deeper insight into their purposes and problems. Professor M. Ia. Kapustin, *Riechi Kazanskogo oktiabrista*, Kazan, 1907, are the speeches of a widely respected Octobrist leader and professor of the Kazan University medical faculty. V. A. Maklakov, *Vlast i obshchestvennost' na zakatie staroi Rossii*, Paris, 1928, 3 vols., are the voluminous memoires of the renowned liberal lawyer who spoke for the right-wing of the Kadet Party. His ideas are also forcefully presented in *Iz vospominaniia. Pervaia gosudarstvennaia duma. Vospominaniia sovremennika*, Paris, 1938. This has been translated by Mary Belkin as *The First State Duma. Contemporary Reminiscences*, Indiana University Publications, Russian and East European Series, Vol. 30, Bloomington, Indiana, 1964. Maklakov's reminiscences on the Second Duma appear in *Vtoraia gosudarstvennaia duma*, New York, 1954. The Kadet leader, and a spokesman for the majority of the Party and Fraction, P. N. Miliukov, collected his speeches in the year of revolution, 1905 in *God borby*, St. Petersburg, 1907. He outlined the efforts by Premiers Witte and Stolypin to draw the Duma leadership into an appointive cabinet in *Tri popytki*, Paris, 1921, and left his extensive memoires in *Vospominaniia*, New York, 1955, 2 vols. A. P. Mendel has edited a part of these memoires covering the period from the spring of 1905 to the summer of 1917 in *Paul Miliukov, Political Memoires, 1905-1917*. The translation is by Carl Goldberg, Ann Arbor, Michigan, 1967. D. N. Shipov has recounted his political experiences and philosophy as a neo-Slavophile leader of the left-wing of the Octobrists and a founder of the Party of Peaceful Renovation in *Vospominanii i dumy o perezhitom*, Moscow, 1928. G. P. Sliozberg, *Diela minuvshikh dnei: zapiski russkago evreiia,* Paris, 1933-1934, 3 vols, are the extensive memoires of an articulate, Jewish spokesman and Kadet.

S. N. Harper, *The Russia I Believe In,* Chicago, 1945, and Sir Bernard Pares, *A Wandering Student,* Syracuse, N.Y., 1948, offer valuable comments on the events they witnessed as newspaper correspondents for the period of the Revolution of 1905 and the first two Dumas. Their interviews with high governmental officials and important "public figures" are especially useful.

NEWSPAPERS AND PERIODICALS

Much of the information offered in this study has been gleaned from the correspondence, reports, editorials, and columns of the daily press of the period 1907-1912 which served as the organs of the various political parties and currents. *Grazhdanin,* St. Petersburg, 1887-1914 was an independent biweekly mouthpiece of the moderate, and betimes, far right in the Russian political scene under the editorship of V. P. Meshcherskii. *Golos Moskvy,* St. Petersburg, 1906-1917 was a daily edited by A. I. Guchkov and served as the organ of the Union of October 17. It is not readily available outside of the USSR, but issues of the period June, 1907, to June, 1912, are to be found at the Columbia University and Oklahoma State University Libraries. *Novoe Vremia,* St. Petersburg, 1887-1917, an independent right-conservative daily, was St. Petersburg's chief newspaper, edited by M. M. Fedorov, 1907-1909. It stood somewhat to the left of the Octobrists, reflecting a suspicion of the sincerity of their constitutionalism.

One of the most famous and enduring of the "thick journals," *Viestnik Evropy,* was founded in 1802 by N. M. Karamzin. It appeared regularly 1886-1912 under the editorship of K. K. Arsenev as the moderately liberal organ of the Party of Democratic Reform. Its contributors included the chief figures of that Party, N. M. Kovalievskii, Professor V. Kuzmin-Karavaev, and M. Stasulevich. Its column-essays on "Domestic Affairs" contained consistently astute analyses of current affairs. *Riech,* nominally independent, was recognized as the chief daily of the Constitutional Democratic Party. It appeared in St. Petersburg from February, 1906, to 1917. Its responsible editor was V. I. Khariton, but its de facto editors were P. N. Miliukov and I. V. Gessen. It tried, with some success, to retain an objective coverage of events, and its columns "Party Affairs" and "News From the Provinces" appeared regularly and proved particularly valuable. They reported on the meetings of all opposition parties and their fractions and groups, and developments among the parties and groups to their right. At times the paper reproduced some significant legislation.

Tovarishch, the organ of the Bersteinist, "legal marxists," appeared in St. Petersburg, 1906-1910. Edited by E. Kuskova and S. N. Prokopovich, it identified itself as belonging to the nonpartisan left but was generally inclined to favor the Kadets. Its reportage on the parties and groups of the left opposition was particularly useful.

The marxist weeklies, *Proletarii*, Moscow, Geneva-Paris, 1906-1909 and *Vpered*, Geneva-Moscow, 1904-1908, were examined for this investigation. *Proletarii* was advertised as the organ of the Moscow and St. Petersburg Committees of the Russian Social Democratic Labor Party but was actually that of the Bolsheviki alone, with Lenin as its chief figure. Its staff included P. Rumiantsev, M. Gorkii, A. Lunacharskii, A. Bogdanov, L. Kamenev, and N. Rozhkov. *Vpered* was issued as the organ of the Moscow, St. Petersburg, Kursk, and Perm Committees of the Social Democratic Party but was recognizable as a strictly Leninist publication.

Index

Absenteeism, in peasant elections, 97-98, 98n; in small landowner elections, 98;, in worker elections to *uiezd* assemblies, 100; in landowner category, 101

Adoratskii, F. N., Octobrist candidate, 23n

Aleksinskii, G. A., Social Democratic leader in Second Duma, 63

Amur Region, no branches of URP in, 8

Anan'ev, I. E., in bureau of Russian National Fraction, 188n

Anenskii, N. F., Popular Socialist leader, 39; excluded from voting lists, 38n

Apathy, Octobrist fight against, 22. *See* Absenteeism

Arkhangel *guberniia*, no clerical electors in, 88n, 102; in Russian North, 113n

Asiatic Russia, reduction of representation from, 6n; defined as an enfranchized area, 113n

Astrakhan *guberniia*, URP in, 8; strength of clergy in, 102; in Volga region, 113n

Astrov, R.I., sounds out public opinion in Tomsk, 85n

Autocracy, URP platform on, 10

Baku, Social Democratic election agreements in, 71; city officials of influence elections, 92

Baku *guberniia*, in Caucasus region, 113n

Balashov, P. N., President of Russian National Fraction, 118n; on Stolypin, 119n

Baltic Region. representation of Germans in, 6n; no branches of URP in, 8; electoral law favors Germans in, 50; Germans in included in Russian category, 89; German electors to

guberniia assemblies in, 104, 105; defined, 113n

Bessarabia *guberniia*, URP strong in, 8; in Southwest Border region, 113n

Black Hundreds, soubriquet of URP, 7; volunteer information on nationality curias, 9

Blocs, Octobrists forbid with anti-constitutionalists, 20; rightist, 59-60; *See* Chap. VI

Bobin, M. P., disqualified as Kadet candidate, 82

Bobrinskii, Count. V. A., Moderate Rightist leader, 113

Bobrishchev-Pushkin, on authentic Octobrist organizations, 16

Bobruisk, registration in, 76

Bobruisk *uiezd*, small landowner lists in, 81

Bogdanov, S. M., in bureau of Russian National Fraction, 118n

Bolsheviki, strength of, 41-42; on trade unions, 44; electors of in St. Petersburg, 70-71

Borderlands, Russian curias in, 50

Borisov, registration in, 76

Boycott of Third Duma, Social Democratic Party on, 45-49

Brianchaninov, A. N., on attitudes of electorate, 85

Bureaucracy, URP platform on, 10

Candidates, opposition, campaign to disqualify, 82-83

Caucasus region, defined, 113n

Central Asia, no branches of URP in, 8; loses representation, 6n

Cherkasov, Baron, N. G., charged with indiscipline, 128; founder of Right Octobrist Fraction, 129

Chernigov, Jewish categories in, 92

Chernigov *guberniia*, strength of clergy in, 102; city categories in, 103; in Dnieper region, 113n

205

Parties, legalized, 7
Parus, forecasts election results, 95
Patrishchev, A. B., Popular Socialist
leader, 37
Pavlograd, rightist-Octobrist bloc·in,
60
Peaceful Renovationists, Fraction of,
creates "Progressive group", 130
Peaceful Renovationists, Party of,
legalized, 7; on government policy,
24; on constitutionalism, 24; differences with Octobrists, 24; foundation
of, 24; on electoral Law of June 3,
1907, 24; program, 24-25; calls for
centrist coalition, 25; differences of
with Kadets, 25; on support for
Stolypin, 25; political tactics of, 25;
suspects zemstvo liberals, 25; weakness of, 25, 142; effort to create Octobrist-Kadet bloc, 61, 61n, 62.
Peasant Category, 4; exclusions from,
81, 81n; official manipulations of
elections of, 90-91, 91n; designation
of deputies from, 101n; electors of
to *guberniia* assemblies, 102, 107
Peasant Non-party Group, 36
Peasants, excluded from landowner
category, 4; URP platform on, 10;
attitude toward Duma, 85n, 98, 150-
151; attitude toward elections, 98;
and Kadets, 145-146
Pensioners, registration of, 78
Penza *guberniia*, clergy in, 102; in
Central region, 113n
Perm *guberniia*, Social Democratic
Party in, 42; landowners in, 101;
clergy in, 102; in Ural region, 113n
Petrokovsk *guberniia*, in Poland, 113n
Petrov, G. S. Father, Bernsteinist sup-
port for, 35n
Pieshekhonov, N. N., Popular Social-
ist leader, 37; excluded from voter
lists, 38n
Pinsk, registration in, 76
Pinsk *uiezd*, small landowner lists
decline in, 8
Planson, V. I. de, Trudovik candidate,
40n
Plekhanov, G. V., Kadet attitude to-
ward, 30; on legal Social Democrat-
ic activities, 44-45; promotes Kadet-
leftist bloc, 67
Plevako, F. N., Octobrist leader, 15n
Plotsk *guberniia*, in Poland, 113n
Podolsk *guberniia*, URP strong in, 8;

clergy in, 102; in Southwest Border region, 113n
Poland, no branches of URP in, 8;
Jewish electorate in, 51-52, 54-56;
Polish electorate in, 51-54; reaction
to Electoral Law of June 3, 1907 in,
52; violation of electoral procedures
in, 90; defined, 113n. See also Vis-
tula Region.
Poles, electors in guberniia assemblies,
105
Polish Kolo, in first two Dumas, 6;
composition of, 53; strength of in
Third Duma, 111; analysis of, 135-
136; R. V. Dmovski leader in. 135;
V. P. Grabski leader in, 135
Polish Krai Party, program, 52-53. See
Kraevists
Polish-Lithuanian-Bielorussian Party,
program, 52; strength in Third
Duma, 111; analysis of, 135
Polish Progressive Party, relations of
with Kolo, 53, 54n
Polish Social Democratic Party, on
Kolo, 52
Polish Socialist Party, on terror, 43-44,
43n; on trade unions, 44n; on boy-
cott, 46, 47; boycotts third elections,
49; on Kolo, 52
Political crime, URP platform on, 10;
Octobrists assail Kadet position on,
14
Polovstov, L. V., expelled from Octo-
brist Fraction, 128
Poltava, rightist-Octobrist blocs in,
59; registration declines in, 76; effects of interpretations of electoral
law in, 76; invalid Jewish category
in, 89; Christian and Jewish categories in, 89n
Poltava *uiezd*, small landowner lists
in, 81
Poltava *guberniia*, clergy in, 102; in
Dnieper region, 113n
Popular Socialist Party, formation of,
37; in Second Duma, 37; enters Third
Duma, 37-38; in third election campaign, 38, 38n; on Social Revolutionary boycott, 41; forms populist
bloc in St. Petersburg, 71; leadership arrested, 83
Plotskii, A. A., in bureau of Russian
National Fraction, 118n
Pravitel'stvo, Social Democratic leaflet
for election campaign, 71

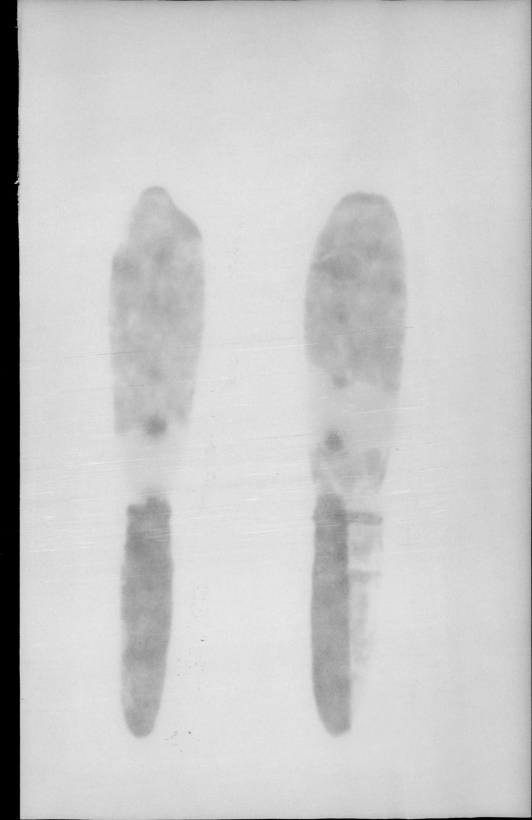

DATE DUE

GAYLORD   PRINTED IN U.S.A.